BARBARA MERVY

# TUDOR REBELLIONS 1485–1603

HODDER EDUCATION
AN HACHETTE UK COMPANY

**Dedication**
With thanks to family and friends for their encouragement and interest, especially my lovely friend Barbara Williamson who sadly did not see the finished book.

**Acknowledgements**
The author and publisher wish to thank Bill Sheils for his advice as academic consultant. All judgements, interpretations and errors remain the responsibility of the authors.

**Photo credits**
Cover © Andrey Kuzmin – Fotolia; © jvphoto / Alamy; **p.3** © The British Library Board, Cotton Roll II (23); **pp.4-7** © Georgios Kollidas – Fotolia; **p.11** © SSPL / Getty Images; **p.14** © Ms.266 fol.10 Henry VII (1457–1509) king of England (1485–1509), from 'Recueil d'Arras' (pencil on paper) (b/w photo), Le Boucq, Jacques (d.1573) / Bibliotheque Municipale, Arras, France / Giraudon / The Bridgeman Art Library; **p.16** *t* © Archivart / Alamy, *b* © TopFoto; **p.18** © APIC / Hulton Fine Art Collection / Getty Images; **p.20** © De Agostini Picture Library / Getty Images; **p.22** © The Art Gallery Collection / Alamy; **p.25** © bpk / Kupferstichkabinett, SMB / Jörg P. Anders; **p.27 & 118** © 2002 Topham Picturepoint / TopFoto; **p.32** © UrbanImages / Alamy; **p.36 & p.40** *t* © The Art Gallery Collection / Alamy; **p.39** *t* © The Granger Collection, NYC / TopFoto, *bl* © National Portrait Gallery / SuperStock; *br* © Photos.com / Thinkstock; **p.40** *b* © Image Asset Management Ltd. / Alamy; **p.44** © FURLONG PHOTOGRAPHY / Alamy; **p.47** © Badge of the Five Wounds of Christ (embroidered textile), English School, (16th century) / His Grace The Duke of Norfolk, Arundel Castle / The Bridgeman Art Library; **p.53** © David Ross / Britain Express; **p.54** © Nando Machado – Fotolia; **p.57** By kind permission of the Battlefields Trust; **p.59** © The British Library Board / Robana via Getty Images; **p.61** © Culture Club / Getty Images; **p.65** © Pontefract Castle, c.1620-40, Keirincx, Alexander (1600-c.1652) / Wakefield Museums and Galleries, West Yorkshire, UK / The Bridgeman Art Library; **p.67** © Topham Picturepoint / TopFoto; **p.68** *t* © *Hulton Archive/Getty Images, b* © 2005 Fotomas / TopFoto; **p.69** *t* © Andy Barker / Loop Images / SuperStock, *b* © Cofiant / Alamy; **p.80** © Kumar Sriskandan / Alamy; **p.82** © World History Archive / TopFoto; **p.83** © The Art Gallery Collection / Alamy; **p.85** © Ivan Vdovin / Alamy; **p.86** © TopFoto; **p.87** © GL Archive / Alamy; **p.89** © 2004 Woodmansterne / TopFoto; **p.90** © The Masters of the Bench of the Inner Temple, Photo: Ian B. Jones; **p.100** © 2003 Topham Picturepoint / TopFoto; **p.104** © Heritage Image Partnership Ltd / Alamy; **p.114** © British Library Board / Robana / TopFoto; **p.130** © Mansell/Time Life Pictures/ Getty Images; **p.136** © Vernon White / http://upload.wikimedia.org/wikipedia/commons/2/2c/DSCN1948PenrynPrayerBookRebellionMemorial.jpg; **p.137** By kind permission of the Battlefields Trust.

**Text credits**
**p.9** Paul Thomas: from *Authority and Disorder in Tudor Times* (Cambridge University Press, 1999); **pp.9, 74, 79, 97, 103** Anthony Fletcher and Diarmaid MacCulloch: from *Tudor Rebellions* 4th edition (Longman, 1997); **pp.9, 32, 43, 84** Alison Wall: from *Power and Protest in England 1525-1640* (Bloomsbury Academic, 2000), reproduced by permission of Bloomsbury Publishing; **pp.20, 26** Michael Bennett: from *Lambert Simnel and the Battle of Stoke* (Palgrave Macmillan, 1987); **p.25** David Beeston: from *A Strange Accident of State: Henry VII and the Lambert Simnel Conspiracy* (Birchwood, 1987); **p.30** Sean Cunningham: from *Henry VII* (Routledge, 2007); **p.30** Ian Arthurson: from *The Perkin Warbeck Conspiracy* (The History Press, 2009); **pp.32, 52, 77, 80, 93, 126** Andy Wood, *Riot, Rebellion and Popular Politics in Early Modern England*, 2002, Palgrave, reproduced with permission of Palgrave Macmillan; **p.37** Christine Carpenter: from *The Wars of the Roses: Politics and the Constitution in England c.1437-1509* (Cambridge University Press, 1997); **pp.44, 49, 54, 119** Geoffrey Moorhouse: from *The Pilgrimage of Grace* (Phoenix, 2002); **p.55** John Guy: from *The Tudors: A Very Short Introduction* (Oxford University Press, 2000); **p.55** Philip Caraman: from *The Western Rising*, 1549 (Halsgrove, 1994); **p.67** Derek Wilson, © Telegraph Media Group Limited 2009; **p.71** David Loades: from *The Mid-Tudor Crisis 1545–1565* (Palgrave Macmillan, 1992); **p.71** Nigel Heard: from *Edward VI and Mary: A Mid-Tudor Crisis?* (Hodder Education, 1990); **p.78** John Walter: from an article on Kett in the *Dictionary of National Biography* (Oxford University Press, 2004); p.86 David Loades: from *The Cecils* (The National Archives, 2012); **p.87** Neville Williams: from *Thomas Howard, Fourth Duke of Norfolk* (Dutton, 1964); **p.88** Roger Turvey and Nigel Heard: from *Change and Protest 1536–88: Mid-Tudor Crises?* (Hodder Education, 2009); **pp.91, 97, 98, 121** David Loades: from *Two Tudor Conspiracies* (Headstart History, 1992; Davenant Press, 2001); **p.93** David Loades: from *John Dudley, Duke of Northumberland* (Clarendon Press, 1996); **p.100** G.R. Elton: from *England under the Tudors*, Third Edition (Routledge, 1991); **p.103** Christopher Haigh: from *Elizabeth I* (Pearson Education, 1988); **p.104** Paul Hammer: from *Elizabeth's Wars* (Palgrave Macmillan, 2003); **pp.110, 112** Colm Lennon: from *Sixteenth Century Ireland* (Gill & Macmillan, 2005); **p.113** Wallace McCaffery: from *Elizabeth I* (Edward Arnold, 1993); **p.115** Steven G. Ellis: from *Tudor Ireland: Crown, Community and the Conflict of Cultures, 1470-1603* (Longman, 1985); **p.127** Geoffrey Woodward: from *Rebellion and Disorder under the Tudors* (Hodder Education, 2010); **p.129** Diarmaid MacCulloch: from *Reformation: Europe's House Divided 1490-1700* (Penguin, 2004); **p.131** Nicholas Fellowes: from *Disorder and Rebellion in Tudor England* (Hodder Education, 2001).

Every effort has been made to trace all copyright holders, but if any have been inadvertently overlooked, the Publishers will be pleased to make the necessary arrangements at the first opportunity.

**The Schools History Project**
Set up in 1972 to bring new life to history for students aged 13–16, the Schools History Project continues to play an innovatory role in secondary history education. From the start, SHP aimed to show how good history has an important contribution to make to the education of a young person. It does this by creating courses and materials which both respect the importance of up-to-date, well-researched history and provide enjoyable learning experiences for students.

Since 1978 the Project has been based at Trinity and All Saints University College Leeds. It continues to support, inspire and challenge teachers through the annual conference, regional courses and website: http://www.schoolshistoryproject.org.uk. The Project is also closely involved with government bodies and awarding bodies in the planning of courses for Key Stage 3, GCSE and A level.

**For teacher support material for this title, visit www.schoolshistoryproject.org.uk.**



Orders: please contact Bookpoint Ltd, 130 Milton Park, Abingdon, Oxon OX14 4SB. Telephone: +44 (0)1235 827720. Fax: +44 (0)1235 400454. Lines are open 9.00a.m.–5.00p.m., Monday to Saturday, with a 24-hour message answering service. Visit our website at www.hoddereducation.co.uk.


First published in 2014 by
Hodder Education,
an Hachette UK company
Carmelite House, 50 Victoria Embankment,
London EC4Y 0DZ

Impression number 10 9 8 7 6 5 4 3 2
Year 2018 2017 2016



Typeset in ITC Usherwook Book 10pt by DC Graphic Design Ltd, Swanley Village, Kent.
Layouts by Lorraine Inglis
Artwork by Barking Dog
Printed and bound in Dubai

A catalogue record for this title is available from the British Library

ISBN 978 1 4441 7871 5

# Contents

# 1 Tudor rebellions – the essentials

## Rebellions before the Tudors

Rebellions did not begin when the Tudors came to power in 1485. British history had already seen many rebellions, going back to Boudicca's rising against Roman rule in AD60. A brief look at three of these rebellions introduces key features of the rebellions of the Tudor period, including whether the word 'rebellion' is the most suitable term for all these events.

Let's begin with the best-known medieval rebellion, the Peasants' Revolt of 1381. This event is portrayed in contemporary accounts by monks and officials as a violent rampage by ignorant peasants, typified by the butchering of the Archbishop of Canterbury and by looting, rioting and arson in London. Unfortunately we have no accounts written by the participants but other records enable historians to create a more complex account.

We now know that many 'rebels' were respectable leaders of their communities in the south-east, men who were local tax assessors and who raised defence forces if the French invaded. It took a great sense of injustice for these men and women (and there were women involved) to ride and march to London, risking death as traitors. Some of their frustrations went back decades, to the Black Death of 1348. Survivors had hoped for higher wages or the freedom to move for higher-paid jobs. Instead their hopes were dashed by new laws punishing anyone seeking such improvements.

More immediate causes lay in the government's failure to prevent French attacks on the coast and in unfair taxes. The new Poll Tax, for example, was resented because everyone, regardless of wealth, paid the same rate. Even so, people didn't protest until pushed to their limit. In 1381 over 20 per cent of taxpayers simply fled to avoid paying yet another tax. It was only when a second group of tax collectors was sent to punish the evaders that the revolt began. Even then the protesters did not aim to depose the young King, Richard II. They emphasised loyalty to the King, blaming his advisers for the poor government. The revolt ended when they refused to confront the King after the killing of Wat Tyler, the rebels' leader. None of this gainsays the violence but it does build up a more complex picture with many hallmarks of protest, not rebellion.

The events of 1381 had many similarities with Cade's Rebellion in 1450. Again a well-organised protest in the south-east led to 'rebels' taking control of London for a few days. The King, the mentally unstable Henry VI, fled to the Midlands. However, again the King was not the target of protests. The protesters blamed the King's 'false councillors' for enriching themselves at the King's expense and for England's problems – corruption in the legal system and the loss of English lands in France. Their actions were also motivated by rising unemployment and falling wages in the south-east but the trigger for the rebellion was the threat by Lord Saye (the royal treasurer) to turn Kent into a wasteland in revenge for the murder of the Duke of Suffolk by unidentified rebels.

Cade punished the men believed to be corrupt traitors. Lord Saye was executed, his naked body dragged round London behind a horse. A handful of others were executed and their homes looted. The violence turned Londoners against Cade and they fought back, forcing the rebels out of the city. Most went home but Cade was caught by the Sheriff of Kent and killed.

Not all 'rebellions' followed this pattern. 1485 saw a rebellion aimed at overthrowing Richard III and replacing him with a new monarch. This rebellion built on a rising in 1483 which began because Richard's opponents believed he had seized the crown illegally from his young nephew, Edward V. The rebels wanted to restore Edward but then, believing he'd been killed, they chose the inexperienced Henry of Richmond (Henry Tudor) as their leader. That rebellion in 1483 failed, partly because of the difficulty of co-ordinating an uprising across the whole of the south of England. In addition, Richard was well-prepared, warned by his spies of what was happening.

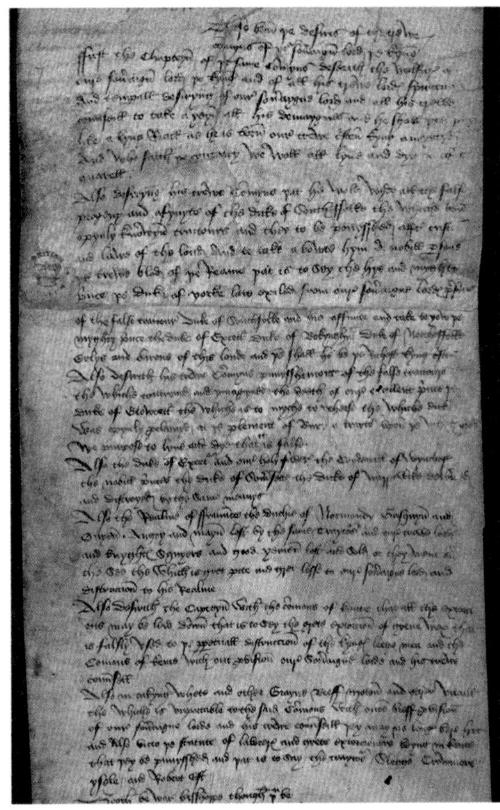

△ **In 1450 Cade's rebels listed their complaints in a petition to the King. They redrafted it several times, repeatedly proclaimed their loyalty to Henry, and distributed copies round the south of England. This shows evidence of sophisticated organisation and leadership. Many of Cade's followers were respectable leaders of their communities. They had a lot to lose so probably thought carefully before joining Cade.**

However, the invasion led by Henry Tudor in 1485 was successful. Richard was well-prepared but was still killed at the Battle of Bosworth and Henry became king. Henry won because of his support from many leading gentry in the south of England and because France provided ships to transport 4000 soldiers including over 2000 French soldiers and 1000 Scots from the King of France's guard. This French aid had made invasion feasible and success in battle far more likely.

What do these events suggest about:

- the causes of rebellions
- the reasons for the successes and failures of rebellions
- the variety of types of rebellions and whether the term 'rebellion' suits all of them?

# The Tudor dynasty

Henry's success at Bosworth saw the Tudors establish themselves on the English throne, a position they held for 118 years. During this period there were perhaps a surprising number of rebellions. Before looking at the rebellions, it helps to have a clear picture of the Tudor dynasty itself.

One feature to note is that there were several occasions when there was uncertainty about who the next monarch would be. Look carefully at the family tree and you will see that:

- Henry VII had only one male heir after 1502 and that heir, Henry VIII, was only 18 when his father died.
- Henry VIII famously struggled to father a male heir and his only son, Edward VI, was just nine when Henry died.
- Uncertainty followed Edward VI's death because his sister, Mary, was Catholic and there was some opposition to Mary becoming queen because she would change the country's religion back from Protestantism to Catholicism.
- Elizabeth never married and throughout her reign there was uncertainty about who her heir would be.

## What's in a name?

Although the Tudors are one of the most famous English dynasties, the historian C.S.L. Davies has shown that people at the time did not refer to the monarchs as 'Tudors'. The family's rise began with an illicit liaison between a Welsh gentleman-servant called Owen Tudor and Katherine of Valois, the widow of King Henry V. Katherine and Owen married and one of their children was Edmund, father of the future Henry VII. As a young man, Henry called himself by his title, Henry, Earl of Richmond but he became more widely known as 'Tudor' in Richard III's propaganda. Richard aimed to insult his rival by calling him Tudor to highlight his comparatively humble background. The name Tudor remains to this day even though the Tudors didn't use it!

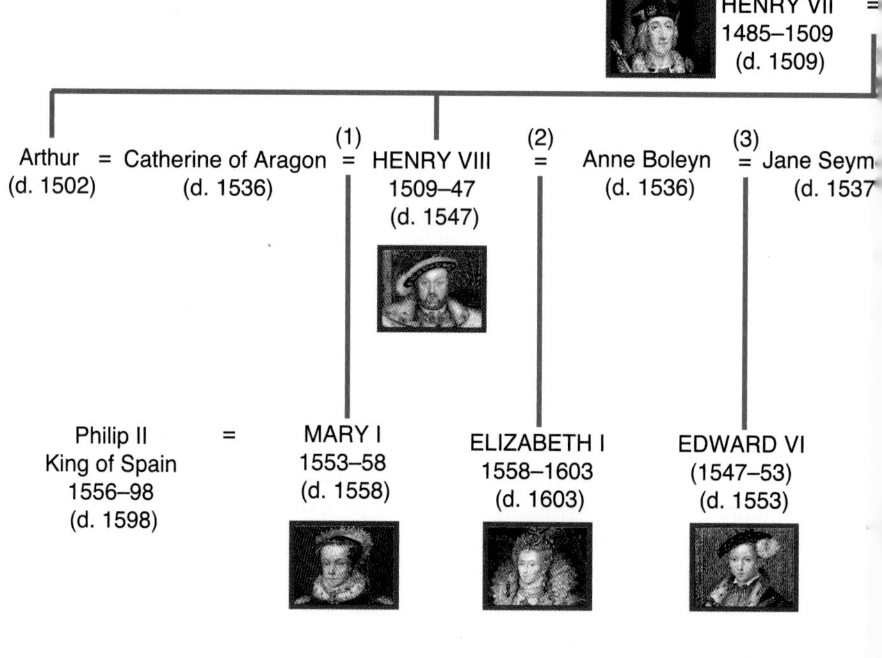

HENRY VII =
1485–1509
(d. 1509)
Arthur = Catherine of Aragon
(d. 1502)
(d. 1536)
(1) =
HENRY VIII
1509–47
(d. 1547)
(2) =
Anne Boleyn
(d. 1536)
(3) = Jane Seym
(d. 1537
Philip II
King of Spain
1556–98
(d. 1598)
=
MARY I
1553–58
(d. 1558)
ELIZABETH I
1558–1603
(d. 1603)
EDWARD VI
(1547–53)
(d. 1553)
Key
1485–1509 years of rule
= married to
(d. 1509) year of death

## Changes of religion

The most significant developments during the Tudor period were in religion. This began with Henry VIII's Break with Rome which secured his divorce in the early 1530s. Henry claimed to be an orthodox Catholic but removed some of the marks of traditional religion, such as shrines, monasteries and images, and placed himself at the head of the English Church. As each of Henry's children followed him to the throne, further religious changes took place. Edward VI introduced a fairly radical Protestantism. Mary returned the country to Catholicism. Elizabeth restored moderate Protestantism. Each of these changes created an atmosphere of uncertainty and worry and provided motives for rebellion for those who put their religious faith before their loyalty to the Tudor dynasty.

## Mary, Queen of Scots

One of the best-known figures of the Tudor period was Mary, Queen of Scots, Elizabeth's cousin. (Note that Mary, Queen of Scots was not the same person as Mary Tudor, Elizabeth's elder sister!) Mary, Queen of Scots was seen by some Catholics as an alternative queen to the Protestant Elizabeth. The most serious rebellion of Elizabeth's reign in 1569 aimed to put Mary on the throne. The family tree enables you to see how Mary had a claim to the English throne through her descent from Henry VII's eldest daughter, Margaret.

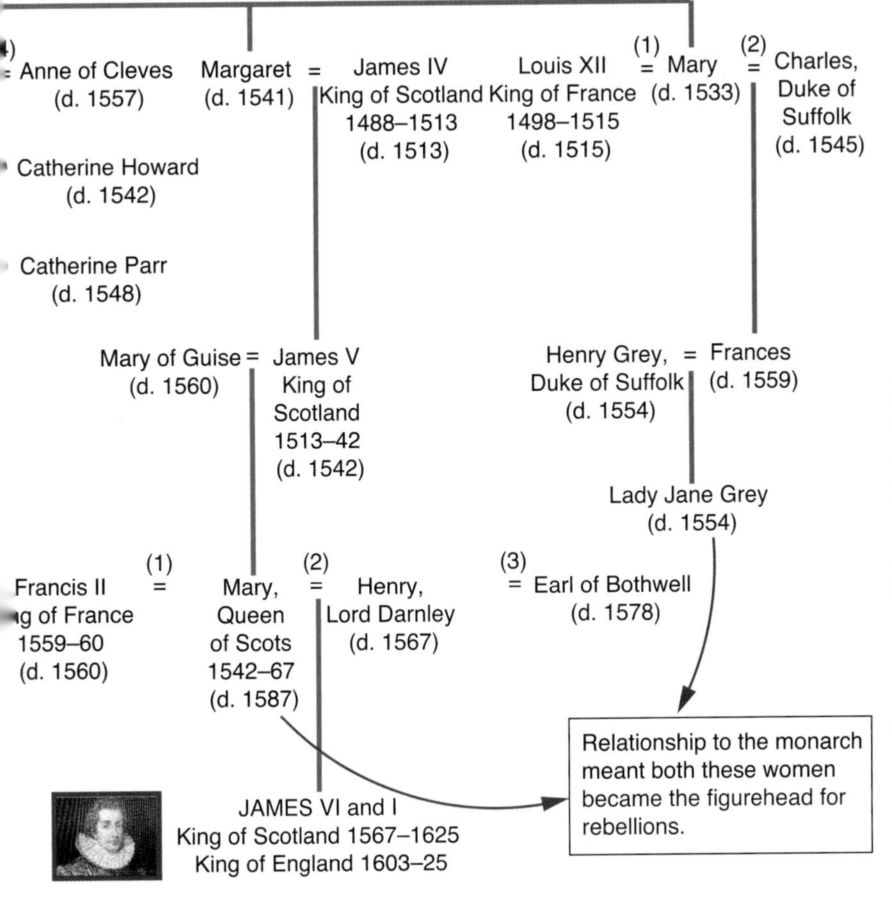

zabeth of York (d. 1503)
4) = Anne of Cleves (d. 1557)
Catherine Howard (d. 1542)
Catherine Parr (d. 1548)
Margaret (d. 1541)
= James IV King of Scotland 1488–1513 (d. 1513)
Louis XII King of France 1498–1515 (d. 1515)
(1) = Mary (d. 1533)
(2) = Charles, Duke of Suffolk (d. 1545)
Mary of Guise (d. 1560) = James V King of Scotland 1513–42 (d. 1542)
Henry Grey, Duke of Suffolk (d. 1554) = Frances (d. 1559)
Lady Jane Grey (d. 1554)
Francis II ng of France 1559–60 (d. 1560)
(1) = Mary, Queen of Scots 1542–67 (d. 1587)
(2) = Henry, Lord Darnley (d. 1567)
(3) = Earl of Bothwell (d. 1578)
JAMES VI and I King of Scotland 1567–1625 King of England 1603–25
Relationship to the monarch meant both women became the figurehead for rebellions.


## Lady Jane Grey

Sometimes known as the 'Nine Days Queen', Lady Jane Grey was briefly a rival to Mary Tudor in 1553 because Protestant plotters wanted to prevent Mary changing the country's religion back to Catholicism. Jane Grey's claim to the throne came through her descent from Henry VII's youngest daughter, Mary (see the right-hand side of the family tree).

# Tudor rebellions – a timeline

This timeline shows the major rebellions that took place during the Tudor period. It provides a reference point for checking the dates and sequence of rebellions and enables you to analyse the patterns of rebellions which in turn helps to introduce the main themes in this book. Think about these questions while analysing the timeline – you may not be able to answer them all at the moment but suggesting possible answers helps to prepare you for the issues ahead.

1 What type of rebellion appeared most frequently before 1530 and why?
2 Why did religious motives only appear after the 1530s?
3 Which periods saw the most outbreaks of rebellion? Why might this have been?
4 Which regions were most frequently the centres of rebellion? Why might this have been?

HENRY VII 1485–1509

HENRY VIII 1509–1547

1485

1505

1525

Mar–May 1486
Lovell and Stafford Brothers, Yorkshire

May–June 1487
Lambert Simnel's rebellion, the North

1491–97
Perkin Warbeck's rebellion, East Anglia, the North, Cornwall

Feb 1486
The Yorkshire rebellion

May–June 1497
The Cornish rebellion

May 1525
The Amicable Grant Rising, East Anglia

Oct 1536–Jan 153
The Pilgrimage of Gra
North of England

1534–35
Revolt of Silken Thor
The Pale

**Key**
**Elite conspiracies**
**Economic**
**Religious**
**Irish rebellions**

## Definitions

**Elite conspiracies**: used to describe rebellions led by members of the noble or gentry classes whose aim was to overthrow the monarch.

**Economic:** used to describe rebellions which sought to persuade the government to introduce reforms which would alleviate social or economic distress.

**Religious:** used to describe rebellions which sought to persuade the government to change its policies on religion.

**The Pale**: an area of approximately 80km surrounding Dublin in Ireland which was the region of Ireland directly under English rule.

EDWARD VI 1547–1553

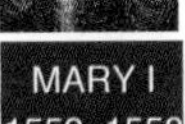
MARY I
1553–1558

ELIZABETH I 1558–1603

5 | 1565 | 1585 | 1603

July–Aug 1553
The Lady Jane Grey Plot,
London and East Anglia

Jan–Feb 1554
Wyatt's rebellion,
Kent and London

Nov–Dec 1569
The Northern rebellion

Feb 1601
Essex's rebellion,
London

July–Aug 1549
Kett's rebellion,
East Anglia

May–Aug 1549
Western Rising,
Cornwall

November 1596
Oxfordshire rebellion

1559–66
Shane O'Neill's rebellion,
Ulster

1569–70
Rebellion of James
Fitzmaurice Fitzgerald,
Munster

1579–83
Rebellion of James
Fitzmaurice Fitzgerald,
Munster

1594–1603
Earl of Tyrone's rebellion,
Ulster

# Was it really so easy to rebel in Tudor England?

The number of rebellions on the timeline on pages 6–7 may suggest that rebellions were common and that people found the decision to rebel easy. However, our quick look at the rebellions of 1381 and 1450 (pages 2–3) suggested that it took a great deal of provocation and frustration before people took up arms in protest or rebellion. Had this changed by the sixteenth century so that rebellion had become easier to contemplate and join? How strong were the pressures against rebellion and under what circumstances could it be justified?

## 1. The role of religion

In the early sixteenth century the Roman Catholic Church enforced shared beliefs and a moral code based on obedience. It had its own law courts and clergy who preached morality and deference at well-attended weekly services. Children were taught that God demanded they obey all those in authority, not only their parents but also the monarch, nobles and other social superiors, employers, clergymen and magistrates.

However, after 1534 the English Reformation meant that religious beliefs could now provide a major motive for rebellion. The crown's seizure of Church property and doctrinal changes were so bitterly resented that people, including some clergy, took up arms in defence of the old faith. Religion therefore could now give legitimacy to rebellions which took on the mantle of religious crusades against heretical rulers.

## 2 Authority and the social hierarchy

The Tudors believed that everyone was expected to obey their superiors and depicted an orderly universe where everyone had their place, from God at the top to plants and rocks at the bottom. This structure was known as the Doctrine of the Great Chain of Being. This ensured obedience to those above and authority over those below resulting in both social harmony and a strong state as described in Shakespeare's *Coriolanus*: 'The kingly crowned head, the vigilant eye, the counsellor heart, the arm our soldier, our steed the leg, the tongue our trumpeter'. The concept was well understood by all as was the chaos that would result if people challenged their place in the hierarchy.

The English people valued a strong king to give them a stable country. As English monarchs had no standing army, regular taxation, or police force, they relied on the ruling classes, in other words the nobility and gentry, to maintain a law-abiding realm. This ruling class prospered most when it could enjoy its wealth and live without fear of loss of position or life.

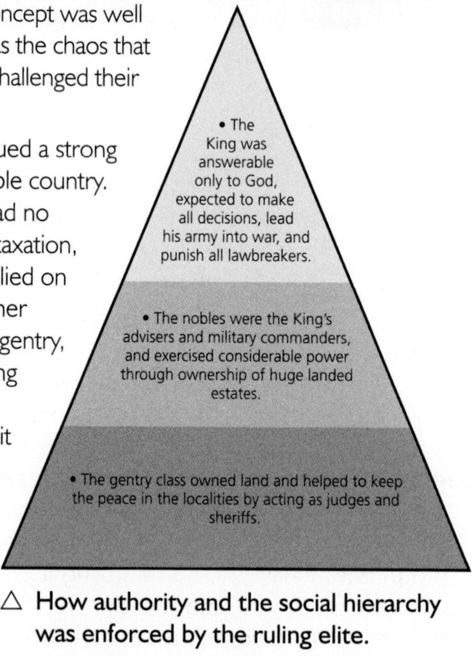

• The King was answerable only to God, expected to make all decisions, lead his army into war, and punish all lawbreakers.
• The nobles were the King's advisers and military commanders, and exercised considerable power through ownership of huge landed estates.
• The gentry class owned land and helped to keep the peace in the localities by acting as judges and sheriffs.


△ **How authority and the social hierarchy was enforced by the ruling elite.**

Peace in fact was in everyone's interest and both the social structure and people's personal preferences reflected this. The system, however, relied for its legitimacy on the respect accorded to the God-anointed monarch. Henry VII's seizure of the throne maintained the uncertainty of the Wars of the Roses, enabling some to challenge Henry's right to be king.

### 3 Quality of life

Like the ruling class, ordinary people had a vested interest in keeping out of trouble, preferring instead to make a secure life for themselves where they could grow prosperous and provide better opportunities for their children. As the historian Paul Thomas has written in *Authority and Disorder in Tudor Times* (1999):

> One should not underestimate the average subject's desire for a quiet life ... it took real provocation to propel most commoners onto the field of battle.

People lived out their lives within local communities in villages and towns and there was a well-established legal system which enabled the resolving of local grievances, provided a lawful outlet for any frustrations and also allowed members of the community an opportunity to take on civic responsibilities and office holding.

The Tudor period provided many opportunities for families to move up the social hierarchy. An unprecedented growth in population, coupled with the spread of literacy and learning, led to some breakdown of the traditional class boundaries as men made their wealth in new ways. In their book *Tudor Rebellions* (1997), Anthony Fletcher and Diarmaid MacCulloch argue that:

> The flood of monastic, chantry and crown lands produced an open and speculative land market. The growth of London and provincial food markets, galloping inflation and increased commercial activity and litigation offered exceptional opportunities for social advancement.

At such a time men had much to lose by participating in rebellion and in the main they did not. According to the historian Alison Wall in *Power and Protest in England 1525–1640* (2000): 'Fear of punishment certainly helped secure obedience. Serious crimes brought execution ... to terrify the public and make them obey'.

However, this same population growth spelled disaster to some: the poor not only grew poorer but there were many more of them. Inflation pushed up prices quickly so the value of wages fell. Poor harvests led to food shortages and price fluctuations led to rapid changes in standards of living and fear of hunger. There was therefore a minority who, despite the eventual introduction of better **Poor Relief**, felt they had nothing to lose by rebellion. As Alison Wall describes:

> Propaganda, participation, surveillance, welfare programmes and punishments provided strong incentives towards order and obedience but they did not always work ... most people obeyed at least as far as keeping out of trouble – though in tougher times more transgressed and more were caught.

**Poor Relief**
Support provided by central or local authorities, which could include employment and shelter. This aimed to alleviate hardships faced by the most vulnerable

■ If, as seems to be the case, few people in Tudor England benefited from taking arms against the monarch, why do you think there were so many rebellions in this period and does this tell you anything about the convictions of the people who took part in them?

## Lessons from the past: why Tudor rebellions are both intriguing and relevant

At the time of writing (2012) the Middle East is in turmoil with people in country after country taking to the streets with some using force to overthrow tyrannical rulers or to promote a particular sect or party in the power vacuum following a successful overthrow. At perhaps the other end of the scale, students in England have demonstrated against the abolition of the Educational Maintenance Allowance and the increase in university tuition fees. An alliance of celebrities and middle-class spokespeople have persuaded the government to change its policy on selling off the UK's national parks and woodland and the public sector has mounted demonstrations against cuts in local government and public services. The summer of 2011 saw violence in major English cities where young people trashed shops and challenged the forces of law and order.

This variety of protests is one selection from one brief period. Similar examples can be found in almost any period, including the reigns of the Tudors. All such events prompt important questions:

- What makes people take to the streets in protest or rebellion?
- What makes a rebellion and how different is rebellion from protest?
- How do governments deal with the threat of rebellions?
- Why do some rebellions succeed while others fail?

Some of the answers to these questions are common to all rebellions in all countries and centuries but it is the complexity of motives and actions, on each side, that makes this study such a rewarding and relevant enquiry. 'The Tudors' is one of the most popular periods of history taught and examined in the sixth form and by asking these questions of events at that time you are being encouraged to think about your own world through the drama of Kett's capture of Norwich, the Northern Earls' attempts to overthrow Elizabeth and replace her with Mary, Queen of Scots or Essex's impulsive dash into Elizabeth's bedchamber.

The rebellions provide a rich opportunity for you to think about those issues which people, including yourself, care enough about to take to the streets in protest. Allied to this are further moral dilemmas about the justification for rebelling against authority, whether central or local, elected or hereditary, and the responsibility of that authority in maintaining law and order and the means used to achieve it. Tudor rebellions also make a gripping read with unlikely leaders thrust to the fore, opportunities taken and missed and rulers rising to the occasion or failing dramatically to do so. This book has a clear focus on the fact that these were real people at a particular moment in time. Examination of all the rebellions will present an opportunity to evaluate the motives of both the people involved in the rebellions and the reactions of the authorities they were directed against. By bringing people and events to life, we hope this book will help to encourage a love of history, a desire to find out more and a sense of the similarities and differences uniting and dividing us from the people in the past.

Before you start your study of Tudor rebellions you should give some thought to what you understand by 'rebellion'. Do you think all the examples described in the first paragraph on page 10 could be classed as rebellions and if not, why not? Alison Wall suggests the following four categories which you might find helpful. In this book, as you have seen on pages 6–7, we also use three categories to define the rebellions and although these are based on the motives of the rebellions you can see from the brackets below that they fit quite well into Alison Wall's framework.

- **'Obedient' protests** where the rioters claimed loyalty to the monarch but were frustrated by, usually, economic grievances. (Economic, for example, the Amicable Grant Rising, 1525)
- **'Single issue' revolts** aimed at the reversal of a policy or removal of a minister, but again stressing loyalty. (Social and economic, for example, Kett's rebellion, 1549)
- **Revolts seeking fundamental change**, usually of religion, with a legitimate mandate to restore previous traditional ways. (Religion, for example, the Pilgrimage of Grace, 1536)
- **'Real rebellions'** where the aim was to change the nature of the government itself or even **overthrow** it. (Elite conspiracies, for example, Lambert Simnel's rebellion 1487, Wyatt's rebellion 1554)

'Dynastic' is often used to describe rebellions where the aim is to **overthrow** the monarch and replace them with a different member of a royal family.

Historians categorise events because it enables the better structuring of narratives and allows for closer analysis through, for example, comparing similarities and differences. Don't be put off by these different categories; they are there to help you understand each rebellion better by considering its most significant factors and to provide a wider perspective of themes and trends over a longer period of time.

As always, it is far easier for us, six centuries later, to analyse and categorise rebellions. Tudor monarchs did not have the luxury of time and perspective and were usually faced with a complex set of issues when determining how to deal with any threat to their authority. For them these events were very real, very immediate and surrounded by rumour and uncertainty. How many rebels were gathering? How were they armed? What did they really want? Rebels and protesters had similar problems. They did not know how the monarch would react or how quickly a royal army would move towards them. Communications for everyone were so slow that events might have changed significantly before a response could be made. What is clear – hopefully – to us was far from clear in the sixteenth century, just as we cannot know what lies ahead tomorrow, next week or next month.

△ Perceptions of rebellions often change over time. The Suffragettes' violent actions before the First World War were condemned at the time and Suffragette protestors were treated as criminals, imprisoned and force-fed. However, their actions which to some at the time seemed like 'terrorism' and 'rebellion' are now seen as understandable and far from extreme. From the descriptions of Tudor rebellions on pages 6–7, are there any which you would similarly see as entirely justified?

Synoptic Activity

# Investigating major Tudor rebellions: how to use Chapters 2–5

Chapters 2–5 provide a detailed study of the rebellions shown in the table opposite. The purpose of these chapters is to enable you to explore the nature of each rebellion, decide what was threatened and how great a threat each rebellion posed.

## Assessing the threat from each rebellion

In order to assess the threat from each rebellion you can use a set of six criteria listed below. Most or all of these criteria needed to be present to give a rebellion a realistic chance of success:

- powerful and effective leadership
- the intention to depose the monarch
- widespread support in England
- a realistic plan of campaign
- effective foreign military support
- a weak or slow government reaction.

In assessing each rebellion against the six threat criteria above you should use a chart like the one given below for the Peasants' Revolt of 1381 which you read about on pages 2–3. This will help you to decide how threatening the rebellion was. Obviously all 'reds' would mean a highly dangerous rebellion while a rebellion that appeared as all green would not amount to much of a threat. It will also enable you to see where the strengths and weaknesses of each rebellion lay.

| | | | | | | |
|---|---|---|---|---|---|---|
| **Very dangerous** | | | | | | 1381 |
| **Fairly dangerous** | 1381 | | 1381 | | | |
| **Slightly/not dangerous** | | 1381 | | 1381 | 1381 | |
| | **How powerful and effective was the leadership?** | **Did the rebels aim to depose the monarch?** | **How widespread was support in England?** | **Was the rebels' plan realistic, having a chance of success?** | **How effective was foreign support?** | **Was the danger increased by a weak or slow reaction from the government?** |

Completing a chart like the one above, summarising the strengths and weaknesses of a rebellion, has to be based on detailed evidence. Therefore, before you complete a chart for a rebellion you will need to make notes collating the evidence relating to each of the six threat criteria. You then use those notes to complete the chart.

Do you agree with the assessments made in the above chart for 1381? Re-read pages 2–3 and decide which evidence supports or challenges the judgements in the chart about the threat posed in 1381.

▽ Overview of Tudor rebellions in England (see pages 6–7 for Ireland).

| Name and main location of rebellion | Type of rebellion | Date | Monarch |
|---|---|---|---|
| Lovell and the Stafford Brothers<br>Yorkshire | Elite conspiracy | March–May 1486 | Henry VII |
| Lambert Simnel's rebellion<br>North of England | Elite conspiracy | May–June 1487 | Henry VII |
| The Yorkshire Rebellion | Economic | February 1489 | Henry VII |
| Perkin Warbeck's rebellion<br>East Anglia. North. Cornwall | Elite conspiracy | 1491–97 | Henry VII |
| The Cornish Rebellion | Economic | May–June 1497 | Henry VII |
| The Amicable Grant Rising<br>East Anglia | Economic | May 1525 | Henry VIII |
| The Pilgrimage of Grace<br>North of England | Religious | October 1536–January 1537 | Henry VIII |
| The Western Rising<br>Cornwall | Religious | May–August 1549 | Edward VI |
| Kett's rebellion<br>East Anglia | Social and economic | July–August 1549 | Edward VI |
| The Lady Jane Grey Plot<br>London. East Anglia | Elitist conspiracy | July–August 1553 | Mary |
| Wyatt's rebellion<br>Kent. London | Elite conspiracy | January–February 1554 | Mary |
| The Northern Rebellion | Elite conspiracy | November–December 1569 | Elizabeth |
| Oxfordshire Rebellion | Social and economic | November 1596 | Elizabeth |
| Essex's rebellion<br>London. | Elite conspiracy | February 1601 | Elizabeth |



## Which rebellions were the most threatening?

The second activity that will help you compare the rebellions is an assessment of which rebellions proved most threatening. One way to summarise your thoughts on this is to draw two 'threat lines' (shown below) and, at the end of each chapter, add the rebellions studied to the relevant line. To do this, you will use the detailed notes you have built up and the completed colour-coded charts on the previous page. Discussing where to place each rebellion on the 'threat lines' is an important way of consolidating your knowledge.

**Rebellions that aimed to depose the monarch**

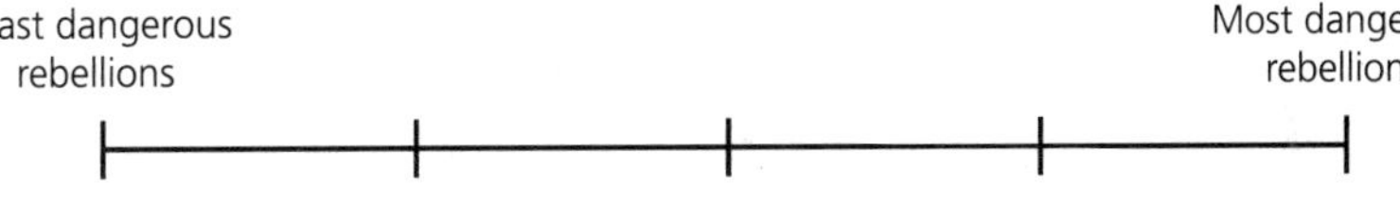
Least dangerous rebellions
Most dangerous rebellions

**Rebellions that aimed to change the monarch's policies or decisions**

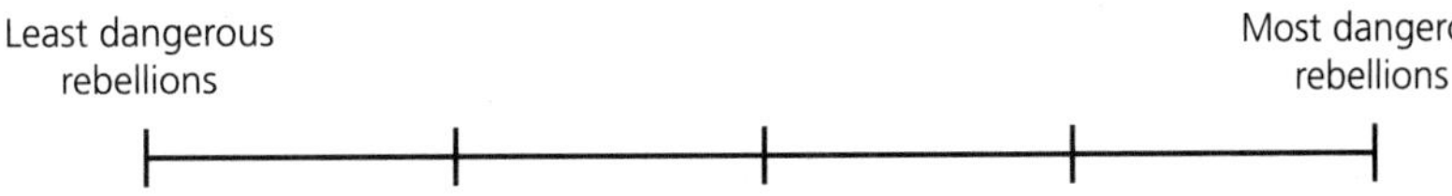
Least dangerous rebellions
Most dangerous rebellions

# Context: The Tudors – the unexpected dynasty

## Who was Henry VII?

The future Henry VII was born in Wales in 1457, the son of Margaret Beaufort and Edmund Tudor (who had died before Henry's birth). Henry was a distant member of the royal family (see the family tree) but no one ever expected him to be king. King Henry VI and his son, Prince Edward, were expected to continue the royal line (the red line in the family tree).

The family tree below shows another reason why Henry was not expected to become king. If you work your way up the green line on the family tree from Henry, Earl of Richmond (Henry VII) you will see that he was descended from King Edward III through Edward's son, John, Duke of Lancaster. However, the Beaufort line (in green) was barred from inheriting the crown by Act of Parliament. This was because the first John Beaufort was illegitimate, born before Lancaster married his mother, Catherine Swynford.

From 1471, when he was fourteen, Henry lived in exile abroad. By now Henry VI and Prince Edward had been killed. The new King, the Yorkist Edward IV was expected to pass the crown securely to his son. However, Edward died in 1483 and his young son was deposed by Richard III (see page 17). This changed Henry's fortunes completely. Suddenly he was chosen by rebels as their leader against Richard III. Henry was now a candidate to be king, despite having lived in exile for fourteen years, being virtually unknown in England and having only the slightest of claims to the throne via the Lancastrian line.

△ **A drawing of the young Henry VII.**

As preparation for Chapter 2 think about these questions:

1 Why was Henry Tudor such an unlikely candidate for the crown?

2 What were the main stages in the transformation of his chances of becoming king?

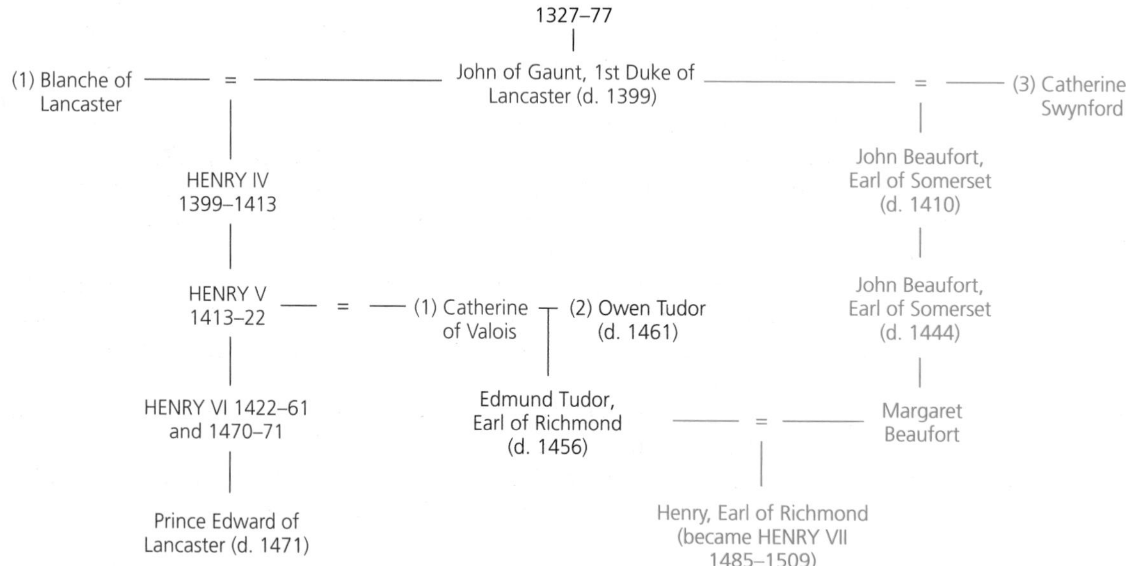
EDWARD III
1327–77
(1) Blanche of Lancaster
=
John of Gaunt, 1st Duke of Lancaster (d. 1399)
=
(3) Catherine Swynford
HENRY IV
1399–1413
John Beaufort, Earl of Somerset (d. 1410)
HENRY V
1413–22
=
(1) Catherine of Valois
(2) Owen Tudor (d. 1461)
John Beaufort, Earl of Somerset (d. 1444)
HENRY VI 1422–61 and 1470–71
Edmund Tudor, Earl of Richmond (d. 1456)
=
Margaret Beaufort
Prince Edward of Lancaster (d. 1471)
Henry, Earl of Richmond (became HENRY VII 1485–1509)

△ **Family tree showing Henry VII's descent from Edward III and his links to the Lancastrian royal family.**

## Henry VII's road to the throne

This graph summarises Henry's road to the throne and how belatedly he became a serious contender to be king.

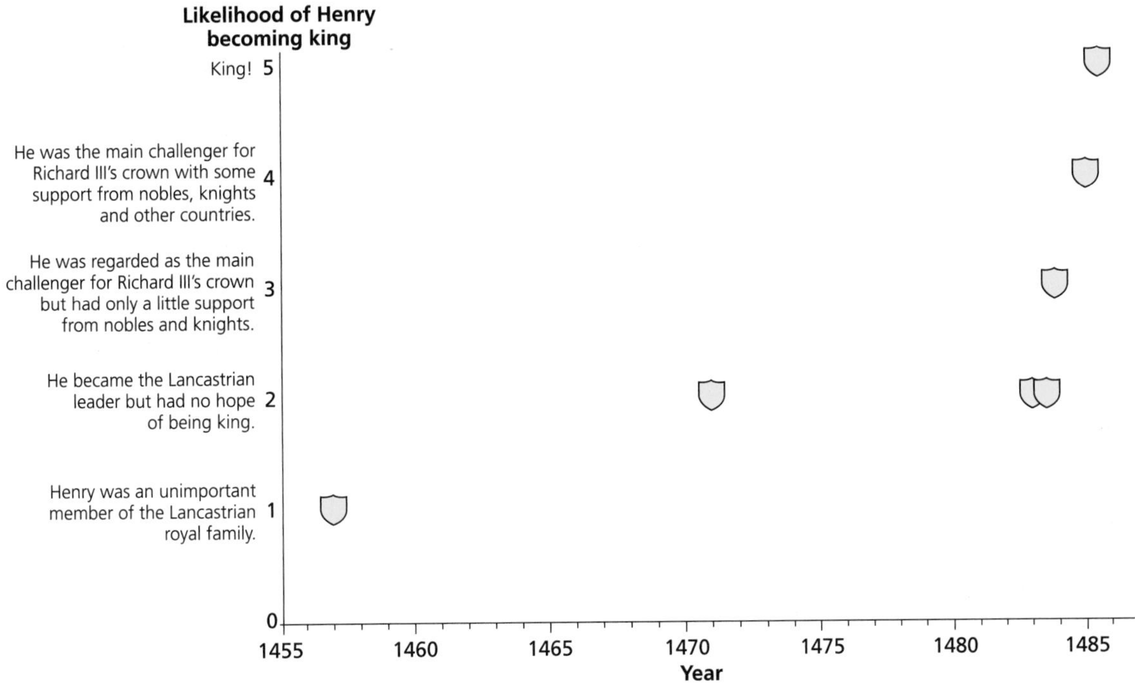

Likelihood of Henry becoming king
King! 5
He was the main challenger for Richard III's crown with some support from nobles, knights and other countries. 4
He was regarded as the main challenger for Richard III's crown but had only a little support from nobles and knights. 3
He became the Lancastrian leader but had no hope of being king. 2
Henry was an unimportant member of the Lancastrian royal family. 1
0
1455
1460
1465
1470
1475
1480
1485
Year


In just two years between 1483 and 1485 Henry Tudor went from being a man with no chance of becoming king to wearing the crown. How did this happen? The graph above shows how sudden his rise was. The information below explains his position at each point on the graph.

| | |
|---|---|
| **1457** | Henry was the son of Margaret Beaufort, the great-great granddaughter of Edward III. He had a distant claim to the crown but no one expected him to become king. |
| **1471** | The deaths of King Henry VI and his heir, Edward of Lancaster, left 14-year-old Henry as the principal Lancastrian claimant. However, he had to flee into exile. Edward IV was secure on the throne. |
| **April 1483** | Edward IV died unexpectedly and his brother Richard seized the throne from his nephew (Edward V). Richard proclaimed himself Richard III. Henry was still in exile. |
| **July 1483** | The sons of Edward IV (Edward V and his younger brother) were imprisoned in the Tower of London and it is likely that these 'Princes in the Tower' were killed sometime in 1483. |
| **Summer 1483** | A rebellion broke out, led by Yorkists who held Richard responsible for the Princes' murder and wanted him to be replaced, even with a Lancastrian. They chose Henry. He announced that he would marry Elizabeth of York, eldest daughter of Edward IV and sister of the Princes. |
| **June 1485** | The King of France feared Richard might invade France so provided Henry with a fleet and approximately 4000 soldiers. |
| **August 1485** | Henry invaded England. Richard and his closest supporters were killed at the Battle of Bosworth in Leicestershire. Henry was now King Henry VII. |

## Context: The 'Yorkist' rebellions – a misleading name?

Three of the rebellions against Henry VII are usually described in textbooks as Yorkist rebellions. These are:

**1486 – Lovell's Rising**. Francis, Lord Lovell had no claim to the crown but may have hoped to replace Henry VII with the Earl of Warwick, the nephew of the Yorkist kings, Edward IV and Richard III.

**1487 – Lambert Simnel's Rising**. Simnel pretended to be the Earl of Warwick who was used as a figurehead by plotters headed by the Earl of Lincoln (see family tree), another nephew of Edward IV and Richard III.

**1490s – Perkin Warbeck** was another pretender, claiming to be Richard, Duke of York, the second son of Edward IV, the younger of the Princes in the Tower.

In addition, during the early 1500s, the Earl of Suffolk went into exile in Europe and seemed capable of posing a threat to Henry's hold on the throne although Suffolk never led an invasion.

As you can see on the family tree opposite all these rebellions had links to the family of the Yorkist kings, Edward IV, Edward V and Richard III. However, thinking of these rebellions as 'Yorkist' rebellions may be misleading as it implies that, after 1485, English nobles were split into two groups, Yorkists on the one hand and supporters of Henry VII and the Lancastrian family on the other. This idea of two equal groups is incorrect.

In assessing these 'Yorkist' rebellions we have to remember that Henry had considerable Yorkist support from Yorkists at Bosworth because Richard III's deposition of Edward V had alienated many of them and driven them to support Henry. Henry then married Elizabeth of York so in many ways he can justifiably be described as a Yorkist king – he would never have won the crown without Yorkist support. Therefore it is misleading to describe these rebellions as 'Yorkist' given that so many supporters of Henry VII had themselves been Yorkist.

The rebellions listed above were primarily the work of a relatively small number of supporters of Richard III who refused to accept Henry VII as king, believing they had no chance of retaining their power and position if Henry remained as king. Therefore we should be careful about calling these rebellions 'Yorkist' – they were the work of a small number of outsiders, not a mass of supporters of the family of the House of York.

△ Edward IV, King of England 1461–83. He was succeeded by his son, Edward V, who was king for just three months before his uncle, Richard, Duke of Gloucester, seized the crown and became Richard III.

△ Richard III, King of England 1483–85.

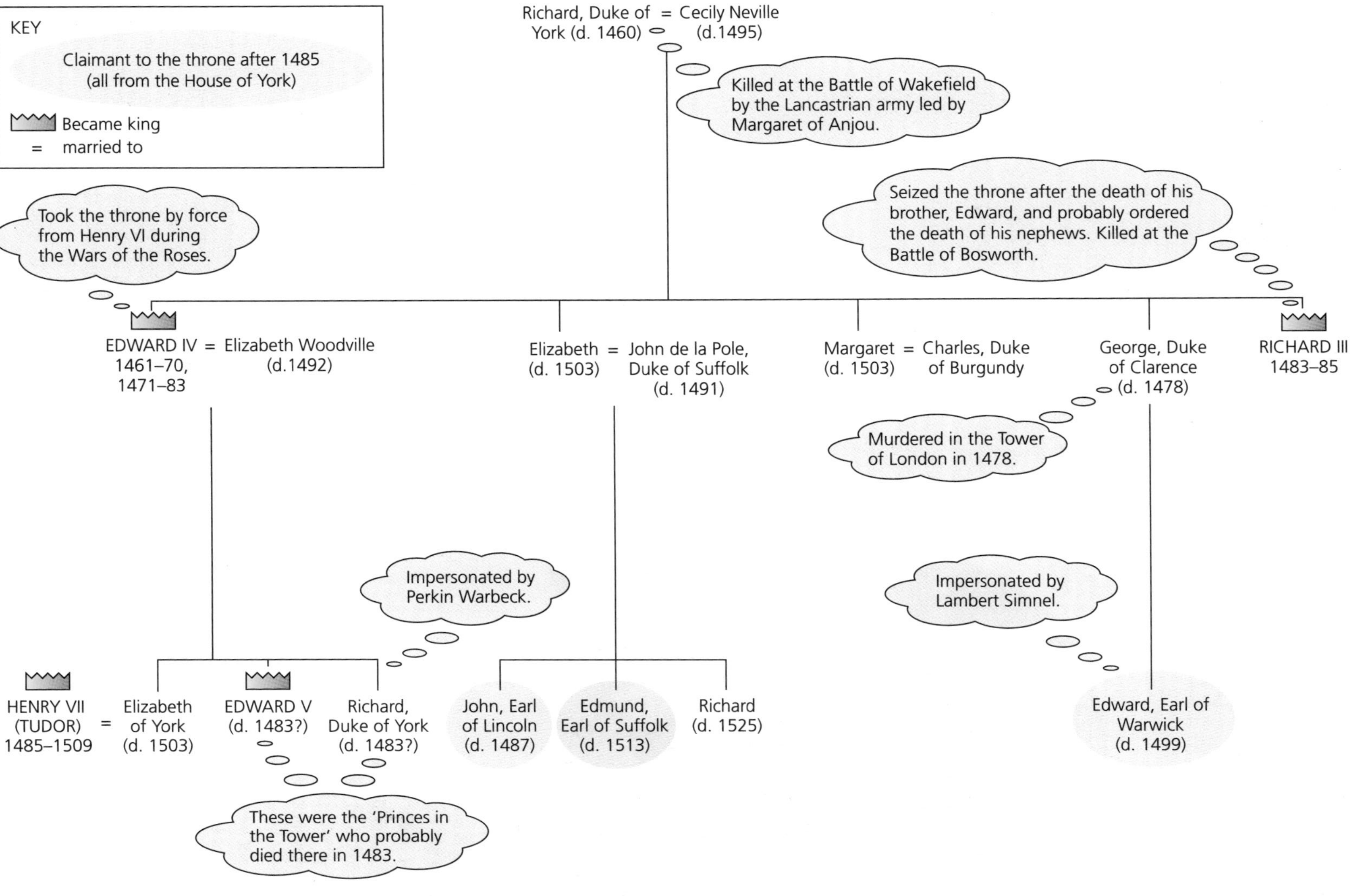
KEY
Claimant to the throne after 1485 (all from the House of York)
Became king
= married to
Richard, Duke of York (d. 1460) = Cecily Neville (d.1495)
Killed at the Battle of Wakefield by the Lancastrian army led by Margaret of Anjou.
Took the throne by force from Henry VI during the Wars of the Roses.
Seized the throne after the death of his brother, Edward, and probably ordered the death of his nephews. Killed at the Battle of Bosworth.
EDWARD IV 1461–70, 1471–83 = Elizabeth Woodville (d.1492)
Elizabeth (d. 1503) = John de la Pole, Duke of Suffolk (d. 1491)
Margaret (d. 1503) = Charles, Duke of Burgundy
George, Duke of Clarence (d. 1478)
RICHARD III 1483–85
Murdered in the Tower of London in 1478.
Impersonated by Perkin Warbeck.
Impersonated by Lambert Simnel.
HENRY VII (TUDOR) 1485–1509 = Elizabeth of York (d. 1503)
EDWARD V (d. 1483?)
Richard, Duke of York (d. 1483?)
John, Earl of Lincoln (d. 1487)
Edmund, Earl of Suffolk (d. 1513)
Richard (d. 1525)
Edward, Earl of Warwick (d. 1499)
These were the 'Princes in the Tower' who probably died there in 1483.

△ **The House of York.**

# 2 Were the Tudors ever really threatened by rebellion before 1530?

△ Painted in 1505 by an unknown artist, the King is known to have sat for this portrait. Henry is usually described as a dedicated and hard-working monarch who brought stability after the Wars of the Roses but whose meanness earned him a reputation for avarice.

In May 1487 Dublin Cathedral was awash with bright colours, sumptuous silks and rich velvets for the coronation of the 'Earl of Warwick' as King Edward VI of England. All the 'royalty' of Ireland was there. The Earl of Kildare, head of the great Fitzgerald clan oversaw proceedings. English support was represented by John de la Pole, Earl of Lincoln, a nephew of Richard III, the last Yorkist king, and by Francis, Viscount Lovell. As 'Edward VI' was escorted to the high altar and a crown placed upon his head many in the congregation hoped that the brief reign of Henry VII was nearly over. The ceremony was followed by a stately procession through cheering crowds to Dublin Castle where days of feasting lay ahead. Coins were struck bearing the new royal coat of arms and proclaiming the start of the reign of a new king of England.

Who was this new 'Edward VI'? He was an imposter! The details of his early life are far from certain but sometime in 1486 Richard Symonds, an ambitious young priest in Oxford, was earning some extra money by tutoring a local teenager. The boy was bright, articulate and confident; probably the son of a local trader. We know him as Lambert Simnel, almost certainly a made-up name since neither 'Lambert' nor 'Simnel' was common in fifteenth-century England. Symonds decided to train the boy to impersonate Edward, Earl of Warwick. As nephew to the last two Yorkist kings Warwick had a high profile and a claim to the throne. Symonds believed discontented nobles would fight to help 'Warwick' regain 'his' throne from Henry.

All this time the real Warwick was in the Tower of London. He'd been there since 1485 when Henry VII, fearful of Warwick's claim to the throne, had ordered his imprisonment. When rumours spread that Warwick had escaped and was now in Ireland, Henry paraded the real Warwick through London's streets to prove that the youth in Ireland was an imposter. However, despite the King's efforts, the youngster crowned in Dublin began to attract support. In 1487 'Edward VI', Lincoln and Lovell, set sail from Ireland for Lancashire, along with 2000 German mercenaries provided by Margaret, Duchess of Burgundy (sister of the Yorkist kings, Edward IV and Richard III) and between four and six thousand Irish provided by Kildare. Was Henry VII about to lose his throne to a boy imposter?

## Enquiry Focus: Were the Tudors ever really threatened by rebellion before 1530?

Simnel's invasion seemed a significant threat to Henry VII and it proved to be only one of a number of invasions and rebellions that he and his son, Henry VIII, had to face. They survived – but was that because the various rebels never had a chance or did the Tudors come closer to defeat in their early years than we might imagine?

Like all the chapters in this book, this one focuses on an enquiry question:

**Were the Tudors ever really threatened by rebellion before 1530?**

At first glance this question may seem to have an obvious answer. There were six rebellions between 1485 and 1530 (see the timeline on pages 6–7) but all of them were defeated. Therefore it appears that neither Henry VII nor Henry VIII was really threatened and you may feel that the hypothesis that they were never seriously threatened will be straightforward to prove. However, think back to what you read on the opposite page. The followers of 'Edward VI' must have been confident to risk their lives and they clearly had a sizeable army when they invaded England. This does not sound like a threat that would be easily beaten.

Therefore, to assess the degree of threat we have to move beyond generalisations about a rebellion being 'a major threat' or 'not a threat' and look closely at each rebellion, analysing the kinds of threat each posed and whether they appeared more dangerous to contemporaries than they do with hindsight. It's worth noting that of the six rebellions in this period three had essentially dynastic causes and three had their roots in economic problems. Were these different kinds of rebellions likely to be equally threatening?

The following steps will help you work through this enquiry and come to your conclusion.

1. Read the account of each rebellion which follows and then complete a chart for each one, like the example on page 12, to assess the degree of threat.
2. Make separate clear notes to justify how you have graded the threat criteria for each rebellion.

At the end of this chapter use the completed charts and the 'threat line' activity on page 13 to reach your overall answer to the question. The evaluation at the end of each rebellion will provide further details to help you to develop your own analysis and reach a conclusion.

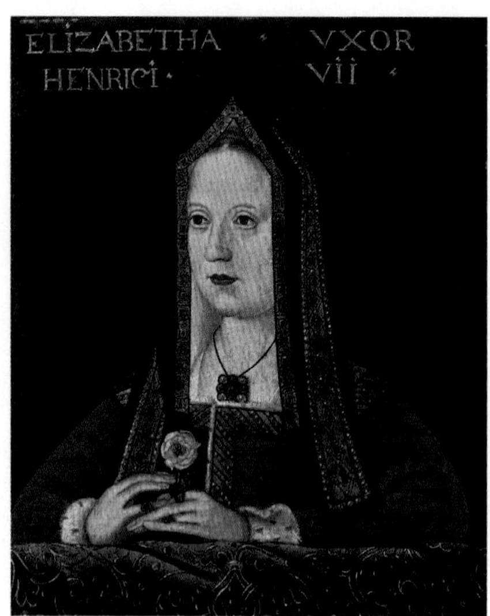
ELIZABETHA · VXOR
HENRICI · VII

△ **Elizabeth of York, daughter of Edward IV and niece of Richard III. She was born in 1466 and died in 1503 on her 37th birthday. Henry married Elizabeth in January 1486, fulfilling a promise he made in exile to win over her Yorkist supporters.**

# 1486 – The Lovell and Staffords' Uprising

Following his victory at Bosworth in August 1485 Henry was crowned king. He married Elizabeth, the daughter of Edward IV in an attempt to ensure the loyalty of former Yorkists but he did not have to wait long for the first rebellion against him, one that developed even before that of Lambert Simnel.

Within six months of becoming king, in February 1486, Henry led a large retinue of nobles and gentry towards the north of England. This was partly a public relations exercise to show the power and authority of the new king, but also aimed to deal with any rebellious subjects who were more likely to be found in the unsettled north. By March, Henry had reached Nottingham Castle and it was here that news reached him of a conspiracy amongst former supporters of Richard III.

The major figure behind this conspiracy was the 30-year-old Lord Francis Lovell, a close confidante of Richard III. In Henry VII's first parliament Lovell had been **attainted** which meant that he had lost all his lands and property and would, in all likelihood, be executed if captured.

He probably felt there was nothing to lose by rebelling. Lovell provided the leadership of this uprising (although as a refugee he had little access to wealth and he also had little military experience) along with Sir Humphrey Stafford, a Midlands landowner and his brother, Thomas. Lovell and the Staffords had been in **sanctuary** at Colchester since the Battle of Bosworth.

**attainted**
The Act of Attainder was used by the Tudors to rid themselves of their opponents. Those convicted under this act could be executed without trial while their titles and possessions passed to the crown

**sanctuary**
A sacred place where, under medieval law, fugitives were immune from arrest

In the spring of 1486 Lovell left sanctuary with the aim of raising support in the north so he could move against Henry VII. The Staffords began to raise forces in the West Midlands. This meant that the King would be threatened from two regions at once. Lovell's plan was to rally the north, seize York and capture the King. According to Michael Bennett in *Lambert Simnel and the Battle of Stoke* (1987), 'the Crowland Chronicle makes mention of a plot to kill King Henry at York'. However, it is not clear who Lovell hoped would become king had he succeeded in deposing Henry.

Lovell and the Staffords were motivated by a combination of loyalty to Richard and fear that Henry would not give them any local power. Such self-interested motives may explain why the leading northern families failed to support Lovell's rising and remained loyal to the King. Thus the rebels received little local support and had no foreign aid at all.

In response Henry reacted quickly, deciding that the threat from the north was greater and began marching towards York. On the way he was joined by the Earl of Northumberland and knights from Yorkshire, some of whom had fought with Richard at Bosworth.

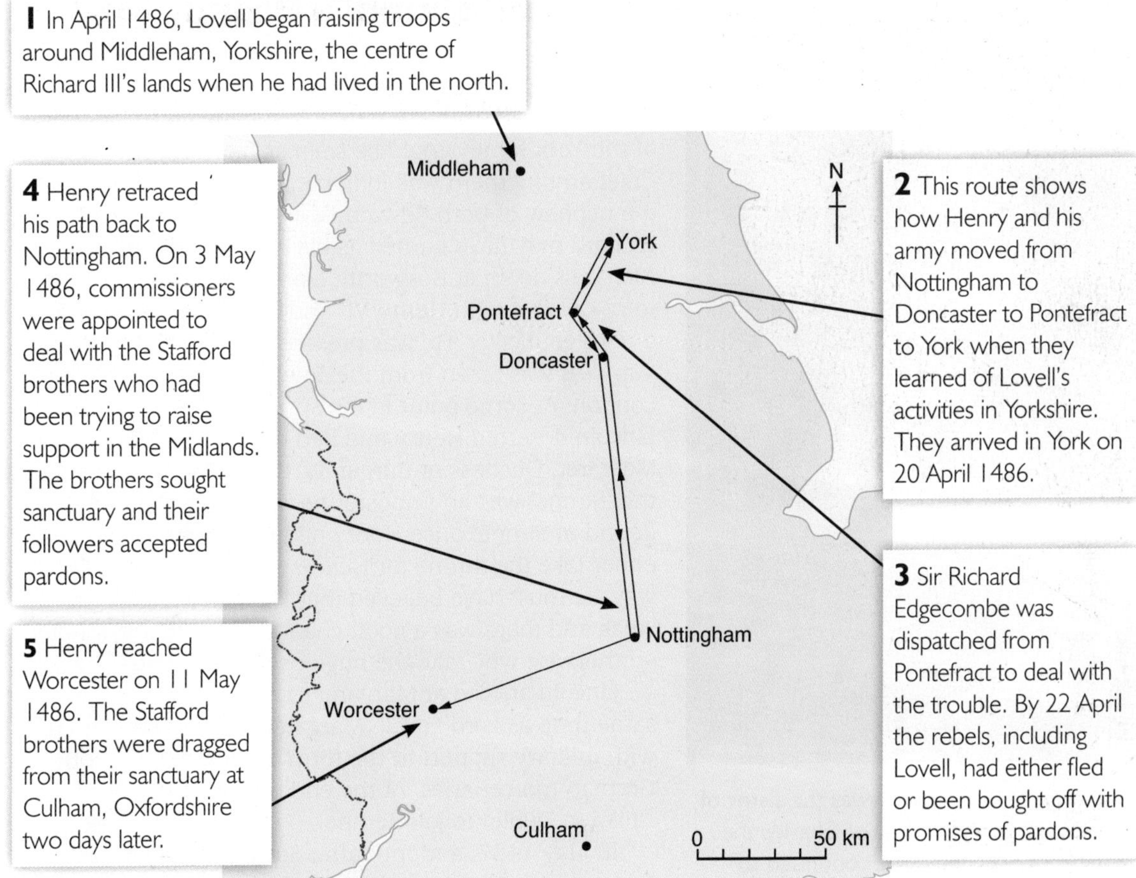
**1** In April 1486, Lovell began raising troops around Middleham, Yorkshire, the centre of Richard III's lands when he had lived in the north.
**2** This route shows how Henry and his army moved from Nottingham to Doncaster to Pontefract to York when they learned of Lovell's activities in Yorkshire. They arrived in York on 20 April 1486.
**3** Sir Richard Edgecombe was dispatched from Pontefract to deal with the trouble. By 22 April the rebels, including Lovell, had either fled or been bought off with promises of pardons.
**4** Henry retraced his path back to Nottingham. On 3 May 1486, commissioners were appointed to deal with the Stafford brothers who had been trying to raise support in the Midlands. The brothers sought sanctuary and their followers accepted pardons.
**5** Henry reached Worcester on 11 May 1486. The Stafford brothers were dragged from their sanctuary at Culham, Oxfordshire two days later.
Middleham
N
York
Pontefract
Doncaster
Nottingham
Worcester
Culham
0
50 km

△ **Escalation of Lovell and the Staffords' uprising.**

In the event Lovell's followers were easily dispersed and Lovell fled to Flanders. As Henry retraced his steps to Worcester the disturbance in the Midlands also subsided. Although the Stafford brothers claimed sanctuary Henry had them dragged out to answer charges of treason. Humphrey Stafford was executed. The uprising had never escalated into a serious rebellion but these events had shown the possibility of co-ordinating regional unrest. Equally important for what happened next in 1487, some rebels were apparently inspired to participate because of rumours that the Earl of Warwick (see family tree on page 17) was about to join Lovell and fight for 'his' throne.

■ Complete a 'threat chart' (see page 12) to evaluate the threat from the Lovell and Staffords' Uprising. Make notes to justify your grading of the threat according to each of the six criteria.

△ Margaret of Burgundy was the sister of Edward IV and widow of Charles the Bold of Burgundy. She continued to reside in Burgundy after Charles' death. Margaret was determined to help any opponents of Henry VII and her court became a focal point for discontented former supporters of Richard III and others, like Lincoln, who had ambitions for the crown and power. As the mother-in-law of the Holy Roman Emperor, Maximilian, Margaret also had the means of providing military support provided it was in Maximilian's interest to destabilise Henry's position in England.

## Lambert Simnel's Rising, 1487

Now we can return to the rebellion introduced on page 18, one which caused Henry considerable anxiety. As you have seen from the family tree on page 17, members of the York family could be seen as heirs to Richard III. Chief among them was John de la Pole, Earl of Lincoln, the nephew of both Edward IV and Richard III, whom Richard may have named as his heir in 1484. After Richard's death at Bosworth, Lincoln initially appeared to co-operate with Henry VII and continued to serve as a royal councillor. He was present when the real Earl of Warwick was taken from the Tower and paraded through London. At some point in the spring of 1487 however, Lincoln deserted Henry and fled to the court of his aunt, Margaret, Duchess of Burgundy. Given that Lincoln knew that Simnel was an imposter he may have planned to get rid of Simnel once Henry had been overthrown and either take the throne himself or restore Warwick. Either way, he must have believed that Henry's position was weak and there was a good chance of him being toppled – otherwise why take the huge risk of rebellion?

Lincoln arrived at Margaret's court at roughly the same time as Lord Lovell. Margaret now provided them with military support in the form of an army of 2000 German mercenaries. At the end of April 1487 this force sailed to Dublin to join Simnel.

In May 1487, a month after Simnel's coronation as Edward VI in Dublin Cathedral, the rebels landed in Lancashire. The foreign military support from Margaret had been strengthened by Irish soldiers provided by the Earl of Kildare. This combined force probably numbered between 6000 and 8000. The plan was to meet up in the north-west with an English army raised by Sir Thomas Broughton, a former supporter of Richard III, collect more support from the north of England and then march on London. The rebel army moved at great speed across England, averaging twenty miles a day. They were joined by some local gentry but the rebellion never attracted the expected English support. Historians have put forward several possible reasons for this lack of support, shown in the diagram opposite They are not in order of importance and are not mutually exclusive.

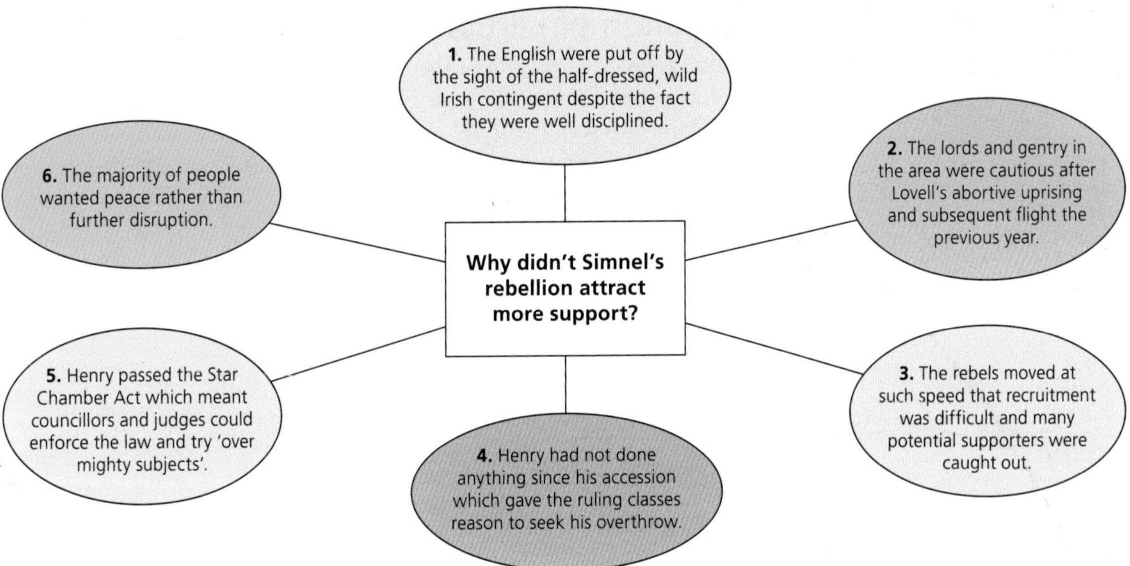
Why didn't Simnel's rebellion attract more support?
1. The English were put off by the sight of the half-dressed, wild Irish contingent despite the fact they were well disciplined.
2. The lords and gentry in the area were cautious after Lovell's abortive uprising and subsequent flight the previous year.
3. The rebels moved at such speed that recruitment was difficult and many potential supporters were caught out.
4. Henry had not done anything since his accession which gave the ruling classes reason to seek his overthrow.
5. Henry passed the Star Chamber Act which meant councillors and judges could enforce the law and try 'over mighty subjects'.
6. The majority of people wanted peace rather than further disruption.

Throughout the early part of 1487 Henry received intelligence of events in Ireland and Burgundy although it must often have been vague and conflicting. However, thanks to existing plans to assemble an army to invade Ireland he was able to respond speedily and had begun **mustering** his troops as early as February. On the 5 June 1487, Henry left Kenilworth Castle in the Midlands, heading north.

**mustering**
Sending out orders for soldiers to assemble

It seems likely that the lack of English support led Lincoln to change his campaign plans. He seemingly believed his only chance of success was one swift decisive battle and he turned the rebel army south towards Newark. By 15 June the rebels had reached Newark and made camp near the little village of East Stoke. In the evening the royal army of 12,000 set up camp ten miles from the rebels. Both sides knew there would be a battle the next day.

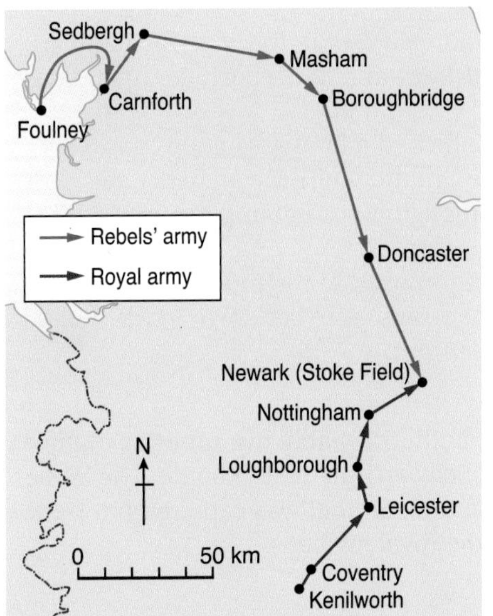
Sedbergh
Masham
Boroughbridge
Carnforth
Foulney
Rebels' army
Royal army
Doncaster
Newark (Stoke Field)
Nottingham
N
Loughborough
Leicester
0
50 km
Coventry
Kenilworth

◁ **The route of the two armies to Stoke Field.**

## The escalation of Lambert Simnel's rebellion

There are few detailed accounts of the Battle of Stoke in existence but the timeline below represents what most historians think happened. It seems clear that despite the superiority of the King's forces there were times during the three hours of hand-to-hand fighting when the outcome seemed to hang in the balance. In addition, the presence of Henry added a further worry. If the King was killed in battle, as had happened at Bosworth, then victory would go to his opponents.

### A likely reconstruction of the Battle of Stoke Field

By about 9a.m. on the morning of 16 June the two armies were drawn up on opposing sides of a ridge just beyond the Fosse Way. The royal army with its standards, banners and armour would have been an intimidating sight.

The rebel army, was possibly split into the three contingents of the Irish under Kildare, the German mercenaries led by Schwarz and the English commanded by Lovell, Lincoln and Broughton, and almost certainly had the advantage of higher ground near Burnham Furlong.

The fighting started when the vanguard of the king, 6000 of Henry's best troops under the Earl of Oxford, advanced slowly releasing a hail of deadly arrows from their longbows while remaining out of range of the rebels' response. The casualties were very high, particularly amongst the unprotected Irish.

The rebels gave up the advantage of higher ground and charged down the slope rather than remain as sitting targets.

For the next three hours the two armies engaged in savage, hand-to-hand fighting. The German mercenaries were particularly formidable. Henry VII was watching anxiously from a safe vantage point and Michael Bennett believes; 'His main fear was that Lincoln had an understanding with some of the lords and knights in the royal host, and that at a crucial juncture sections might either defect or simply withhold their support'. Time however was on the King's side.

The sheer weight of numbers eventually began to swing the battle in favour of Henry as Oxford's vanguard began to push back the main body of the rebel force.

At about 11a.m the royal army launched a final assault on those rebels who had regrouped on higher ground while the archers and cavalry picked off any stragglers, although fierce fighting continued for another hour.

Somewhere around midday, Henry moved to the top of Burnham Furlong to claim victory. Many of the rebels were cut down in the Red Gutter, trying to flee across the River Trent.

Source materials for Lambert Simnel and the Battle of Stoke are very few and are limited. The main account of the battle by Polydere Vergil was written twenty five years later and represents the official government view. Why do you think this is the case? What does this tell you about the extent of Simnel's threat and Henry's reaction to it?

At least 6000 men were killed in the battle, probably five times as many as at Bosworth. Lincoln, Fitzgerald and Schwartz all died in battle. The bodies of Lovell and Broughton were never found. Simnel was captured but Henry spared him and put him to work in the royal kitchens.

## How threatening was Lambert Simnel's rebellion?

The leadership of the rebellion appeaed strong. Although the nominal leader, Lambert Simnel, was clearly an imposter, he nevertheless provided a figurehead for York interests who were ready to manipulate him. The presence of Lord Lovell, and more particularly, the Earl of Lincoln, at the head of the rebellion brought to it the status which Simnel lacked. David Beeston in *Henry VII and the Lambert Simnel Conspiracy* (1987) suggests that Lincoln's defection meant that: 'The rebels now had the support of an authentic claimant to the throne, who would give even greater credibility to the pretender Simnel'.

However, despite Henry's fears of wider noble involvement, Lincoln and Lovell were the only noblemen to support this rebellion. The rebels also failed to recruit large numbers of gentry. The leadership of the rebellion was therefore limited in numbers and power despite Lincoln's presence.

The aim of the rebellion had the advantage of clarity as it was a dynastic rebellion aiming to overthrow Henry VII. The rebels may have intended to rule the country through their puppet, Lambert Simnel posing as the Earl of Warwick, or for a surviving member of the York family such as Warwick or Lincoln to take the throne. Either way the result would be the same, the restoration of the York monarchy. However, to many, this aim must only have promised more upheaval and uncertainty, creating the likelihood of further warfare. The quantity of support for Henry, even though he had been on the throne for less than two years, suggests that further disruption was not what the nobles and gentry wanted.

The strategy of the rebel leaders was to land their forces in the north-west, march south gaining as much support as possible and then march on London. Unlike many of the rebellions which you will read about in later chapters, this one anticipated the use of force and bloodshed with no negotiations. When the likelihood of a successful march on London faded, the idea was replaced by the decision to engage the King in a pitched battle from which only one victor would emerge. To the rebel leaders it must have appeared a realistic plan.

This failure to attract widespread English support meant that the bulk of the rebel forces consisted of foreign military help. The 2000 German mercenaries, provided by Margaret of Burgundy, were commanded by Colonel Martin Schwartz, a former mercenary who had earned a reputation for boldness in wars in the Netherlands and was now in the service of the Holy Roman Emperor, Maximilian. The Earl of Kildare provided between 4000 and 6000 Irishmen. Although lacking experience and body armour, and armed mainly with Gaelic daggers, these troops were enthusiastic and eager to see action. Support from England came from Sir Thomas Broughton, with a small company of

1521

△ **This engraving, thought to be from the sixteenth century, gives an idea of what Irish soldiers and peasants would have looked like as they marched through the north of England in 1487.**

former supporters of Richard III, but overall fewer than 1000 Englishmen joined the rebellion. The rebel army probably added up to about 8000 (more than Henry VII had at Bosworth), but it was lacking in cavalry, archers and a cannon. Henry's army, by contrast, may have contained as many as 15,000 men as nobility and gentry showed their loyalty to the King.

The response of Henry to the news of Lambert Simnel's rebellion was immediate. There was no attempt at negotiations or offers of deals. Like the rebel leaders, Henry knew this rebellion would end in violence unless the rebels fled. While Lincoln and Lovell were still in the Netherlands Henry sent out the musters to raise the royal army. He appointed his uncle, Jasper Tudor, Earl of Bedford, and the Earl of Oxford as his leading generals. Both men had been with him in exile in Brittany and had fought at Bosworth. The majority of the English nobility and gentry, including former Yorkists, showed their loyalty to the King and joined him, rather than the rebels, as he marched north. Henry's preparations were timely. The royal army outnumbered the rebels at the Battle of Stoke but the outcome was never a foregone conclusion. Certainly Henry never regarded it as such as he did not know, until very late in the course of events, the extent of support for the invaders nor could he have forgotten how close the outcome at Bosworth had been.

Contemporaries and historians have tended to undervalue this rebellion by focusing on the unlikely person of Lambert Simnel and comparing his threat unfavourably with that posed by Perkin Warbeck which, in part, seems more threatening because of its longevity. More recent analysis however, has stressed the fact that, like other kings of the fifteenth century, Henry could have lost both his throne and life on the battlefield. To quote Michael Bennett again:

> However, it was later viewed, the rising of 1487 was, at the time, taken very seriously indeed. For three months, from the middle of February to the middle of May, the conspiracy and the threatened invasion were the main pre-occupation of Henry and his government. For the best part of the following month the King was in harness and the nation was in arms. Even after the enemy army had been annihilated at Stoke, there was no immediate respite. Throughout the long summer the King moved through areas of possible disaffection.

■ Complete a 'threat chart' (see page 12) to evaluate the threat from Lambert Simnel's rebellion. Make notes to justify your grading of the threat according to each of the six criteria.

# Introducing Perkin Warbeck's rebellion, 1490–99

Henry VII did not have to wait long before his throne was again threatened by dynastic rebellion with another young man plucked from obscurity to pose as a Yorkist prince and claim the crown of England. In his later confession Perkin Warbeck stated that he was born in Tournai and as a youth had travelled in Europe as an apprentice in the silk trade. On his arrival in Cork, Ireland in 1491 he said he was firstly mistaken for the Earl of Warwick and then for Richard of York, the younger of the two Princes in the Tower.

Like Simnel, Warbeck was taken in hand by a Yorkist sympathiser, this time one John Taylor, and tutored to impersonate a prince of the House of York. Taylor had been a yeoman in the households of both Edward IV and Richard III. Five years after Bosworth, many former Yorkists were now in the service of the King but Taylor had been unable to work for Henry VII and had seen his former post given to another. Taylor devoted himself to turning Warbeck into Richard of York. Warbeck was a good actor and made a plausible royal prince. He had the additional advantage that since Richard of York had disappeared after entering the Tower of London in 1483, Henry could not display him in the streets of London.

Taylor's plan was for his claimant to attract enough English and foreign support to overthrow Henry and restore the House of York. The map on pages 28–29 shows Warbeck's attempts to raise foreign support and his three subsequent failed invasions of England. He did attract some Englishmen to his cause who moved round Europe with him but, as you will see, Warbeck's rebellion was always weakened by a lack of support from nobles and gentry. However, in 1495 when he did finally receive military support from Maximilian I, the **Holy Roman Emperor**, and had the potential to link up with scheming nobles in Henry's household, Henry moved too quickly for him and Warbeck failed to capitalise on the opportunities. His landing in Cornwall two years later was similarly disastrous.

The **Holy Roman Emperor** ruled a collection of states stretching over most of central Europe and comprising about 20 million subjects. Maximilian, King of the Romans, and head of the House of Habsburg, became Emperor in 1493 and was therefore a force to be reckoned with, particularly as he had acquired the lands of Burgundy (the Netherlands) through marriage.

◁ A sketch of Perkin Warbeck who was said to resemble Richard, Duke of York and his father, Edward IV.

## The escalation of Perkin Warbeck's rebellion

**1** In 1491 Warbeck started his campaign to gather popular support, like Simnel, in Ireland where the Fitzgeralds could usually be relied upon to welcome opponents of the King of England. This time however the Irish lords concluded they had more to gain from continuing to work with Henry. Warbeck was popular with the ordinary people of Cork but it was military support from the ruling classes that he needed.

**2** Warbeck next travelled to France, in 1492, to try to get some foreign support. At first he was welcomed as a prince by King Charles VIII who saw an opportunity to put pressure on Henry, as the two Kings were in conflict over the future of Brittany. Once Charles and Henry had settled their differences however, France refused to give any support to Warbeck.

**3** After the Treaty of Etaples was signed between England and France in 1492, Warbeck and Taylor were forced to flee to the Netherlands. Warbeck's arrival at the court of Margaret of Burgundy provided a much needed boost. Margaret treated Warbeck as her nephew, Richard of York, and therefore increased the seriousness of his threat to Henry. More importantly both Margaret and the Holy Roman Emperor, Maximilian, provided Warbeck with the military support which was so essential for his success.

N
SCOTLAND
6
IRELAND
Waterford
5, 7
1
Cork
Cornwall
8
0 100 km

**Philip** of Burgundy was the son of Maximilian I, the Holy Roman Emperor. In 1482 he inherited the Duchy of Burgundy/Netherlands from his mother Mary of Burgundy (daughter of Charles the Bold) but he pre-deceased his father.

**4** In July 1495 Warbeck's force of fifteen ships set sail from the Netherlands. His military operation was planned and led by a Flemish contingent under the command of experienced captains from the armies of Maximilian and **Philip**.

The leadership of the English force is less clear but it was probably led by Sir Richard Harleston who had commanded forces under Edward IV. The plan was to land in East Anglia and meet up with English supporters. Some of Henry's own household, as you will see on page 31, had already been plotting with Warbeck but Henry had learnt of this and dealt with the ringleaders. The rebels were also unlucky in that the weather ensured that the force came ashore at Deal on the better protected Kent coastline instead of East Anglia as planned. Although the commanders suspected a trap, the landing party was tricked by Henry's forces. One hundred and fifty rebels were cut down by a hail of arrows as they waded ashore. Warbeck and his commanders fled from the carnage. Their ships were driven by the prevailing winds to Ireland.

NETHERLANDS
3
Deal
4
2
Paris
FRANCE

**5** After unsuccessfully laying siege to Waterford for a month, the rebels were driven off by Sir Edward Poynings. Although at this stage the rebellion seemed to be lacking any strategic planning, the decision to set sail for Scotland marked the beginning of its most serious phase.

**6** James IV, the new and ambitious King of Scotland, was keen to prove himself against his more powerful neighbour. He proclaimed Warbeck as Prince Richard of England and in January 1496 married him to one of his relatives. He also provided Warbeck with 1500 troops. This potentially crucial foreign support meant Henry was now faced with a hostile army on his northern border. In September 1496 Warbeck invaded England for a second time, this time riding with the army of the King of Scotland. They received no support from the English however and they soon retreated back across the border.

**7** In July 1497 as James IV and Henry signed the Truce of Ayton, Warbeck was forced to leave Scotland and returned to Waterford for two months.

**8** In September 1497 Warbeck and Taylor now planned to capitalise on the rebellion against taxation in Cornwall. This might have worked three months earlier. However, the King had had a victory over the Cornish rebels at Blackheath in June which resulted in the collapse of the already limited noble and gentry support for the Cornish rebels. Warbeck's own force, numbering 1500 men when he left Flanders, had dwindled to about 300 and no longer included the Flemish commanders. Warbeck gained support from about 6000 aggrieved Cornish, largely farmers and miners, but rather than wait to see if any noble support was forthcoming, Warbeck showed poor tactical judgement by trying to capture the now heavily defended towns of Exeter and Taunton. He finally abandoned his supporters and claimed sanctuary in Beaulieu Abbey. He was persuaded to give himself up and was brought before Henry at the beginning of October 1497.

## How threatening was Perkin Warbeck's rebellion?

It is possible to regard Perkin Warbeck as a far greater threat to Henry VII than Lambert Simnel had been. Sean Cunningham in *Henry VII* (2007) describes his rebellion as:

> ... one of the most protracted and dangerous conspiracies faced by an English monarch ... [an] almost catastrophic challenge to the King. ... Warbeck's credibility was perceived as genuine by enough influential people to shake the foundations of the Tudor regime.

Aged 25, Warbeck was significantly older than Simnel when he invaded England, looked more the part of a Yorkist prince and was more likely to take decisions independently of his Yorkist backers. Unlike Simnel's rising however, this rebellion did not have the leadership of a noble such as the Earl of Lincoln, and therefore lacked presence and influence at its head. Therefore the need to raise foreign military support with experienced commanders was even more essential.

The origins of Warbeck's rebellion are vague but it is likely that Margaret of Burgundy was central and aimed to restore a Yorkist heir to the throne even if this was at the expense of her niece, Elizabeth of York, Henry VII's queen. According to Warbeck's confession, the conspirators, including Taylor, said they were guaranteed support from the Irish lords, Desmond and Kildare, and would attract international support, particularly from France whose agents were in touch with Yorkist dissidents. Ian Arthurson, in *The Perkin Warbeck Conspiracy* (1994), believes 'what John Taylor wanted to promote was an English rising on behalf of Edward, Earl of Warwick' leading to 'a French-backed version of the Stoke invasion complete with Irish rising, important past political figures and another pretender'. As with other elite conspiracies the aim was the capture of the King or his death in battle. However, Warbeck's rebellion never came close to challenging Henry on the battlefield.

Warbeck never gained widespread or even significant localised support in England. Sean Cunningham states that:

> ... overwhelming evidence was needed if the groups targeted by plotters were to be pushed into treason. Those on the cusp of rebellion shared the King's urgent search for the hard facts of Warbeck's identity.

He did attract Irish interest, although less than expected and largely confined to the town of Cork. Those Englishmen who joined him abroad were disaffected supporters of Richard III, merchants unhappy at trade embargos with Flanders and renegade Scottish, Irish and Flemish adventurers. In 1492 they numbered only about 100. For the rebels to succeed, their invasion from across the channel needed to join forces with allies in England and to this end correspondence was exchanged between Warbeck and two powerful English nobles, Lord Fitzwalter, steward of the royal household, and Sir William Stanley, Henry's step-uncle and Lord Chamberlain. They co-ordinated a miscellaneous group, united only by growing frustration at what they saw as a lack of their due rewards for serving Henry. Henry soon learned of this conspiracy within his own household and took appropriate action before Warbeck landed in 1495. The conspiracy is a timely reminder that there were still some men of status near to Henry who believed that the King was vulnerable although subsequent events were to prove otherwise. When Warbeck landed in Cornwall in 1497 he attracted support from about 6000 miners, farmers and artisans but not from nobles or gentlemen and the reason for their support was a set of quite different grievances (see page 33).

All four of Warbeck's military campaigns were failures. In 1495 he walked into a trap at Deal where his followers were dispatched with ease by the King's forces. In Ireland his force of several thousand was unable to capture Waterford or maintain a siege for more than eleven days. In 1496 his invasion of England from Scotland lasted only two days. Finally, in 1497, his poorly-armed followers in Cornwall were unable to capture Exeter and faded away at the sight of the royal army. None of Warbeck's expeditions did more than 'puncture the outer defences of the Tudor state' and perhaps even this is an exaggeration.

The main danger to Henry came from the international situation. At times Henry's relations with France and Scotland were poor and both countries used Warbeck to put diplomatic pressure on the English King. However, Henry's signing of The Treaty of Etaples with Charles VIII in 1492 ended French support for the rebels. Despite Henry's trade embargo with the Netherlands, Warbeck did receive some military support from Margaret of Burgundy and the Holy Roman Emperor. The force that invaded England in 1495 was led by Rodigue de Lalaing, a Count of the Holy Roman Empire, who had fought for Maximilian. Scotland provided military aid of 1500 troops and King James rode alongside Warbeck when he crossed the border in 1496. Such foreign support made Warbeck's attempted invasions possible and prolonged his threat, but lack of support within England meant he never posed a serious threat to Henry.

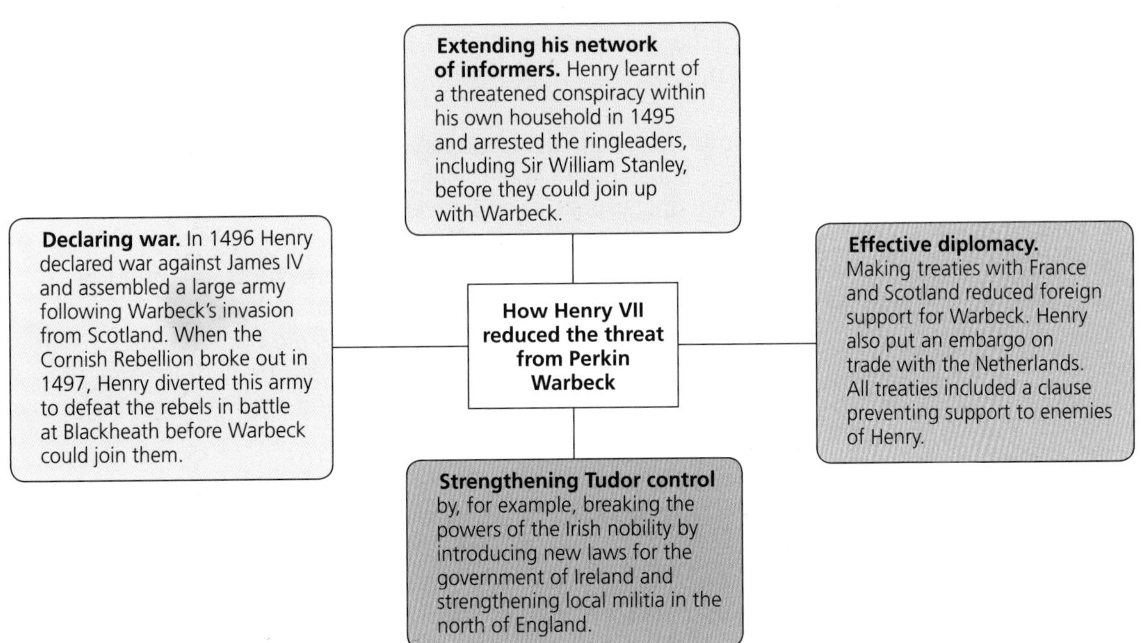
How Henry VII reduced the threat from Perkin Warbeck
**Extending his network of informers.** Henry learnt of a threatened conspiracy within his own household in 1495 and arrested the ringleaders, including Sir William Stanley, before they could join up with Warbeck.
**Declaring war.** In 1496 Henry declared war against James IV and assembled a large army following Warbeck's invasion from Scotland. When the Cornish Rebellion broke out in 1497, Henry diverted this army to defeat the rebels in battle at Blackheath before Warbeck could join them.
**Effective diplomacy.** Making treaties with France and Scotland reduced foreign support for Warbeck. Henry also put an embargo on trade with the Netherlands. All treaties included a clause preventing support to enemies of Henry.
**Strengthening Tudor control** by, for example, breaking the powers of the Irish nobility by introducing new laws for the government of Ireland and strengthening local militia in the north of England.

Complete a 'threat chart' (see page 12) to evaluate the threat from Warbeck's rebellion. Make notes to justify your grading of the threat according to each of the six criteria. Would your answer have been the same if this was 1493?

Henry always kept one step ahead of Warbeck and this helps to explain why the rebellion did not escalate into a greater threat. The chief strategies Henry used are shown in the diagram on page 31.

After his failure in Cornwall in 1497, Warbeck gave himself up and was imprisoned in the Tower of London. His rebellion had lasted far longer than Simnel's and had more foreign recognition but it never succeeded in forcing Henry into battle so ultimately providing a weaker challenge to the King. This of course is easy to state with the luxury of hindsight. Henry did not know if people would be convinced by Warbeck's claims; whether there would be support in England to enable a fully-fledged Yorkist challenge to the throne, or the extent of armed forces from abroad. Henry was vulnerable, and knew it, particularly at the beginning of Warbeck's decade. Even with Warbeck's imprisonment however, Henry was still unable to relax. There were constant rumours of a plot within the Tower to free both Warbeck and the Earl of Warwick. Meanwhile the Earl of Suffolk, who like Warwick had a claim to the throne, had fled from England to join Philip and his step-mother, Margaret of Burgundy. Again Henry's reaction was swift. Both Warbeck and Warwick were executed for treason. Suffolk was secured from Philip and, although Henry VII spared his life and imprisoned him, in 1513 Henry VIII ordered the execution of this surviving nephew of Edward IV.

## Introducing the rebellions of 1489 and 1497

Rebellions against the Tudors before 1530 were not only driven by dynastic motives. Those of 1489 and 1497 had economic causes although this did not mean they were equally threatening or saw similar outcomes. In *Riot, Rebellion and Popular Politics in Early Modern England* (2002), Andy Wood states:

> The most prominent cause of rebellion in pre-Reformation Tudor England was taxation ... whereas the rebellion of 1489 involved relatively little violence, rebellion in 1497 ended with significant bloodshed.

Did economic motives make these rebellions more or less threatening than dynastic rebellions? Alison Wall is clear that this kind of rebellion aimed to overthrow unpopular policies and advisers rather than the monarch.

> (This) kind of revolt arose when economic pressures seemed too great, when additional burdens – tax demands for war ... – became too hard for some to endure. These protests did not seek to overthrow the regime ... These were the most obedient in tone, the rioters claiming loyalty to the state and 'aimed at reversing a single policy'.

Unlike the dynastic rebellions, these rebellions had no military support from foreign powers and no pre-planned campaign other than presenting the rebels' grievances to the monarch.

However, the problem for Henry VII was the context in which these rebellions occurred. The Yorkshire Rebellion of 1489 was still early in his reign when anxiety about elite conspiracies continued. The fact that Yorkshire was the power base of Richard III only added to the government's fears. The Cornish Rebellion of 1497 came in the midst of the threat from Perkin Warbeck. This may well have appeared to increase the likelihood of each rebellion gaining more widespread support. In addition their outbreak in the distant regions of Yorkshire and Cornwall meant that the distance from London delayed both hearing about the rebellions and dealing with them.

## The events of the rebellions

The first of these economic rebellions broke out in Yorkshire in 1489. The King's officer, the Earl of Northumberland, had been sent to collect the new **Subsidy Tax**, approved by parliament to finance the war against France. Northumberland was murdered, probably by Sir John Egremont, when he went to investigate a disturbance. There is no evidence to prove that this started as anything more than a protest against taxes led by local gentry and it never escalated beyond the gathering of large crowds following the murder of Northumberland. Yorkshire was a poor county and had recently suffered bad harvests. The people resented this additional tax being imposed, particularly when their security did not seem to be at risk from the French. The intensity of Henry's reaction however suggests that he was worried that Egremont's known sympathies for Richard III's cause meant that this was another attempt to dethrone him rather than genuine popular anger about taxation. His anxiety is shown by the large army he sent north under the Earl of Surrey. Unsurprisingly the rebels rapidly dispersed. This was not the case however with the rebellion that broke out in May 1497.

Subsidy Tax
A tax of a fixed amount on land or goods granted by parliament to increase the value of the crown's standard source of taxation, the tenth and fifteenth, whereby towns represented in parliament paid a tenth on their landed property and the rest paid a fifteenth

In 1497 Cornwall was fiercely independent with its own language and parliament, the Stannary, but was also a poor county. The people of Cornwall, like those in Yorkshire, resented paying a new tax for an issue which had little to do with them, this time the defence of the north of England against an invasion from Warbeck and the Scottish King. However, because this rebellion was caused by and therefore coincided with Warbeck's rebellion it appeared to have the potential to be bigger and more serious than the one in Yorkshire. The rebellion was led by Lord Audley, a local lawyer called Thomas Flamank, and the physically imposing Michael the Blacksmith. Between them they had no problem in whipping up local support before setting off on an extraordinary march across England to London. The rebels' force as they approached London was bigger than the hastily diverted royal army

▽ This plaque on the north side of Blackheath is a memorial, in Cornish and English, to the leaders of the 1497 Cornish Rebellion.

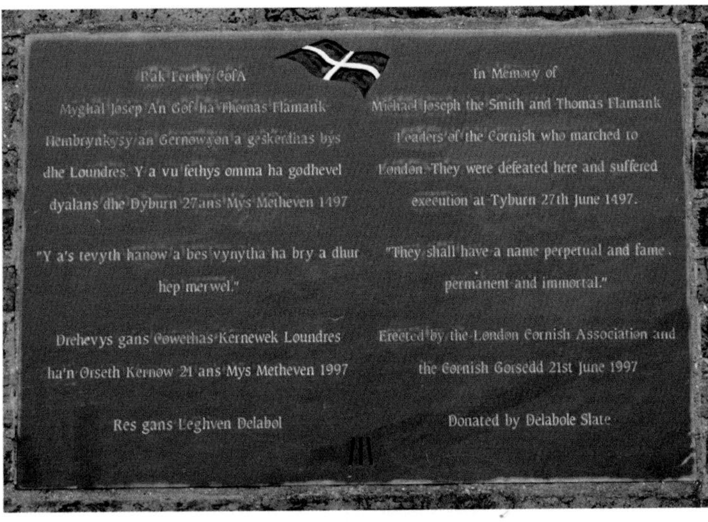
In Memory of
Michael Joseph the Smith and Thomas Flamank
Leaders of the Cornish who marched to
London. They were defeated here and suffered
execution at Tyburn 27th June 1497.
"Y a's tevyth hanow a bes vynytha ha bry a dhur
hep merwel."
"They shall have a name perpetual and fame
permanent and immortal."
Drehevys gans Cowethas Kernewek Loundres
ha'n Orseth Kernow 21 ans Mys Metheven 1997
Erected by the London Cornish Association and
the Cornish Gorsedd 21st June 1997
Res gans Leghven Delabol
Donated by Delabole Slate

under Lord Daubeney. The leaders reiterated their complaints against the King's 'evil counsellors', Morton and Bray, who they blamed for the taxes. The King played for time so that reinforcements could arrive. At this point however, support for the rebels began to collapse as many men deserted to return to Cornwall. Some were disappointed by the lack of support from Kent, which had been the focus of rebellion in 1381 and 1450, while others never intended to take up arms against the King. When the two sides met at Blackheath Henry's army numbered about 25,000 men. The cavalry and archers made short work of the rebels whose losses were about 1000. Lord Audley and the two local leaders were executed.

## The escalation of the Cornish Rebellion, 1497

**1** Rebellion broke out in Penryn, west Cornwall in May 1497.

**2** Led by Michael the Blacksmith and Flamank the Lawyer the rebels reached Exeter by the end of May.

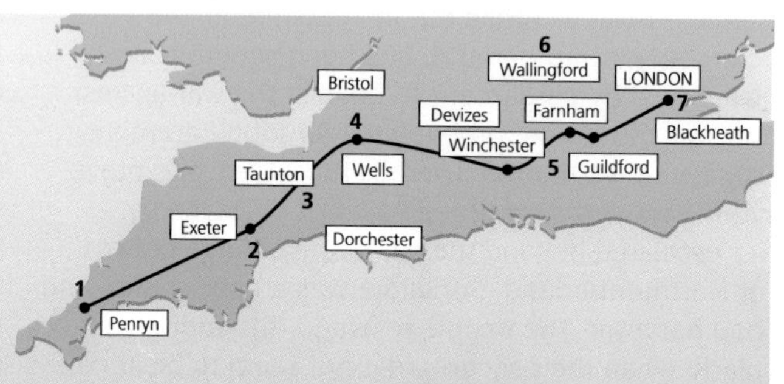

6
Wallingford
LONDON
Bristol
4
Devizes
Farnham
7
Blackheath
Winchester
Taunton
Wells
5
Guildford
3
Exeter
Dorchester
2
1
Penryn


**7** The two sides met on 14 June at Blackheath.

**6** Henry moved to Wallingford and sent for reinforcements.

**3** The rebels crossed Devon and at Taunton were joined by Lord Audley. There was unrest in Devizes, Dorchester and Winchester.

**4** The rebels entered Wells at the beginning of June. Support was declared in Bath and Bristol.

**5** The main body of the rebels, now estimated at between 15,000 to 40,000 marched on London via Winchester, Farnham and Guildford.

## How threatening was the Cornish Rebellion?

The two Cornish leaders, Michael the Blacksmith and the lawyer Thomas Flamank, the son of a gentleman, were quickly joined by local gentry and clergy. In Taunton they acquired the support of the noble who would become their leader, Lord Audley, who was an experienced soldier. He brought in other gentry from south-western counties who were angry at Henry for excluding them from local rewards while over-rewarding other local men such as Daubeney who'd been with Henry in exile before he became king. The leadership was small and localised but encapsulated all social classes and showed skill and determination in leading the rebellion out of Cornwall.

The leaders' stated aim was to present the rebels' grievances over the tax levy to the King. Later rebellions which aimed for redress of grievances usually built up local support, often capturing a key town, and awaited the arrival of royal officers to begin negotiations. However, the Cornish rebels at some point decided to march on London. This gave Henry VII the chance to claim in his proclamations that the rebels sought to overthrow him and cause insurrection throughout the land. Henry's claims have tended to be seen as propaganda to justify the harsh repression of defeated rebels but it is worth remembering that Perkin Warbeck was still at large and the Earl of Warwick still alive in the Tower of London.

The rebellion did not attract much support from neighbouring Devon but once the rebels arrived in Somerset they were joined by a wide cross-section of the local population. This broad support shows a united opposition to royal policies which was absent in the other rebellions. Divisions amongst the local gentry also gave the rebels a chance to reach London. These men should have stopped the rebels but failed to do so. The rebel force had swelled to 15,000 by June, although some estimates are as high as 40,000. The size and speed of the rebellion shocked Henry and his government.

Having issued their proclamation of grievances and marched across the south of England unopposed, the rebel leaders were no nearer gaining any concessions from the King. Presumably at some point they realised that their only choices now were to retreat or risk military action. Many did return to Cornwall, showing that their intention had never been to challenge the King. Others were persuaded by Flamank that in order to put more pressure on Henry they should try to raise support in Kent. When this appeal failed the remaining rebels resigned themselves to meeting the King in battle. A force of between 9000 and 10,000 left Guildford and set up camp at Blackheath near London.

The success of the rebels' tactics caught Henry exposed and unawares in London having dispatched the bulk of his forces to the north. He was pre-occupied with Warbeck and the threat from Scotland and expected that the Cornish rebels would be easily dealt with by local leading families. This lack of speedy reaction from the King and his officials made the rebellion appear to be a greater threat than would otherwise have been the case. Nevertheless the recalled royal army of 25,000 that faced the Cornish on 17 June heavily outnumbered them. The Cornish also lacked both cavalry and artillery. This time Henry was determined that there would not be a three-hour contest with the verdict hanging in the balance. Unlike his successors, Henry did not negotiate with, or make concessions to, rebels. All protests were dealt with in the same way regardless of what 'type' of rebellion they may have been or how threatening they were. It is worth noting however that, despite their defeats, both the rebellions of 1489 and 1497 against Henry's taxation demands were successful in that the taxes were not collected from either Yorkshire or Cornwall.

■ Complete 'threat charts' (see page 12) to evaluate the threat from the Yorkshire Rebellion and the Cornish Rebellion. Make notes to justify your grading of the threats according to each of the six criteria.

## The Amicable Grant Rising of 1525

We now need to move forward nearly 20 years. By 1525 Henry VIII had been king for 16 years but, like his father in 1489 and 1497, was about to face a rebellion against a new tax intended to raise money for an unpopular military campaign. Henry was eager to invade France (as he had done in 1513) and saw his chance as the French King was fighting in Italy. Henry ordered his chief minister, Cardinal Wolsey, to raise the money to fund this invasion. Wolsey had already collected £260,000 through a **Forced Loan** in 1522 and a Subsidy Tax that had been approved by parliament as recently as 1523 was still being collected. Wolsey's new Amicable Grant imposed a tax of one third and one sixth respectively on the annual revenue or goods (whichever was the greater) of the clergy and laity, with the poor charged proportionately less. The Grant was unpopular from the start with both clergy and gentry, usually supporters of the

**Forced Loan**
This was raised by putting pressure on richer subjects in times of emergency but not always fully repaid by the monarch

CARDINAL

◁ Wolsey graduated from Oxford University before entering the Church and becoming Henry VII's chaplain. Under Henry VIII, Wolsey had a meteoric rise joining the King's Council in 1510, becoming Archbishop of York in 1514, and Cardinal and Lord Chancellor in 1515. Although he had to back down over the Amicable Grant, he served Henry effectively as his chief minister until the King asked Wolsey to secure him a divorce from Catherine of Aragon which led to Wolsey's fall from power and his death.

government, claiming they could not raise the money. Severe resistance in Warwickshire, particularly from the gentry, resulted in the government exempting that county from payment. In April, Wolsey announced to the council that instead of the fixed rate he would ask people to pay what they could afford. This had the effect of strengthening resistance.

Discontent came to a head when the Dukes of Norfolk and Suffolk tried to collect the Grant in Suffolk and Essex. This area was already suffering economically through a drop in the price of wool and was still struggling to pay the Subsidy Tax. A gathering of 4000 aggrieved cloth workers in Lavenham made rebellion a very real possibility. Unrest now spread over several counties and had support across social classes. The usually loyal citizens of London had recently announced that they too would not pay the Amicable Grant. Although the rising itself was not led by nobles, the two Dukes proved instrumental in mediating between the rebels and the government. The rebels always claimed to be loyal to the King and were reluctant to resort to violence but felt they were being pushed into poverty by Wolsey's demands. The Dukes took these grievances to the King and persuaded him of the need to act promptly to prevent outright rebellion.

■ Complete a 'threat chart' (see page 12) to evaluate the threat from the Amicable Grant Rising. Make notes to justify your grading of the threats according to each of the six criteria.

Henry VIII's response was to blame the Grant on Wolsey, cancel both the tax and his proposed invasion of France, and pardon the rebels. Henry thus emerged as the hero of the hour. This makes it difficult to assess the seriousness of the rebellion as it was never really allowed to develop. The royal reaction, however, and, more importantly, the fact that Henry retreated needs considering when you evaluate the extent of the threat.

## Concluding your enquiry

There were times before 1530 when both Henry VII and Henry VIII felt threatened by rebellion. Henry VII in particular never seems to have relaxed. He had taken the throne by force and therefore feared danger from similar attacks, those described by Alison Wall (see page 11) as 'real rebellions' in which the aim was to overthrow the ruler and replace him with another monarch.

However, none of the rebellions before 1530 received the degree of foreign support Henry had enjoyed in 1485. (It's interesting to note that even in 1485 foreign support had been short-lived – if Henry had delayed his invasion by a month then French support might have been withdrawn.) Henry was also greatly helped by the fact that almost all the nobles and gentry remained loyal to him. Unlike Richard III, who was suspected of killing the Princes in the Tower, he did nothing to provoke widespread outrage in his early years as king. In addition, nobles and gentry greatly preferred peace and stability to the risks created by warfare so there was little incentive for them to rebel. However, while that sounds as if Henry had little to fear, he did not know for certain that important nobles were not hoping to replace him with a descendant of the Yorkist kings.

As Christine Carpenter has argued in *The Wars of the Roses: Politics and the Constitution in England c.1437–1509* (1997), even as late as 1538 Henry VIII executed members of the Pole and Neville families:

> In the 1530s the Wars of the Roses were still going on in the mind of the King, as the last descendants of rival claimants were murdered by his orders.

Henry VIII's fears in the 1530s help us to understand the extent of Henry VII's anxieties 40 years earlier.

Other rebellions fit largely into Wall's category of 'obedient rebellions' where even the rebels proclaimed their loyalty to the King. However, for the Kings themselves, such divisions were not at all clear. Economic causes might well have led to the commons backing elite conspiracies or making them much more threatening, as appeared to be happening in 1497. This anxiety must have seemed justified to Henry VII given that on two occasions he had to take to the field of battle to put an end to rebellions.

## Concluding your enquiry

1. Review the six 'threat charts' and the notes you have made. Make sure they are complete and you have the evidence to justify your conclusions.
2. Compare the six 'threat charts'.
   **a)** Which of the criteria were most important in this period for increasing the level of threat from rebellions? Why was this?
   **b)** Which criteria do most to explain the failures of these rebellions to threaten the Tudor Kings?
3. Place each rebellion on your own version of the 'threat line' on page 13. This cannot be a precise choice and involves generalising about the degree of threat but it creates a general picture of the comparative threats posed by rebellions before 1530. Add brief annotations to give the major reasons for where you place each rebellion.
4. On page 19 a hypothesis was put forward suggesting that 'The Tudors were never seriously threatened by rebellions before 1530'. Write a short answer explaining whether your work supports or challenges this hypothesis. Make sure you identify the evidence that supports your view. You may also wish to discuss whether any of these rebellions achieved their aim without threatening the Tudor dynasty.

Insight

# Context: Religious reforms – the potential for rebellions

## How important was religion in the lives of the people of England in 1500?

During the reign of Henry VII no one would have expected religion to become a major cause of rebellion. The Church in England was a loyal part of the Roman Catholic Church headed by the Pope and had been for 900 years. Religion dominated the lives of the English people. They were expected to attend church on Sundays and holy days to hear Mass and to confess their sins to the priest who gave forgiveness. The majority seem to have done this. The Catholic service was in Latin but the sound of the words was familiar and reassuring. Services embraced all the senses from the smell of incense to the colours on the clergy's robes to the touch of Holy Water and taste of bread. Support for parish churches was high. Between 1490 and 1529 significant numbers of churches and chapels were built, funded by individuals' donations and bequests.

The Church added a welcome physical and spiritual richness to the often harsh lives of people in the sixteenth century. The cycle of Church festivals was closely entwined with village life. Harvest Festival was celebrated in church; **Michaelmas** heralded both the paying of rents and slaughtering of animals ahead of the winter months; people's behaviour in **Lent** was monitored by both Church and government officials; festivals such as Christmas and Easter occasioned celebrations and rituals which took over the village. All rites of passage were sanctioned by Church **sacraments** from baptisms to marriage to the last rites. After the death of a loved one their family and friends would intercede to speed the progress of an individual soul through **Purgatory**. As a result both **chantries** and religious guilds dedicated to a particular saint were extremely well supported, often through money left in wills, as they would organise prayers and Masses on behalf of the souls of the dead.

The Church was responsible for ensuring people led a good life to shorten time in Purgatory and make it more likely the soul would reach Heaven. Sins were confessed to the local priest and penances undertaken in atonement. Parishioners were expected to donate a tenth of their income or belongings to the Church and to pay dues, for example, for burials. There is a great deal of evidence from wills that people were deeply loyal to the Church and did leave money, not only to pay for Masses but also decorations such as windows and religious carvings and ornaments and for church building and improvements.

As preparation for Chapter 3 think about these questions:

1. Why was religion so important to individuals and communities?
2. Why might individuals and communities have felt threatened by religious changes under Henry VIII and Edward VI?
3. How do you think religious beliefs might have affected the aims, methods and support for rebellions after 1534?

**Michaelmas**
The Feast of St Michael the Archangel at the end of September. It represented the beginning of the 'autumn term' for law students and the start of preparations for the harvesting and storing of food for the winter

**Lent**
Forty days of fasting in the period before Easter, starting with Ash Wednesday

**sacraments**
The Catholic Church believes in seven sacraments: baptism, the Mass or communion service, confirmation, penance, marriage, ordination and the last rites, where the wording and rituals mean the participant receives God's blessing

**Purgatory**
Catholics believe that individual souls are judged upon death. Purgatory is a place of waiting for the souls of the dead who cannot be admitted to Heaven until they have undergone penance for their sins and become pure

**chantries**
Chapels in which Masses for the dead were said

# Henry VIII and the beginnings of religious change

## 1 State of the English Church and reformist ideas in Europe

△ Henry VIII.

Although the people of England were loyal to the Roman Catholic Church, that did not mean there was no criticism of it. In the fourteenth century John Wycliffe, whose followers became known as Lollards, had attacked the Catholic Church for losing sight of the scriptures and becoming too ritualistic. Although Lollards were persecuted by both Church and state and driven underground, their ideas played a role in the English Reformation of the sixteenth century. This too began with an individual criticising the state of the Catholic Church, this time in Germany. In 1517, a monk in Wittenberg, Martin Luther, nailed 95 Theses to the door of the cathedral, the usual way of instigating religious debates. Within a decade Luther's analysis of the faults and corruption within the Catholic Church attracted followers within Germany who became known as Protestants, whose ideas then spread along the trade routes across the North Sea to England. The number of Protestants in England was small but they had some influence through the positions they held in the universities, London and even the King's court and church. These early Protestants both drew influence from and emphasised their continuity with the Lollards. Even so, given the King's outspoken opposition to Luther's teachings, few people would have thought it possible that Henry would overthrow the Pope's authority in England.

## 2 Henry VIII and the need to secure the Tudor dynasty

△ Catherine of Aragon.

Henry VIII had succeeded his father in 1509 and raised hopes of a more dynamic and colourful reign. The familiar pictures of an overweight and overbearing middle-aged monarch show few signs of the vigour and excitement that the young King promised in 1509. The seventeen-year-old Henry was athletic, handsome, an accomplished horseman and gifted musician. As the younger brother, Henry had not expected to become king. It was Arthur who had been groomed since birth for this role, not least through his marriage to Catherine of Aragon. Yet five months after this wedding in 1502 Arthur was dead and his widow lined up for marriage to Henry, so reluctant was Henry VII to lose the alliance with Spain. A special dispensation was granted by the Pope to enable Catherine to marry her dead husband's brother and after his accession in 1509 she and Henry were married. All that was needed now was a male heir.

## 3 The King's 'Great Matter'

△ Anne Boleyn.

Catherine gave birth to a daughter, Mary, in 1516 but no other children survived beyond a few days. The lack of a son to succeed him was a serious blow to Henry who became increasingly obsessed with remedying the situation. It is probable that Anne Boleyn attracted Henry's attention around 1525 but she refused to become his mistress. The extent to which Henry's subsequent actions were due to his need for a son or his desire for Anne Boleyn remains debateable. Henry was increasingly worried by his conscience and convinced that his marriage to Catherine was against God's law and therefore cursed by a lack of male heirs. This was not just a convenience. Henry had already shown how important his Catholicism was and had been given the title Defender of the Faith by the Pope in 1521 for writing a book attacking Luther. Popes routinely agreed to royal divorces but special papal permission had been given for Henry to marry Catherine in the first place. Henry therefore decided to appeal to the current Pope against that ruling, citing a chapter in Leviticus which appeared to forbid a widow marrying her brother-in-law. Even in the late 1520s a split from Rome was unthinkable.

### 4 Thomas Wolsey and the King's divorce

The man entrusted with the job of securing Henry his divorce was his chief minister, Thomas Wolsey (see page 36). As a cardinal of the Church, Wolsey seemed well placed to go to Rome and plead Henry's cause but the circumstances of European politics conspired against him. The recent sack of Rome by the Emperor Charles V, nephew of Catherine of Aragon, meant that the Pope, Clement VII, was not in a position to grant an annulment. Instead Cardinal Campeggio was sent to London to conduct hearings at which Catherine gave evidence. By 1529 Henry had had enough. He dismissed Wolsey and began to put pressure on the Pope to speed up his divorce. This new strategy brought to the fore Thomas Cromwell, an inventive and determined man who'd been one of Wolsey's leading officials.

CARDINAL
WOLSEY

△ Thomas Wolsey

### 5 Thomas Cromwell and the Break with Rome

Although the Church in England was no more corrupt than elsewhere in Europe, it gave way under the King's demands and the growing opposition to the clergy's privileges held by some of the politically influential. Between 1531 and 1534 Cromwell steered nine acts through the House of Commons, as a result of which England broke away from the Roman Catholic Church. In 1534 Henry became Supreme Head of the newly established Church of England. His Archbishop of Canterbury, Thomas Cranmer, ruled against Henry's marriage to Catherine. Henry's marriage to a now pregnant Anne Boleyn was declared legal. The succession was altered to favour children of this marriage and a Treason Act passed to prevent opposition to these changes on pain of death.

△ Thomas Cromwell.

The religious revolution that had been unthinkable 30 or even 5 years earlier had taken place by 1534 much to the shock and surprise of the English people. How would they react? Would they put their loyalty to their religion before their loyalty to their king?

## The changing pattern of religious reform under Henry VIII and Edward VI

Religion had not been a cause of rebellions before Henry VIII's Break with Rome. However, once monarchs became head of the Church of England and introduced changes, they risked angering those of their subjects who feared that change was endangering their chances of reaching Heaven. The reforms of Henry VIII and Cromwell in 1534 were not the end of change. They were followed by:

1 **The Dissolution of the Monasteries 1536–39**

Under Henry VIII the new Church of England was not vastly different from its Catholic predecessor. For many people the greatest change came when Henry VIII attacked the monasteries mainly to secure their wealth. The best of the monasteries however provided charity, hospitality and even education as well as their spiritual function. Their loss was keenly felt in some communities particularly in the north.

2 **The advance of Protestantism – Edward VI's Reformation 1547–53**

Far greater religious change came in the reign of Henry VIII's son. The two Prayer Books, enforced by Edward VI, ordered the replacement of the Catholic Church services with Protestant ones said in English. The appearance of churches changed considerably as the colourful statues, shrines and wall paintings were replaced with bare whitewashed interiors. Traditions which people had held dear for centuries, particularly praying for the souls of the dead in chantries, were overturned in a couple of years causing many people real distress.

3 **The return to Catholicism under Queen Mary 1553–58**

The staunchly Catholic Queen Mary reunited England with Rome and introduced heresy laws which enabled the execution of Protestants who would not renounce their faith. This created a crisis of conscience for all those who believed in the new Protestant Church and wanted to remain loyal to Protestantism. About 284 people were ordered to be burnt at the stake, becoming known as the Marian Martyrs and earning the Queen the unshakeable nickname of 'Bloody Mary'.

4 **Back to the middle-ground? The Elizabethan Settlement 1558–1603**

Elizabeth established a Church of England which at first sight combined Catholic appearance and tradition with a form of service that was moderately Protestant. In fact the English Church was always more Protestant than it looked and Roman Catholics could not accept either the loss of the Pope's authority or the accession to the throne of Elizabeth whose mother (Anne Boleyn) had been the cause of the Break with Rome and thus, in their eyes, was not legally married to Henry. For all Elizabeth's attempts at moderation many people opposed her religious reforms.

After 1534 religion was a factor in nearly all the remaining Tudor rebellions. While some of the rebels saw the opportunity presented by religion to pursue worldly ambitions, there were many more who genuinely feared that these changes were preventing their souls from going to Heaven. Did this depth of motivation make the succeeding rebellions more threatening to the Tudors?

# 3 Did their religious motives make the rebels of 1536 and 1549 serious threats to the Tudors?

On the evening of Wednesday 4 October 1536 a young lawyer set out from his sister's house in East Yorkshire to make the journey to London for the start of the law term. He never arrived. Instead the lawyer, Robert Aske, embarked on a series of meetings that was to change the course of his life and transform local uprisings into a major rebellion – the Pilgrimage of Grace.

After leaving his sister's house, Aske and three of his nephews headed for the ferry to take them across the River Humber to get to the Great North Road and London. By the time they reached the opposite bank the ferryman had told them all the local gossip about an uprising in Lincolnshire. The group then headed south, intending to break their journey by spending the night with relatives. Before they could reach their destination they were stopped by a group of rebels. Their leader, one George Hudswell, demanded that the travellers swore an oath of loyalty to the King. (You'll find out how they could be both loyal and rebels later!) At this point Aske thought it best to return home but his way was blocked by rebels and so he spent the night with his relatives. The following morning he had further conversations with the rebels and accompanied them to their camp at Hambleton Hill, near Market Rasen, where he met the main leaders. After this Aske was allowed to return home but over the next few days he continued to cross the Humber into Lincolnshire to find out what was happening.

There was nothing in Aske's conventional background that suggests he would grow into a highly effective rebel leader. His family were typical Yorkshire gentry with landed estates near Aughton in the East Riding of Yorkshire and Robert was the third son. In 1527 he was admitted to the Inns of Court in London to train as a lawyer where he had a rigorous education designed to develop his intellectual abilities and debating skills.

It seems likely that Aske was drawn into the rebellion by deep sympathy with its aims and a belief that there were many people who were prepared to rebel but who lacked organisation and leadership. Religious changes in the north were central to the grievances he felt. Before the end of the month he had issued a proclamation calling upon every man to muster in order to 'preserve the Church of God from spoiling'. Aske was never to see London's Inns of Court again.

## Enquiry Focus: Did their religious motives make the rebels of 1536 and 1549 serious threats to the Tudors?

You learned in Chapter 2 that before 1530 the Tudors had faced two types of rebellions:

**a)** Henry VII faced serious dynastic rebellions with a royal figurehead and foreign forces but with little support from ordinary English people.

**b)** Henry VII and Henry VIII faced rebellions which enjoyed some popular and gentry support but no foreign aid. Unlike the dynastic rebellions these did not seek the overthrow of the monarch but were directed against new taxes and the ministers responsible for them.

The motives behind the rebellions of 1536 and 1549 were different, as witnessed by their names which reveal more than do rebellions called after people (Warbeck) or places (Cornish). The name of the 1536 rebellion – The Pilgrimage of Grace – shows straightaway the importance of religion. Here 'Grace' is used in its religious meaning and refers to the kindness and forgiveness, including the gift of eternal life, which God grants to mankind even though it may not be deserved. Not only did this rebellion have a religious title but all the rebels called themselves pilgrims, swore an oath of loyalty to 'God, the King and the commons', and marched behind religious banners and crosses. The 1549 rebellion is known as either the Western Rising or the Prayer Book Rebellion, the latter again a clear indicator of the importance of religion in its development.

These rebellions of 1536 and 1549 had something in common with the second group of earlier rebellions described above as they claimed loyalty to the state. However, Alison Wall sees these rebellions as more dangerous than those caused by economic grievances because they 'sought fundamental change, spurred by religious ideology that was opposed to that of governments. They tried to force the government to accept the views of the rebels, claiming legitimacy and a return to previous religion'. The religious rebels of 1536 and 1549 were fighting for their immortal souls and were convinced they were right and had God on their side. In an age when the monarch and the rule of law, now including divine law, were one and the same, the threat posed by these rebels cannot be underestimated because they also claimed to be loyal to the King.

This enquiry therefore asks you to evaluate the threat posed by each of these two rebellions and particularly whether the religious motives of the rebels made these rebellions more threatening.

1. Read the account of each rebellion and then complete a chart for each one, like the example on page 12, to assess the degree of threat.
2. Make separate clear notes to justify how you have graded the threat criteria for each rebellion.

At the end of this chapter use the completed charts and the 'threat line' activity on page 13 to reach your overall answer to the question. The evaluation at the end of each rebellion will provide further details to help you to develop your own analysis and reach a conclusion.

## The beginnings of rebellion – the Lincolnshire Rising

Now let's return to the story of the Pilgrimage of Grace that we began on page 42. Opposition to the policies of Thomas Cromwell had broken out in September 1536. Geoffrey Moorhouse in his book *The Pilgrimage of Grace* (2002) describes Cromwell as the 'most hated man in England' because he was the author of the legislation which established the Break with Rome and Henry as Supreme Head of the Church. He was appointed Vicegerent by the King in 1535, with powers to visit religious houses in England and Wales to determine their fate, and it was widely feared that Cromwell would use this power to attack church property to raise money for Henry's foreign policy. Initial protests in Louth in Lincolnshire began when local people believed their parish church was under threat. They took up arms against Cromwell's commissioners, imprisoning several of them, and encouraged insurrection throughout the area through the ringing of bells and lighting of beacons. The Louth rebels were quickly joined by local gentry with their followers and a force estimated at between 20,000 and 40,000 occupied Lincoln in October 1536. Here they drew up a list of grievances, though throughout they protested their loyalty to the King.

The speed and size of this rebellion meant it could not be dealt with by local forces, many of whom were sympathetic to the rebels anyway. When Henry promised to consider their petition if the rebels lay down their arms, they did so, returning to their homes before the royal army reached Lincoln. The Lincolnshire Rebellion, which had made such an impact on Robert Aske, had lasted only two weeks but was a blueprint for the far larger and more dangerous Pilgrimage of Grace which followed.

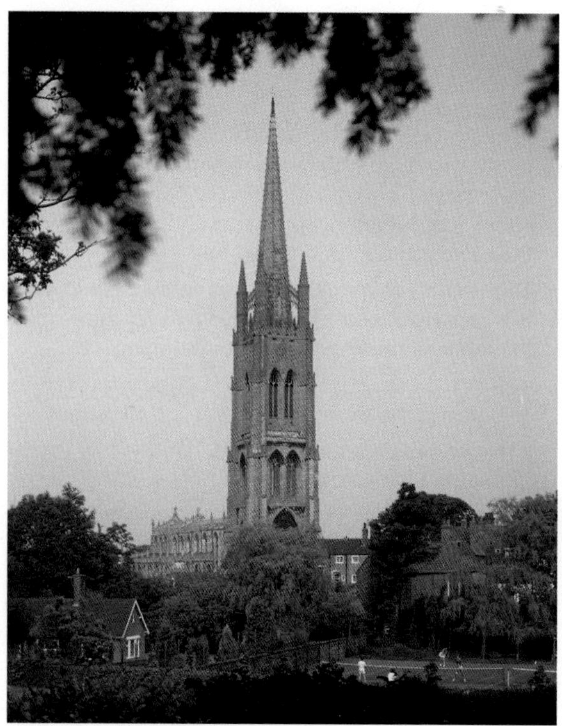

▷ The parish church of Louth in Lincolnshire, the starting point of the rebellions of 1536. As recently as 1515 great celebrations had marked the building of the church's new steeple but in 1536 the parish was engulfed in rumours of the cancellation of most holy days (people's holidays), of new taxes and of the confiscation of the church's treasures. All this was blamed on Thomas Cromwell and when one of his men arrived in Louth, anger turned to rioting and then into the Lincolnshire Rebellion.

## The Pilgrimage of Grace

The Pilgrimage gathered pace in the early weeks of October 1536 and lasted until 6 December. The focus of the rebellion moved from Lincolnshire to Yorkshire after 11 October but, as you can see from the map of the uprising on pages 46–47, there were rebel forces taking up arms across the north of England. The main force however was that raised by Robert Aske in Yorkshire, after his meeting with the Lincolnshire rebels that had both inspired him and changed his life. It was Aske who composed the oath all the pilgrims had to swear which called on them, out of their love for God and his Holy Church, to preserve the King's person by expelling from his Privy Council, evil and heretical advisers. By 16 October, Aske had marched his force of 10,000 rebels from Howden to the region's capital, York. By now Aske had drawn up the rebels' five main grievances in a document known as the York Articles which would be presented to the crown's representative. The aim of the pilgrims was to pressurise the government, through both the scale of their numbers and the implied threat of future violence, into remedying these grievances by reversing its policies.

In all, nine regional uprisings (see the map on pages 46–47) took place across the north of England in those first three weeks of October, led by nobles and gentry. Most, but not all, of these uprisings joined the main rebels' army giving Aske 30,000 well-armed men. By 21 October the rebels' army had taken control of Pontefract Castle, the major fortress in the north, which Lord Darcy surrendered to them.

### The main events of the Pilgrimage of Grace

This chronology box, together with the map on pages 46–47, provides an outline of the main events of the uprisings in October 1536 and some idea of their localised nature.

**1536**

| | |
|---|---|
| 1 October | Lincolnshire Rising began at Louth, Lincolnshire |
| 4–10 October | Robert Aske learned of the rising and began raising the force in Yorkshire that became the Pilgrimage of Grace |
| 11 October | 10,000 Lincolnshire rebels assembled at Lincoln but dispersed after the appearance of a government herald |
| 16 October | Aske led his force of about 10,000 to York. Over the next five days Aske articulated the rebels' grievances in the York Articles. He then directed all rebel forces to march to Pontefract. When Aske and his followers arrived there themselves they brought the number of rebels to about 40,000. |
| 21 October | Lord Darcy surrendered Pontefract Castle to the pilgrims |
| 27 October | A truce was signed after negotiations with the Duke of Norfolk |
| 4 December | Aske presented the Pontefract Articles to Norfolk. The rebels were pardoned |

**1537**

| | |
|---|---|
| 16 January | Bigod's Uprising gave Henry the chance to hunt down the rebels, execute the leaders and subdue the north over the following six months |

## The progress of the Pilgrimage of Grace

On the map and text boxes on these pages you can see the regional uprisings, which of them joined Aske's Pilgrimage of Grace and what the others did instead.

① On 8 October the main rebel force of about 10,000 under Robert Aske assembled at Howden before taking York.

② A second rebel force mustered at Beverley, under William Stapulton, a lawyer, before capturing Hull on 19 October. This force arrived in Pontefract on 22 October with between 2000 and 3000 men.

③ The North Riding also rose in the week of the 11 October, assembling at Richmond with Robert Bowes, a lawyer and member of the gentry, as their captain. Bowes sent out summons to Durham, Westmoreland and Cumberland and took St Cuthbert's banner from Durham as the Pilgrimage's flag. When they arrived in Pontefract, Bowes had between 4000 and 10,000 men.

④ Thomas Percy, the brother of the Earl of Northumberland, raised 5000 men at Seamer and arrived in Pontefract two days ahead of Aske.

⑤ On 21 October Aske moved the main force from York to Pontefract which Lord Darcy promptly surrendered. Aske was joined by most of the nine regional forces with their captains. By the end of October about 40,000 men had taken up arms against the King.

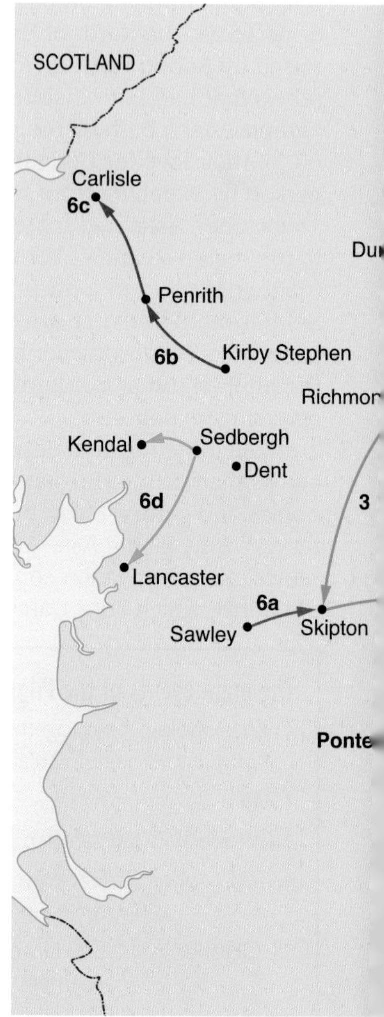

SCOTLAND
Carlisle
6c
Penrith
6b
Kirby Stephen
Richmon
Kendal
Sedbergh
Dent
6d
3
Lancaster
6a
Sawley
Skipton
Ponte
Du


Pilgrims or rebels? What should we call them? Most books call Aske and his followers 'rebels' although Aske always said he was not a rebel. To him they were 'pilgrims' who were loyal to the King so how could they be rebels? Today we would call such people protesters. What do you think they should be called?

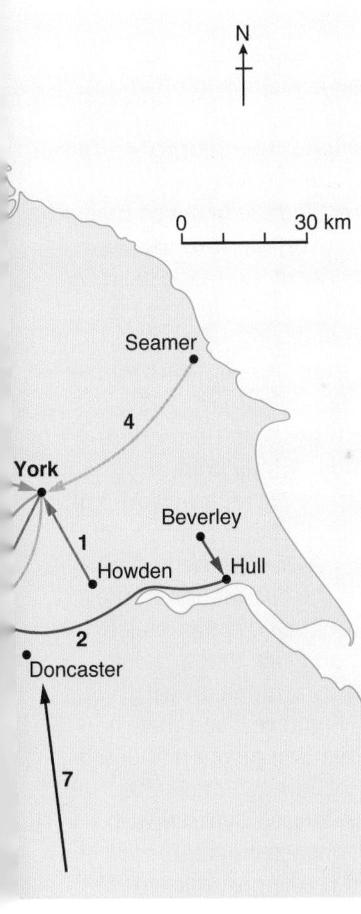
N
0
30 km
Seamer
4
York
Beverley
1
Howden
Hull
2
Doncaster
7

(6) The remaining regional uprisings pursued local grievances and strategies of their own and made no attempt to join up with the main rebels led by Aske. This gives some indication of the complexity of Aske's task and equally the scale of his achievement. These other uprisings centred on:

**a** Sawley Abbey. Sir Stephen Hammerton was the captain. About 6000 stayed at Sawley, the rest joined rebels led by Sir Thomas Tempest in attacking Skipton Castle.

**b** Kirby Stephen. The leaders were Robert Pulley, a commoner, and Nicholas Musgrave a yeoman who led their force to Penrith.

**c** Carlisle. The city withstood an assault by the force from Penrith now led by four commoner captains who called themselves Charity, Faith, Pity and Poverty.

**d** Sedbergh and Dent provided a force which gained control of Kendal and Lancaster.

(7) The royal army led by the Duke of Norfolk reached Doncaster on 27 October. Norfolk met Aske and the rebels' leaders at Doncaster Bridge.

▷ The Pilgrims' badge showing the five wounds of Christ. Religious imagery was very important in the sixteenth century and the wounds Jesus received at the crucifixion, represented here, were particularly emotive. This badge, thought to have originally come from the Darcy family, also enabled the pilgrims to identify one another and united them in a common cause.

It was 27 October before a royal army of 8000 reached the north, led by the **Duke of Norfolk** who followed Henry's orders to play for time.

> Thomas Howard, Third **Duke of Norfolk**, was the most powerful noble in the country, a close companion of the King and a renowned military commander. He fought in the wars against the Scots in 1513 and France in 1522. His offices, by 1536, had included Lord Lieutenant of Ireland, Lord Treasurer, President of the Council, Earl Marshall and Lord High Steward. His niece, Anne Boleyn, was the King's second wife.

Norfolk met Aske and the rebels at Doncaster Bridge and a truce was agreed whereby Henry agreed to pardon all but the leaders, two of whom were to travel to London and put their case. By early December the rebels' leaders had finalised all their demands in the twenty-four Pontefract Articles. Aske gave these to Norfolk who promised there would be a northern parliament set up to discuss them. The rebels now believed that Henry had listened to them and that they had won. Norfolk, however, had no intention of keeping his word. In a letter to Henry he made clear that whatever promises he made to the rebels 'surely I shall observe no part thereof'.

The pilgrims began to disperse and go back to their homes. Aske met the King in London where he was treated like a hero. By January 1537 however, impatience was setting in across the north because Henry had taken no action to implement the pilgrims' demands. At this point the King was aided by the actions of one rebel, Sir Francis Bigod, a powerful, if incompetent, Yorkshire landowner. Bigod had originally been a supporter of Thomas Cromwell and as an adherent to the reformed faith he had been appointed by Cromwell as a commissioner in the Dissolution of the Monasteries. Having been pressed into action by the host of pilgrims led by Robert Bowes, he underwent a change of heart and saw that at least his own economic difficulties might best be solved by a rebellion which secured Cromwell's removal. When Henry stalled, Bigod realised that the King was going to betray the pilgrims and on his own initiative engineered a new uprising to capture the towns of Hull and Scarborough and seize the Duke of Norfolk. This ill-conceived plot was repudiated by Aske who was striving to keep the north united behind the Doncaster Agreement. Although Bigod was swiftly captured, Henry seized the opportunity to move against the rebellion's leaders. Martial law was declared. Around 100 of the pilgrims, largely from the ruling class and including Aske, were put on trial in London and found guilty of treason.

## Why did the Pilgrimage of Grace take place?

The causes of the Pilgrimage of Grace were many and complex, reflecting a wide cross-section of people throughout the north of England. Some were felt more keenly in some areas, and by different social classes, than others. They were formulated by Robert Aske into a set of grievances, firstly in the York Articles, and then in the lengthier Pontefract Articles of December 1536 which he gave to the Duke of Norfolk. They are summarised in the chart below.

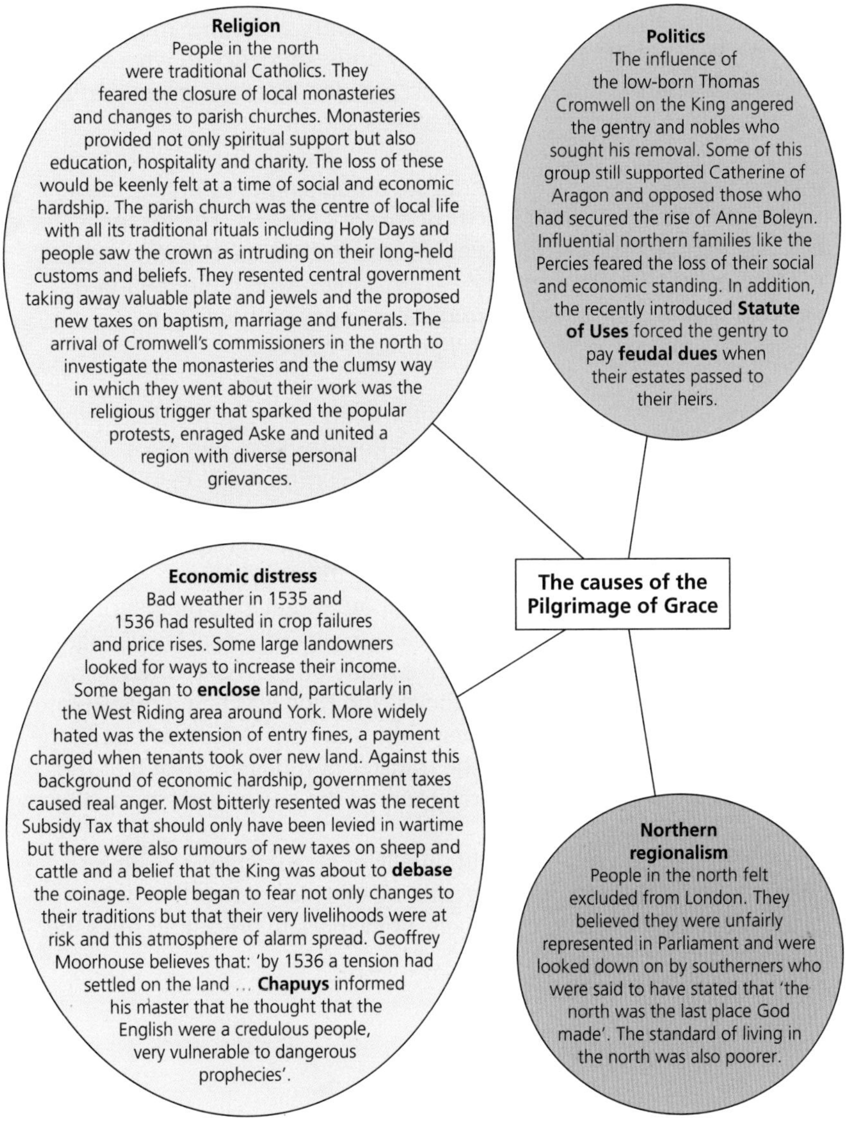

**The causes of the Pilgrimage of Grace**

**Religion**
People in the north were traditional Catholics. They feared the closure of local monasteries and changes to parish churches. Monasteries provided not only spiritual support but also education, hospitality and charity. The loss of these would be keenly felt at a time of social and economic hardship. The parish church was the centre of local life with all its traditional rituals including Holy Days and people saw the crown as intruding on their long-held customs and beliefs. They resented central government taking away valuable plate and jewels and the proposed new taxes on baptism, marriage and funerals. The arrival of Cromwell's commissioners in the north to investigate the monasteries and the clumsy way in which they went about their work was the religious trigger that sparked the popular protests, enraged Aske and united a region with diverse personal grievances.

**Politics**
The influence of the low-born Thomas Cromwell on the King angered the gentry and nobles who sought his removal. Some of this group still supported Catherine of Aragon and opposed those who had secured the rise of Anne Boleyn. Influential northern families like the Percies feared the loss of their social and economic standing. In addition, the recently introduced **Statute of Uses** forced the gentry to pay **feudal dues** when their estates passed to their heirs.

**Economic distress**
Bad weather in 1535 and 1536 had resulted in crop failures and price rises. Some large landowners looked for ways to increase their income. Some began to **enclose** land, particularly in the West Riding area around York. More widely hated was the extension of entry fines, a payment charged when tenants took over new land. Against this background of economic hardship, government taxes caused real anger. Most bitterly resented was the recent Subsidy Tax that should only have been levied in wartime but there were also rumours of new taxes on sheep and cattle and a belief that the King was about to **debase** the coinage. People began to fear not only changes to their traditions but that their very livelihoods were at risk and this atmosphere of alarm spread. Geoffrey Moorhouse believes that: 'by 1536 a tension had settled on the land … **Chapuys** informed his master that he thought that the English were a credulous people, very vulnerable to dangerous prophecies'.

**Northern regionalism**
People in the north felt excluded from London. They believed they were unfairly represented in Parliament and were looked down on by southerners who were said to have stated that 'the north was the last place God made'. The standard of living in the north was also poorer.

**Statute of Uses**
This removed an individual's right to leave his land to whoever he wanted and increased the amount of taxation payable when an estate changed hands

**feudal dues**
Money paid to the crown in accordance with tradition and usually based on land ownership. For example relief was paid to the king as land was inherited

**enclosure**
Putting fences around common or arable land to use new farming methods such as the selective breeding of animals

**Debase**
Debasing the coins meant reducing the gold or silver content by increasing the proportion of base metals. The government pocketed the difference but confidence in the value of English money dropped, with harmful effects on trade

**Chapuys** was the ambassador to England of the Holy Roman Emperor, Charles V between 1539 and 1545.

## How threatening was the Pilgrimage of Grace?

■ By now you should have begun to fill in your 'threat chart' for the Pilgrimage of Grace using pages 43–49. Review your conclusions to date then complete the chart using the further analysis on the following pages (50–54). Remember to make more detailed notes to support the summary conclusions in your chart.

The leadership of the Pilgrimage included gentry and some members of noble families and this brought authority and experience to what was, essentially, a popular protest. However 'popular' does not mean that the rising was disorganised. As Alison Wall has shown:

> They followed traditional procedures, organising musters by the usual methods in divisions, as if for military service. The lesser local leaders of village and township, the yeomen and tradesmen accustomed to minor authority as constables, and churchwardens, played a vital role in co-ordinating the risings. Without them, mustering would not have raised so many men.

These methods of raising and organising support were similar to those used by the 'rebels' of 1381 and 1450. In other words, they used existing systems of raising men for national defence.

The Church and clergy helped the gentry to organise the rebellion, with some clerics taking up arms and leading their flocks to join Aske. The Church also provided funds and channels of communication to help speed the mobilisation of men.

The rebellion was made more dangerous by the high quality of Robert Aske's leadership. Religious belief gave Aske the conviction to sustain a long campaign and the empathy to support and inspire the pilgrims. Although religion was one of several reasons why this local lawyer agreed to take charge, it was a crucial one. Like many others, Aske could also see the poverty of the north and believed the King was being misled into introducing policies that would worsen the situation. Aske was one of the few people who understood that the transfer of monastic wealth to the south would increase the impoverishment of the north, both spiritually and financially, for decades to come.

Aske provided the rebellion with intelligent leadership throughout with outstanding skills in debating and organisation. At York he was instrumental in drawing up the rebels' grievances to present to the King, summarised in the following chart.

1. *The suppression of the monasteries.*
2. *The Statute of Uses which stopped landowners from leaving their land to their heirs unless they paid tax on it.*
3. *Taxes on sheep and cattle coming on top of two years of disastrous harvests.*
4. *The power and position of Thomas Cromwell, who was of 'low-birth'.*
5. *The behaviour and reformist teachings of particular bishops including Lincoln, Worcester and Dublin.*

◁ The York Articles. A summary of the pilgrims' grievances written up by Robert Aske, at York, on 15 October 1536. They were developed into the lengthier Pontefract Articles which were presented to the government in December.

Aske led his followers as befitted a rebellion which was sanctioned by the Pilgrims' Oath and had the trappings of a religious crusade. He ensured strict discipline throughout the city of York and insisted that all goods procured by his army were paid for and that the men conducted themselves quietly. They were organised into companies as if they were a regular army, daily musters were held and a watch kept. Under Aske's leadership the rebels' council acted as an unofficial **Council of the North** as it oversaw money and supplies and debated grievances. Above all Aske brought coherence and purpose to what were initially localised regional uprisings. By uniting the pilgrims, keeping them together for a substantial period and winning wider support through his refusal to resort to violence, Aske made it difficult for Henry to portray the pilgrims as rebels.

The aim of the Pilgrimage of Grace was to put pressure on the King to force him to reverse many of the policies introduced since 1534 by Thomas Cromwell. The grievances of the pilgrims were (see page 49) many and varied but the crucial motive was to overturn recent religious changes. Religious grievances united all the rebel groups, creating a regional rather than local rising, because of the common anger created by Henry's breach with the papacy, his attack on the traditions of the Roman Catholic Church and on its beliefs, liturgies, wealth, monasteries and other social structures. Religion acted as a unifying force, forging these diverse grievances into something approaching a spiritual crusade. The opportunities presented by this were not lost on Robert Aske who, during the march to York, first began to speak of the rising as a pilgrimage.

**Council of the North**
This was set up by Henry VII to exert central control over the unsettled border areas. It was staffed by lawyers and civil servants who administered royal lands and exercised wide criminal and civil jurisdiction and was under the Presidency of either a noble or bishop

The language and imagery of the Church were used to underline the righteousness of the rebels' cause and provide inspiration, as shown by Andy Wood in *Riot, Rebellion and Popular Politics in Early Modern England* (2002):

> The rebels in the north marched behind banners depicting the 'Five Wounds' of Christ, and presented themselves as pilgrims, seeking their monarch's grace to maintain their established religion. The rebels swore oaths to maintain the commons, the King and the Church against the 'enemies of the commonwealth' (that is, the King's advisors), and circulated handbills and ballads which were attached to church doors, market crosses, or were sung aloud in ale-houses or on the march.

The aims of the Pilgrimage of Grace in themselves do not appear unduly violent but, in attracting huge popular support and in challenging royal policies, they represented a formidable threat to Henry VIII's ability to govern.

The popularity of the motives behind the Pilgrimage of Grace and its appeal to peaceful protest explain the escalation of the Pilgrimage across the north (see the map on pages 46–47). The nature of this widespread support is summarised below.

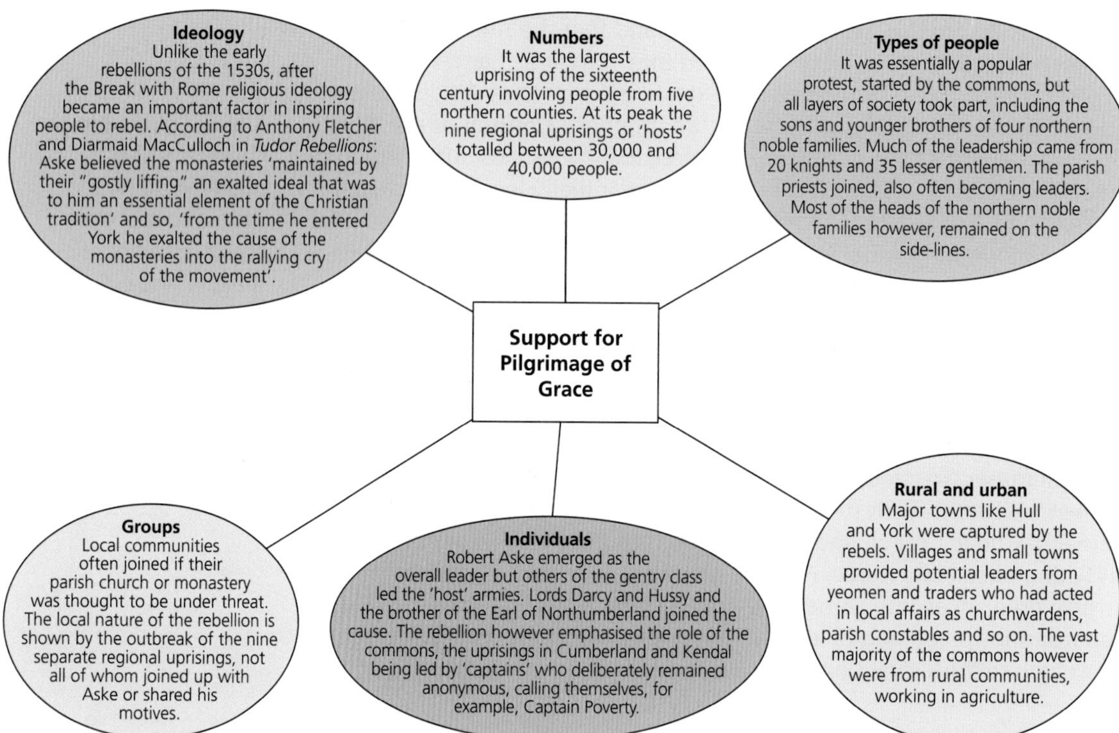
Support for Pilgrimage of Grace
Ideology
Unlike the early rebellions of the 1530s, after the Break with Rome religious ideology became an important factor in inspiring people to rebel. According to Anthony Fletcher and Diarmaid MacCulloch in *Tudor Rebellions*: Aske believed the monasteries 'maintained by their "gostly liffing" an exalted ideal that was to him an essential element of the Christian tradition' and so, 'from the time he entered York he exalted the cause of the monasteries into the rallying cry of the movement'.
Numbers
It was the largest uprising of the sixteenth century involving people from five northern counties. At its peak the nine regional uprisings or 'hosts' totalled between 30,000 and 40,000 people.
Types of people
It was essentially a popular protest, started by the commons, but all layers of society took part, including the sons and younger brothers of four northern noble families. Much of the leadership came from 20 knights and 35 lesser gentlemen. The parish priests joined, also often becoming leaders. Most of the heads of the northern noble families however, remained on the side-lines.
Groups
Local communities often joined if their parish church or monastery was thought to be under threat. The local nature of the rebellion is shown by the outbreak of the nine separate regional uprisings, not all of whom joined up with Aske or shared his motives.
Individuals
Robert Aske emerged as the overall leader but others of the gentry class led the 'host' armies. Lords Darcy and Hussy and the brother of the Earl of Northumberland joined the cause. The rebellion however emphasised the role of the commons, the uprisings in Cumberland and Kendal being led by 'captains' who deliberately remained anonymous, calling themselves, for example, Captain Poverty.
Rural and urban
Major towns like Hull and York were captured by the rebels. Villages and small towns provided potential leaders from yeomen and traders who had acted in local affairs as churchwardens, parish constables and so on. The vast majority of the commons however were from rural communities, working in agriculture.

△ Adam Sedbar, who was the sixteenth Abbot of Jervaux in Wensleydale, carved his name on the wall of his cell in the Tower of London while awaiting his execution for participating in the Pilgrimage of Grace.

Aske's plan of campaign was very clear from the outset. He had no intention of leading an army south to overthrow Henry VIII but believed he was using the traditional methods of seeking redress of grievances from the monarch. Aske's plan therefore was to increase his support, particularly from the ruling class, take control of key cities, articulate the rebels' grievances and take these, backed by the threat of force, to negotiate with the King. Aske's belief that they were protesting to restore the old religion from the changes introduced by Cromwell kept him loyal to the King. Not all the rebels wanted negotiations rather than military engagement. Some of the commoners feared that the gentry would let them down. Not all of the nine uprisings had joined Aske in York. Nevertheless it was Aske's authority and campaign plan which kept the movement united and made it appear such a threat to Henry's authority. He persuaded the pilgrims at the Pontefract meeting to negotiate rather than fight, in keeping with their religious image. Ironically Aske's greatest strength turned out to be also the greatest flaw in that this strategy gave the devious Henry the time he needed. Unlike the dynastic rebellions of Henry VII's reign, the Pilgrimage of Grace was not prepared to attack the person of the King and this ultimately was its great weakness. Religious beliefs had a considerable impact on both its leadership and support but may have weakened planning and strategy in that Aske's refusal to consider force played into Henry's hands.

For all the size and scale of the rebellion the response of the government was slow. The King was simply caught out by the spread and size of the rebellion and was forced to play for time. Many of his forces were still in Lincolnshire while the royal army under the Earl of Shrewsbury was at Nottingham. Henry therefore, although he had no intention of accepting the pilgrims' demands, promised a pardon while requesting more information. While Norfolk and the rebel leaders continued negotiating, the majority of the now pardoned rebels drifted home. The rebels in fact believed that Henry had granted their demands but Bigod's rising in January 1537 gave the King the excuse he was looking for and showed the scare he had been given. The intensity and cruelty of Henry's reaction shows he saw the threat of the Pilgrimage of Grace as a direct challenge to his royal authority as Supreme Head of the Church of England, however much the pilgrims might profess their loyalty to him personally.

◁ Clifford's Tower in York, the site of Robert Aske's execution in July 1537.

When Robert Aske received the summons to attend Henry in London in March 1537 he was told by Norfolk to expect a warm reception. Instead Aske found himself housed in the Tower and fighting for his life in an examination by jury. Despite the gravity of his situation, the evidence shows Aske's willingness to reflect on and talk openly about his role in the Pilgrimage. Although in hindsight this appears naive, he chose to answer all questions accurately. Aske was found guilty of treason on 16 May but Henry ordered that his sentence, and those of other rebel leaders, should be carried out in places with which they had connections. The sorry group was taken north, stopping at Lincoln and Hull for the executions of Lord Hussey and Sir Robert Constable respectively. Aske was taken onto York where the execution was scheduled for market day to ensure a sizeable crowd.

On the 6 July 1537 Robert Aske was taken from his cell to his death on a gallows at the top of Clifford's Tower. Unusually, Henry allowed him to die before the body was cut down but it was then hung by chains from the castle walls as a deterrent.

**1** Complete your 'threat chart' (see page 12) to evaluate the threat from the Pilgrimage of Grace. Make notes to justify your grading of the threats according to each of the six criteria.

**2** 'The religious motives of the participants made the rebellion a greater threat to Henry.' List the main arguments for and against this statement. You will have the opportunity to develop this further at the end of this enquiry.

**3** Place the Pilgrimage of Grace on your own version of the 'threat line' on page 13, alongside the rebellions from the previous enquiry. Add brief annotations to give the major reasons for where you placed the Pilgrimage.

**4** Geoffrey Moorhouse in the *Pilgrimage of Grace* (2002) describes the rebellion as 'the nearest thing to civil war that the Tudors ever had on their hands, which at one stage even threatened Henry's grip on the throne'. To what extent do you agree with his conclusion?

## The Western Rising (or Prayer Book Rebellion) of 1549

Although Henry had established the Church of England by 1534, he had no intention of replacing the Catholic Church service. According to John Guy in *The Tudors* (2000), 'the King was a doctrinal conservative with largely orthodox views on the sacraments ... overall, Henry imagined a "Church of England" which would retain Catholic doctrine, but curtail the influence of the clergy'. The 1539 Act of Six Articles therefore upheld Catholic services and the sacraments and stated that after Henry's death these could only be changed by an adult king. Henry's son and heir, Edward, was only nine when Henry died in 1547, but with the **Lord Protector**, the Duke of Somerset, and Archbishop Cranmer, he embarked on the destruction of Catholic practices and ritual. This included, in December 1548, an act abolishing chantries. Philip Caraman in *The Western Rising* (1994) suggested this affected people more than the loss of the monasteries. Chantries were sited in towns, so more people had access to them, and often included bequests providing education or nursing care, as well as prayers for the souls of the dead. 'Within a matter of months the people were deprived of the ancient symbols of their faith which had been familiar to them from childhood.'

**Lord Protector**
Title of a nobleman who runs the country on behalf of a king who is only a minor, also known as a regent

Unrest at these changes was not confined to the West Country. In 1548 and 1549 there were outbreaks of violence throughout the country with some areas adding agrarian grievances to those of religion. The common people were suffering from high rent increases, debasement of the coinage (see page 49) and inflation. Andy Wood has argued there was also a heartfelt resentment against men of the gentry class who had profited from the sale of Church lands and were now occupying positions of authority in central and local government; '... the dissolution of chantries and sale of their assets after 1547 were felt to benefit a class of "rich oppressors" while simultaneously depriving "the commons" of cultural identity, spiritual salvation and material succour'.

In Devon and Cornwall agrarian discontent was less, there were virtually no enclosures. Cornwall though was particularly devoted to the old faith. Place names such as St Neots still show us the importance of local saints, many of whom had Celtic origins. When the government imposed the **Prayer Book of 1549** the men of Cornwall rose up against the introduction of church services in English, a language that was far more mysterious to them than the familiar rhythms of the Latin Mass. What happened next is told on the next page.

Although the Common **Prayer Book of 1549** retained many of the rites and ceremonies of Catholic ritual, it was perceived as Protestant. In addition it came after the issuing of Protestant sermons for the clergy to preach, the destruction of chantries, the removal of images from places of worship and the whitewashing of church walls.

# The main stages of the Western Rising, May to August 1549

**3** At Whitsun the citizens of Sampford Courtenay in Devon rebelled when the new service was used in their church. A member of the gentry who intervened was killed. This force then marched to Crediton where Arundell and his Cornish force of about 6000 had established themselves and fortified the town. The government sent a small force under Sir Peter Carew with instructions from the Duke of Somerset to show leniency in dealing with the rebels. Carew made the situation worse, he failed to meet with the rebels and the accidental burning of Crediton barns increased tension.

**4** Instead of marching towards a poorly defended London, Arundell decided to capture the largely sympathetic and strategic town of Exeter. Those citizens most supportive of the rebels now left the city to join them, thus weakening the prospect of a successful uprising within the city, not least by reducing the pressure on the limited amount of food so enabling Exeter to hold out longer. Meanwhile, led by the mayor, John Blackaller, the town officials' fear of committing treason overcame their sympathies with the rebels. The result was a lengthy siege which swung one way and then the other for six weeks.

**2** In spring 1549 the imposition of the New Prayer Book led to protests across Cornwall which came together under the leadership of Humphrey Arundell at Bodmin.

**1** The first sign of trouble came the year before the outbreak of the rebellion proper, at Helston in April 1548, when the much-hated government commissioner William Body visited the town to oversee the destruction of church images. In the ensuing riot Body was murdered. Ten men were ordered to be hung, drawn and quartered and the brutality of the government's response caused widespread resentment.

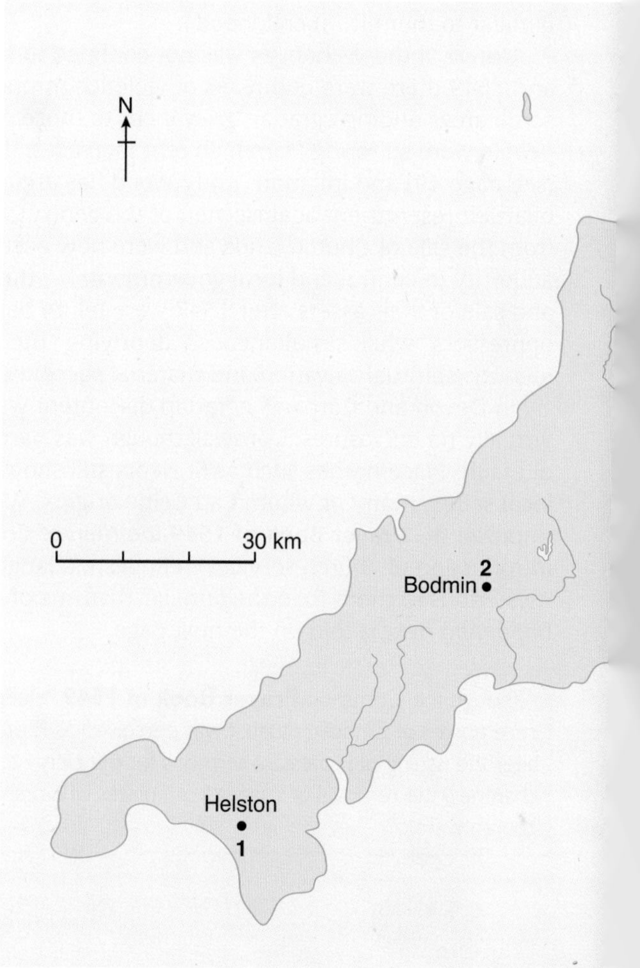

▷ This map shows you the main stages of the Western Rising from its outbreak in May 1549 to its suppression four months later in August.

**5** Meanwhile the Protector, the Duke of Somerset had replaced Carew with Lord John Russell, who was the Lord High Admiral and President of the Council of the West. Russell based himself at Honiton throughout July 1549. His force was probably less than a hundred. He was not strong enough to attack the rebels and was forced to wait for reinforcements.

**6** On 3 August the arrival of further forces under Lord Grey enabled the royal army to march on Exeter. The rebels were defeated in clashes at Fenny Bridges, Clyst St Mary and Clyst Heath. Finally on 6 August Russell relieved the city of Exeter as further government forces under William Herbert arrived.

**7** On the 16 August Russell led a royal army of 8000 men against the rebels who had reformed at Sampford Courtenay. It required a three-pronged attack by Russell, Grey and Herbert before the rebels fled. In total about 4000 West Country men lost their lives in the battle or the hunting down that followed it.

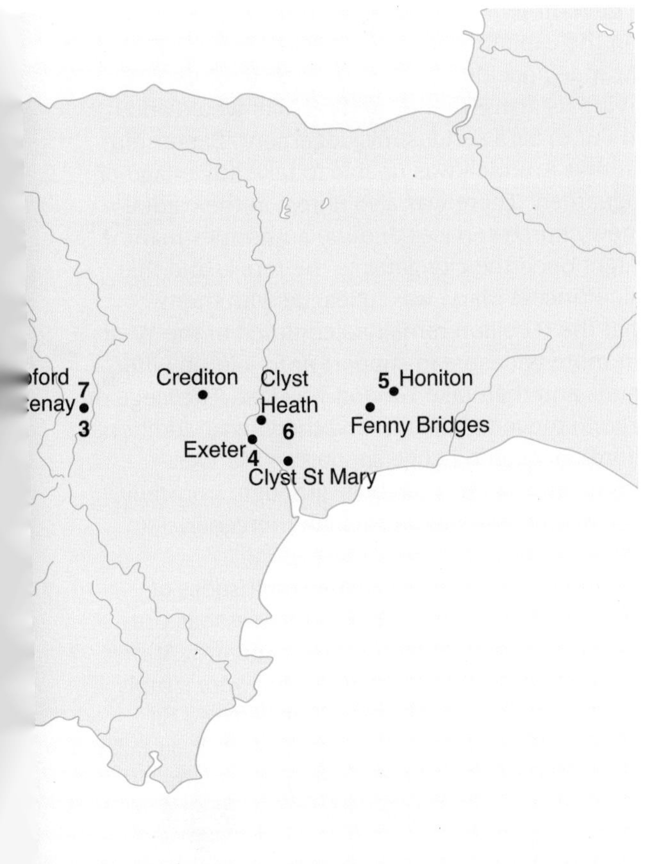

7
3
Crediton
Clyst
Heath
6
5 Honiton
Fenny Bridges
Exeter
4
Clyst St Mary


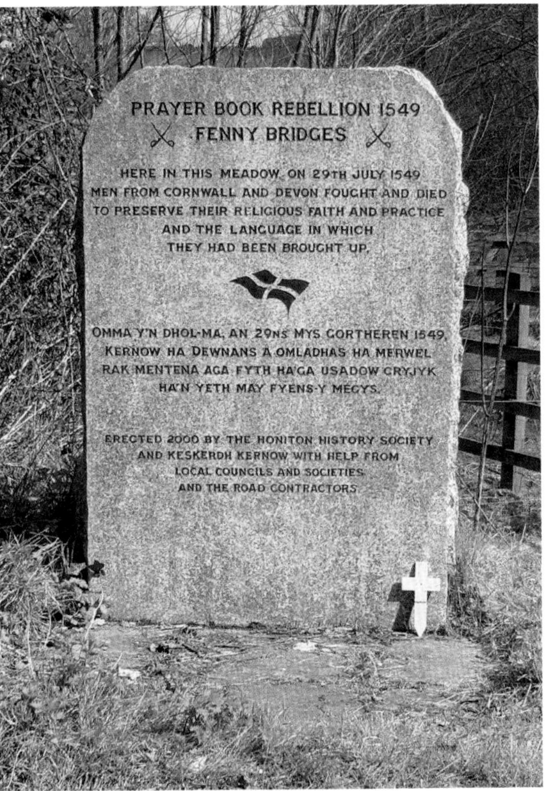

PRAYER BOOK REBELLION 1549
FENNY BRIDGES
HERE IN THIS MEADOW ON 29TH JULY 1549
MEN FROM CORNWALL AND DEVON FOUGHT AND DIED
TO PRESERVE THEIR RELIGIOUS FAITH AND PRACTICE
AND THE LANGUAGE IN WHICH
THEY HAD BEEN BROUGHT UP.
OMMA Y'N DHOL-MA, AN 29NS MYS GORTHEREN 1549,
KERNOW HA DEWNANS A OMLADHAS HA MERWEL
RAK MENTENA AGA FYTH HA'GA USADOW CRYJYK
HA'N YETH MAY FYENS-Y MEGYS.
ERECTED 2000 BY THE HONITON HISTORY SOCIETY
AND KESKERDH KERNOW WITH HELP FROM
LOCAL COUNCILS AND SOCIETIES
AND THE ROAD CONTRACTORS


△ Memorial stone for the Battle of Fenny Bridges.

By now you should have begun to fill in your 'threat chart' for the Western Rising using pages 55–57. Review your conclusions to date, and then complete the chart using the further analysis on this page. Remember to make more detailed notes to support the summary conclusions in your chart.

## How threatening was the Western Rising of 1549?

The alternative name for this uprising, the Prayer Book Rebellion, encourages comparison with the Pilgrimage of Grace. There are many similarities. The protests in the West Country turned into a rebellion because of strong leadership. Like Aske, Humphrey Arundell was a gentleman with considerable tactical skills. By June 1549 his support had built up until he commanded a force of about 6000 men, centred on Bodmin, and representing all social classes. Again, Arundell kept control and discipline by ordering that the rebels were divided into military detachments under the control of colonels, majors and captains or clergy. The aims of the rebels were clearly expressed in the Eight Articles largely written by the clergy, all but one of which called for the return of the old religious beliefs and practices. Like the 'pilgrims', their plan was to send their grievances to the Council, while protesting their loyalty to Henry VIII's wish that there would be no religious changes until Edward came of age. In one way, however, Arundell appeared to differ from Aske. He was determined to march on London to make sure the government both met his demands and kept its word. Again, although this rebellion was not a dynastic threat in that it was not seeking the overthrow of the monarch, the impact on the regency government of being brought news of a rebel force intending to march on the capital needs to be considered.

In the event however, Arundell decided to capture Exeter before advancing to London believing its arms, money and recruits would add to his strength. This turned out to be a serious misjudgement. Exeter did not surrender which meant that Arundell was unable to take advantage of London being relatively unguarded. There was also unrest in the capital over the preaching of the new church services and the authorities feared both that the Londoners might open the city gates to the rebels and that Edward's sister, the Catholic Princess Mary, was in league with them. Arundell's error ensured that the rebellion remained confined to the West Country. The chance to win more widespread support or to join up with disturbances in other counties and then take London was lost. The siege of Exeter also gave Russell time to move to Honiton and then await additional forces. The rebellion therefore only gained huge support in the West Country. There was no foreign support for the rebels although, ironically, foreigners were involved when Somerset paid for Italian mercenaries to fight on the government's side.

The reaction of the government does not reveal the seriousness of this rebellion. It was slow to react decisively because Somerset was pre-occupied with economic issues and looming war against Scotland. At first Somerset took the view that the people in the West Country were simply misguided and could be shown the error of their ways. He ordered Sir Peter Carew, the Sheriff of Devonshire, to deal with the rebels, but he failed to do so. Somerset then, under pressure from hardliners in his council to abandon his strategy of leniency, replaced Carew with Lord Russell who had a reputation for brutality and who eventually succeeded in harshly putting down the rebellion. However, for all its delay there was never any chance that the government would agree to the rebels' grievances because overturning the Catholic religion and replacing it with Protestantism was at the heart of this government's policies.

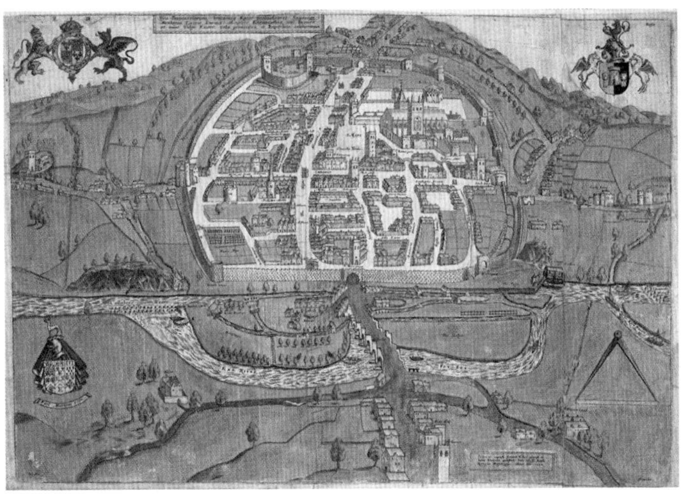

◁ This illustration of the city of Exeter comes from John Hooker's vivid account of the siege of 1549. Hooker was in the city at the time and, although he was a supporter of the government's Protestant reforms, he proudly described the courage of the citizens of Exeter in defending their city. John Hooker's life combined restoring and reviving historical texts and writing books, particularly on the history of Devon, with public service. He was elected MP for Exeter in 1571 and wrote a treatise on parliamentary practice.

**1** Complete your 'threat chart' (see page 12) to evaluate the threat from the Western Rising. Make notes to justify your grading of the threats according to each of the six criteria.

**2** 'To what extent were the religious motives of the participants the main reason why the Western Rising appeared threatening?' List the main arguments for and against this statement. You will have the opportunity to develop this further at the end of this enquiry.

**3** Place the Western Rising on your own version of the 'threat line' on page 13, alongside the Pilgrimage of Grace and the rebellions from the previous enquiry. Add brief annotations to give the major reasons for where you placed the Western Rising.

Later rebellions (see Chapters 4 and 5) also contained religious elements as this chart summarises.

| Rebellion | Summary | Role of religion |
| --- | --- | --- |
| **1549: Kett's rebellion** | Primarily a rebellion caused by economic and social discontent in East Anglia. | The rebels stressed their Protestantism to demonstrate their loyalty to Somerset. Their articles criticised the clergy and called for speedier government reforms. |
| **1553: Lady Jane Grey Plot** | Masterminded by the Duke of Northumberland to prevent Mary Tudor from succeeding to the throne when it became clear that Edward VI was dying. | Mary was a Catholic and both Edward and Northumberland feared she would overturn their Protestant reformation and restore the Pope if she became queen. |
| **1555: Wyatt's rebellion** | Led by courtiers aiming to replace Mary Tudor with her Protestant half-sister, Elizabeth, when Mary began marriage negotiations with the Catholic and Spanish Philip II. | Religion was a factor in that Mary was Catholic and most rebels Protestant, but Wyatt played this down, believing he would attract more support by focusing on English fears of being ruled by a Spaniard. |
| **1569: Northern Rebellion** | Aimed to replace the Protestant Elizabeth with her Catholic heir, Mary, Queen of Scots, although the northern nobility also had personal and political grievances against the centralised Tudor government. | A rebellion with clear religious objectives. Mary, Queen of Scots would restore the Catholic religion if Queen of England. The loss of the Catholic Church and monasteries was felt most in the north. |

## Concluding your enquiry

In 1538 Henry ordered an English translation of the Bible be placed in every parish church. The King blamed inaccurate interpretations of the scriptures for the Pilgrimage of Grace and was determined that there should be no further confusion. As you can see on the page opposite, this title page carried a subtler message that would not be lost on his subjects. The King is on his throne receiving the Word of God which he bestows upon his bishops and archbishops who deliver it to the priests. When this is passed on to the people they cry 'God save the King'. The power and semi-divine majesty of the King is clearly shown as is a social hierarchy of respect and order, all underpinned by religion. However much religious rebels protested their loyalty to the King, this picture makes clear Henry's view. Religious protests challenged the monarch's position, relationship with God and the status quo. They were dangerous.

All the rebellions which broke out after 1534 (except that of the Earl of Essex in 1601) included elements of religion. This meant there was a great likelihood of attracting more popular support because changes to Church traditions had an immediate significance for ordinary people. Such rebellions, fought in the name of religion could acquire the characteristics of a holy crusade with people inspired by the rightness of the cause even if, as in 1536 and 1549, they made clear that they did not want to depose the monarch. However, as monarchs believed that they were appointed by God, their belief that they also were following God's wishes ensured such rebellions would ultimately have to face the might of the Tudor government and all the forces at its disposal.

### Concluding your enquiry

1. Use your notes to list the evidence that suggests that these rebellions:
   **a)** were a serious threat
   **b)** were NOT a serious threat.
2. Did the rebels' proclamations of loyalty to the crown make these risings seem less of a threat to the governments?
3. Which factors were most important in:
   **a)** making these rebellions appear a threat to the crown
   **b)** explaining the failure of these rebellions?
4. Use your threat charts and answers to the questions above to plan an essay answering our enquiry question:

   Did their religious motives make the rebels of 1536 and 1549 serious threats to the Tudors?

The Byble in Englyshe, that is to saye the content of all the holy scrypture, bothe of ÿ olde and newe testament truly translated after the veryte of the Hebrue and Greke textes, by ÿ dylygent studye of dyuerse excellent learned men expert in the forsayde tonges.

Prynted by Rychard Grafton & Edward Whitchurch.

Cum priuilegio ad imprimendum solum.

1539.

VIVAT REX
GOD SAVE THE KYNGE

△ The title page of Henry VIII's English Bible of 1539.

Synoptic Activity

# Investigating Tudor rebellions – the story so far

## Developing some initial conclusions

By now you know a good deal about the rebellions discussed in Chapters 2 and 3. This interim summary section enables you to explore the patterns that are emerging and think about initial answers to two core questions that we will return to at the end of the book in Chapters 7 and 8:

- **Why were some rebellions perceived to be especially dangerous to the monarch?**
- **Why did the rebellions fail?**

1 Make brief notes explaining how each factor shown on the cards helps to explain why some rebellions appeared so dangerous? Use your notes and completed threat charts and threat line from Chapters 2 and 3 together with the information on pages 63–67 and your reading of other books. Make sure you include examples from the rebellions you have studied.

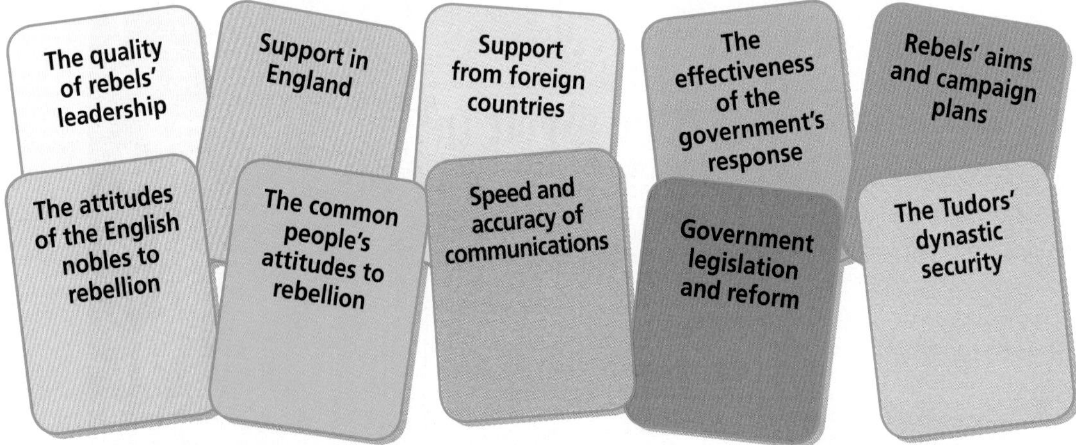
The quality of rebels' leadership
Support in England
Support from foreign countries
The effectiveness of the government's response
Rebels' aims and campaign plans
The attitudes of the English nobles to rebellion
The common people's attitudes to rebellion
Speed and accuracy of communications
Government legislation and reform
The Tudors' dynastic security

2 Create your own set of the ten factor cards. Lay them out in a circle on a sheet of A3, then draw lines between any that you think are linked and write brief notes on the lines to explain the links.

3 Organise the cards into a pattern (perhaps similar to the one on the right) in which the factors that were most important in creating a sense of danger are at the top and those least important at the bottom.

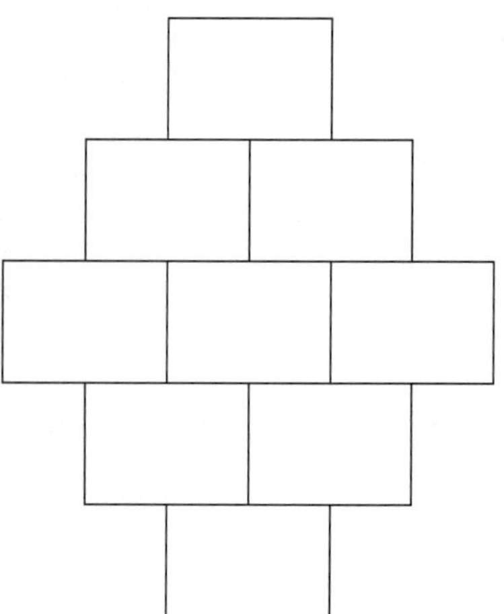

4 Use this pattern and the links to write a short answer to the question 'Why were some rebellions perceived as especially dangerous to the monarch?'

5 Think carefully and make notes about what you are not sure about in your answer. What will you look for when reading Chapters 4 and 5 on later Tudor rebellions that will help answer this question?

6 Repeat questions 1–5 above for the second question 'Why did the rebellions fail?'

# Explaining the dangers and failures of rebellions against the Tudors



## The quality of rebels' leadership

You will already have seen in the dynastic rebellions against Henry VII that where there was a challenge to the legitimacy of the monarch, it needed to be led by a relative with royal blood whose claim to the throne was at least as strong. All rebellions needed members of the nobility and gentry at their head. In a hierarchical society nobles could bring status and authority to an uprising in addition to military strength and experience of command. Gentry who were university educated, particularly with a legal training like Robert Aske, brought the skills needed to articulate and debate the rebels' grievances. Class alone however did not guarantee successful leadership; the threat posed by any leader came from their ability to organise, unite and inspire their followers. Where both status and leadership skills were lacking, rebellions were likely to be directionless and incapable of attracting widespread support. The leaders of a rebellion therefore were just as likely to contribute to its failure as its success.

## Support in England

The support which a rebellion attracted in England threatened the monarch in two ways. The anticipated number of rebels and speed with which they joined was a major concern when it took considerable time for a king to summon and move a royal army of sufficient strength, as you have seen with the Pilgrimage of Grace. Equally important though was the quality of that support. Only nobles had the financial means and military expertise to put well trained and equipped retainers into the field. Rebellions like the ones you have seen which protested against taxes, were more likely to be spontaneous uprisings of commoners whose threat was much reduced by the lack of noble or gentry participation. In the event most Tudor rebellions, as will be illustrated in more detail in Chapters 7 and 8, were local and regional rather than national, and never very large. That was likely to be of little comfort to a king faced with dealing with them however. When a rebellion broke out, the monarch could not know either the size or quality of the potential support.

## Support from foreign countries

This was arguably the most valuable and therefore most feared kind of support which a rebellion might receive. Foreign troops were likely to be mercenaries with experience of fighting in battles in European theatres of war and led by experienced and capable commanders. Both Edward IV and Henry VII had seized the English throne with military forces provided by the Netherlands and France respectively, so Henry was more aware than anyone of the dangers posed by foreign support when both Lambert Simnel and Perkin Warbeck appeared to threaten his rule. European rulers involved themselves in English rebellions, or not, according to their own self-interest and priorities but these tended to be largely confined to those rebellions which challenged the position of the monarch, which in itself would impact on the balance of power of Europe. There was no foreign aid therefore for rebels who were fighting for social and economic causes. As the Tudors established themselves more firmly on the throne, through alliances and marriage with European powers, foreign intervention became more of a hope held by the rebels than a realistic expectation.

## The effectiveness of the government's response

The speed with which a government responded to the outbreak of a rebellion depended on its intelligence of events which themselves depended on the nature of the rebellion itself. Thus Henry VII, who had been expecting a Yorkist rebellion to materialise in the north of his kingdom, maintained an army in the Midlands in the spring of 1487. Henry VIII by contrast was taken completely unawares by the outbreak and spread of the Pilgrimage of Grace. The lack of a standing royal army, and the cost and political implications of keeping one on 'stand-by' was something of a royal juggling act. Once the army was on the road, however, it was far more powerful and better equipped than any rebel force, as the reaction of several rebel leaders when faced with this reality shows. However, both Henry VII and Henry VIII were powerful enough to enforce military decisions. In the mid-Tudor period, particularly during the regency of Edward VI, that authority and focus was lacking to the detriment of the government's response.

## Rebels' aims and campaign plans

Rebels' aims can often be seen in a negative light – as grievances about disruptions to daily life – or as selfish – seeing an opportunity for personal advancement. While this may be true in many cases this view overlooks the importance that ideology and belief (including faith) played, particularly, but not exclusively, in the religious rebellions. There were many in the Pilgrimage of Grace who believed that Henry VIII's divorce and the Break with Rome were morally wrong and against God's law. The notion that they were fighting for 'the right' against 'the wrong' inspired such rebels with the legitimacy of their cause and often underpinned and strengthened the more obvious causes of unrest.

You will be well aware by this stage that rebels' aims and campaign plans depended on both the quality of their leadership and support but more importantly on what type of rebellion it was. While some aimed to depose the monarch others professed loyalty, desiring only to change a minister or policy. In the case of the former, the rebels needed to seize control of both London and the person of the monarch, possibly through success on the field of battle, and to have a legitimate claimant with which to replace them. Protests against unpopular policies and ministers tended to focus on applying pressure through the capture of a key town such as Exeter in 1549, although the Cornish Rebellion of 1497 did not follow this pattern when the rebels decided to take their grievances to the King in London. Campaign plans needed to be both strategic and flexible, able to respond to the complexity of self-interests owned by the rebellion's supporters, to re-adjust when the duration of the rebellion was longer than expected and to capitalise on any mistakes or weaknesses shown by the crown. Aims and plans did not always work well together. Robert Aske did not take advantage of the slow response of Henry VIII in 1536 because he was not aiming to depose the King.

## The attitudes of the English nobles to rebellion

Both Henry VII and Henry VIII expected and feared the involvement of the nobility in rebellions. This is why Henry VII attainted fourteen and executed four members of his household who he believed to be working for Perkin Warbeck in 1495 and why Henry VIII used the excuse of the Pilgrimage of Grace to execute the surviving members of the House of York in 1538. In fact your studies will already have shown you that there were actually few nobles who supported rebellions, as the leaders of Lambert Simnel's rebellion learnt to their cost in 1487. The lack of English noble involvement in all the rebellions undoubtedly weakened them for reasons which have already been highlighted in this section. The reasons why the nobility decided to serve the Tudors rather than fight them are explored in detail in Chapter 8 but their decision meant that, with the exception of Ireland, as the century went on the leaders of the rebellions were far more likely to come from the gentry class, from the ranks of lawyers and local government officials.

## The common people's attitudes to rebellion

If you look back at pages 8–9 you will remember that 'it took a great deal of provocation and frustration before people took up arms in protest or rebellion'. The impact of both religious teachings and a social hierarchy epitomised by the Great Chain of Being combined to ensure that people knew and kept their place and were extremely reluctant to challenge their social superiors, including the King, to whom they owed obedience and respect. Hence the decision by some rebel leaders to claim loyalty to the King by exposing local grievances or to hide from their followers their true intentions.

△ Pontefract Castle was the most important castle in the north of England and was a symbol of the King's military and political power in the region. The fact that the castle was surrendered by Lord Darcy to Robert Aske therefore had a significance which could only have increased the threat of the Pilgrimage in Henry's eyes. This oil painting by the Dutch artist Alexander Keirincx is from 1625–30 and so shows the castle in the early seventeenth century.

## Speed and accuracy of communications

The comparative difficulty of communications in the sixteenth century played a part in the failure of the Tudor rebellions in several ways. Rebels found it difficult to communicate their aims and strategies to others beyond their locality. The time taken to build major support reduced any prospect of rebellions taking the government by surprise – even when the government was caught unawares, as in 1497, the length of time it took the rebels to maximise their threat gave it a breathing space. In this case Henry was able to divert Daubeney's army from its march to Scotland to take on the rebels at Blackheath. Rebels did not know in advance who else might rally to them and this would have an impact on how they planned to achieve their aim – the Earl of Lincoln's frequent change of tactics in the summer of 1487 were a direct response to the lack of support from the north which finally caused him to risk all on bringing the King to battle in the Midlands. Poor communications affected the crown as well. Not knowing what was happening or how many were involved added to the sense of threat. The government was often slow to hear of rebellion and therefore slow to assemble forces and move to deal with the rebels.

## Government legislation and reform

The frequency of rebellions declined throughout the sixteenth century. A key reason for this was the recognition by all the Tudors that they needed to use the law to strengthen their own position and to bring about reform to alleviate the social and economic grievances that caused the poor and unemployed to rebel. You will find a detailed summary of all government legislation and reform in Chapter 8 but it has already played a key role in these earlier rebellions. Henry VII steadfastly weakened potential noble opposition by setting up the Star Chamber (see page 132), passing an Act of Livery and Maintenance and restoring royal authority over the north. Henry VIII passed new treason laws to defend his Break with Rome which included an oath of loyalty to be sworn by all officeholders on threat of pain of death. Later monarchs, particularly Elizabeth, had more freedom to focus on social and economic reform.

## The Tudors' dynastic security

The Tudors were not a secure dynasty with an unchallenged right to the throne and where the crown passed seamlessly from father to son. The lack of strong male heirs was a concern for all Tudor monarchs and gave their opponents, particularly in the reigns of Mary and Elizabeth, some justification for rebellions which claimed to be in the national interest. All the Tudors were aware of this potential weakness however and made considerable efforts to ensure they stayed on the throne, using a combination of propaganda and self-advertising to elevate their authority and power. Henry VII ensured his profile, which was unknown to most of his subjects in 1485, appeared on all coins of the realm, while Henry VIII wrote, and had circulated, his response to the demands of the pilgrims in 1536. This exploitation of the authority of majesty and use of all available forms of media to complement the peoples' innate deference was a key reason why Tudor rebellions failed.

▷ This portrait of Henry VIII was painted by Hans Holbein the Younger in 1536–37. Although the original was destroyed by fire the best known copy, probably commissioned by Edward Seymour, is in the collection of the Walker Art Gallery, Liverpool.

Derek Wilson, the author of *Henry VIII – Reformer and Tyrant* asked 'Was Hans Holbein's Henry VIII the best piece of propaganda ever?' in an article printed in *The Daily Telegraph* on the 12 April 2013.

All other representations have been shouldered aside by the aggressive, defiant, bull-like figure, staring straight out at us, feet spread, fists clenched, shoulders padded, codpiece thrusting – every sumptuously adorned, jewel-encrusted inch proclaiming his self-assured magnificence. This, we have come to believe, is Henry VIII. It isn't. …

Holbein flattered his subject outrageously. The profusion of jewels, from the collar set with fabulous rubies to the gems on the King's cap and worked into his doublet, was the ultimate in 'bling'. The padded-out shoulders added forcefulness to the composition and obliged the artist to lengthen the royal legs to preserve balance. But it is the pose that was so sensational. It has been described by one expert as a 'fantastic amalgam of the static and the swaggering', and is 'unique in royal portraiture …'

And the truth? At the age of 45 Henry was on the brink of old age. The athletic youth who had revelled in tiltyard sports was a figure of the past. Thrombosed legs were causing him increasing pain and would soon turn him into a semi-invalid. He was becoming fat and unwieldy. In 1537, Henry VIII, far from being the man he wished others to see, was insecure. The past was a depressing panorama of expensive and inglorious military adventures; of 28 years of married life without a son to show for them. The present was a skin-of-the-teeth survival from defeat at the hands of unruly subjects; of continued threat from people who regarded him as a tyrant.

# Context: Mid-Tudor England – a time of crisis?

Historians have often described the period between the death of Henry VIII and the accession of Elizabeth I as the 'mid-Tudor crisis'. This idea of crisis stemmed from a range of problems which all occurred within the short period of the brief reigns of Edward VI (1547–53) and Mary Tudor (1553–58). This page introduces two linked aspects of this 'crisis' – economic problems and class conflict – and shows how some classes prospered while others moved into poverty.

△ **This illustration from 1577 (Holinsted's Chronicles) shows workers labouring in the fields to harvest the wheat in time**

△ **This woodcut from 1567 shows a vagabond being flogged as a punishment for begging.**

**Social a**

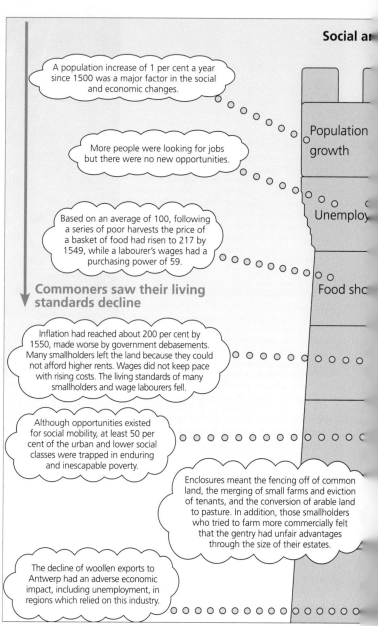

A population increase of 1 per cent a year since 1500 was a major factor in the social and economic changes.

Population growth

More people were looking for jobs but there were no new opportunities.

Unemploy

Based on an average of 100, following a series of poor harvests the price of a basket of food had risen to 217 by 1549, while a labourer's wages had a purchasing power of 59.

Food sh

**Commoners saw their living standards decline**

Inflation had reached about 200 per cent by 1550, made worse by government debasements. Many smallholders left the land because they could not afford higher rents. Wages did not keep pace with rising costs. The living standards of many smallholders and wage labourers fell.

Although opportunities existed for social mobility, at least 50 per cent of the urban and lower social classes were trapped in enduring and inescapable poverty.

Enclosures meant the fencing off of common land, the merging of small farms and eviction of tenants, and the conversion of arable land to pasture. In addition, those smallholders who tried to farm more commercially felt that the gentry had unfair advantages through the size of their estates.

The decline of woollen exports to Antwerp had an adverse economic impact, including unemployment, in regions which relied on this industry.

As preparation for Chapter 4 read pages 68–71 and then think about these questions:

1 What were the most likely causes of rebellion between 1547 and 1558?

2 Which groups of people were most likely to rebel at this time?

3 Why might the ruling classes be reluctant to rebel during this period?

4 Why might government responses to rebellion be slow during Edward VI's reign?



**: changes**

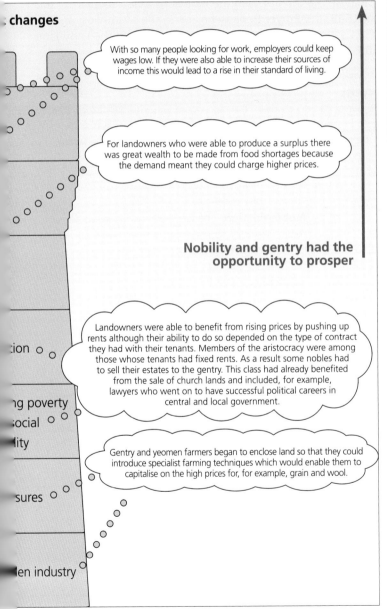

With so many people looking for work, employers could keep wages low. If they were also able to increase their sources of income this would lead to a rise in their standard of living.

For landowners who were able to produce a surplus there was great wealth to be made from food shortages because the demand meant they could charge higher prices.

**Nobility and gentry had the opportunity to prosper**

:ion

Landowners were able to benefit from rising prices by pushing up rents although their ability to do so depended on the type of contract they had with their tenants. Members of the aristocracy were among those whose tenants had fixed rents. As a result some nobles had to sell their estates to the gentry. This class had already benefited from the sale of church lands and included, for example, lawyers who went on to have successful political careers in central and local government.

ıg poverty
;ocial
lity

Gentry and yeomen farmers began to enclose land so that they could introduce specialist farming techniques which would enable them to capitalise on the high prices for, for example, grain and wool.

sures

len industry

△ A restored Elizabethan yeoman's house. Yeomen were wealthy farmers and their houses were the most visible sign of their place in the village social order.

△ After enclosure the open fields, including the common land, were parcelled into units or farms with boundary walls.

Insight

The causes of **sweating sickness** remain debateable and it does not exist today but it was responsible for several epidemics in both Tudor England and Europe between 1485 and 1551. Symptoms included shivering, headaches and hot sweats and the disease could kill within hours. It seems to have been more prevalent in London (20,000 people died there during the 1563 epidemic) and amongst the higher classes.

## Mid-Tudor crisis: more problems

Economic problems were not the only aspects of this period to create a sense of crisis. During the years from the mid-1540s to the late 1550s the people of England also experienced wars, rebellions, religious change and uncertainty over who would wear the crown. As if this was not enough there were severe outbreaks of '**sweating sickness**' and plague in 1551–52, of influenza from 1556–58 and smallpox four years later, all of which had high mortality rates.

Your understanding of these broader events and of the debate on whether there was a 'mid-Tudor crisis' will give you a framework within which you can analyse the threats from the rebellions that took place – the two rebellions of 1549 (the Prayer Book Rebellion in the south-west and Kett's rebellion in East Anglia), Wyatt's rebellion of 1554 and the Lady Jane Grey Plot of 1553.

**Dynastic Insecurity**. Henry's death in 1547 left the throne to his nine-year-old son, Edward. If Edward had no children, the next in line were his half sisters, Mary and then Elizabeth. History seemed to suggest that if the monarch was not an adult male then the prospect for strong and stable government was considerably reduced. This belief induced anxiety over how effectively England would be governed and what problems might ensue.

**Religion**. Henry VIII's establishment of the Royal Supremacy in the 1530s allowed his son's government to establish a Protestant reformation between 1549 and 1552. However, the succession of Mary Tudor, a staunch Roman Catholic, meant that these changes were short lived. These rapid about-turns in religion led some people to oppose and rebel against their monarch on religious grounds and added to the sense of royal insecurity.

**Noble Faction**. The fact that a boy king would need a regency council to govern for him led to an increase in **faction** during the last years of Henry VIII, as leading nobles jockeyed for position. Henry's will stipulated that there should be a Regency Council but in 1547 the Earl of Hertford quickly established himself as Lord Protector and took the title of Duke of Somerset. Within two years however Somerset had been overthrown in a coup led by the Earl of Warwick who, as the Duke of Northumberland, became Lord President of the Council. Northumberland then attempted to change the succession so that the dying Edward would be succeeded by the Protestant Lady Jane Grey and not by the Catholic Mary Tudor.

**Faction** describes the division of the government/court into rival groupings dominated by powerful nobles, each jockeying for position and trying to win the favours of the monarch. After the 1530s these opposing alignments usually included religious differences. A strong monarchy could keep the nobles in check and so faction was always at its most intense when the monarch was weak or distracted. Faction is an important consideration in any analysis of a rebellion, particularly those categorised as elite conspiracies. People were likely to be more willing to rebel when they perceived weakness at the centre and faction was clear evidence of that.

**Foreign Policy.** There was no glorious victory in foreign policy to raise people's spirits. Somerset continued the war against France and Scotland to force the latter to honour the marriage treaty between Edward VI and Mary, Queen of Scots but his fruitless pursuit of military success almost bankrupted the government. Northumberland withdrew from foreign commitments but at the cost of losing English-controlled Boulogne to the French, which represented a considerable humiliation. When Mary Tudor became queen, her support for her Spanish husband's war against France led to the loss of Calais, the last English garrison abroad. Meanwhile, the hostility of the Holy Roman Emperor to Edward's Protestant reformation caused him to threaten the exports of English cloth to Antwerp with disastrous results for the English cloth industry.

## Crisis, what crisis?

As you have seen above, there seems to be plenty of evidence to explain why historians have often described the period between the mid-1540s and the late 1550s as the 'mid-Tudor crisis'. However, historians writing within the last twenty years have challenged this 'crisis' label. They see the fact that the Tudor state faced disastrous foreign wars, internal rebellions, religious change, epidemics and economic and financial collapse and yet still emerged stable and with the monarch able to govern effectively, as a sign of strength rather than weakness. They also argue that this checklist of problems was typical of those faced by many governments and was not unique to the reigns of Edward and Mary. Why do you think that recent historians have become suspicious of general labels like 'crisis'?

The development of this debate is exemplified below, summarising the views of some of the historians who have contributed to it. All are well worth reading.

1 In the first edition of *England under the Tudors* (1955), G.R. Elton portrayed the succession of Edward VI and the prospect of a minority government as threatening the stability of a government which was already divided by faction based on religious differences. This made the country ripe for both internal unrest and possibly foreign invasion. He believed therefore that the death of Henry VIII triggered a crisis.

G.R. Elton

2 In the early 1990s David Loades challenged this view and claimed that historians liked to use the word 'crisis' because it made a period seem more exciting than it actually was in order to 'catch the readers' attention'. In *The Mid-Tudor Crisis 1545–1565* (1992) he characterised this period as one of change, development and continuity, less dramatic perhaps but ensuring each of Henry's children was able to succeed to the throne in turn; 'the true significance of the reigns of Edward VI and Mary lies less in what happened than in what did not happen'.

David Loades

3 Nigel Heard was another historian who disliked the use of 'crisis'. In *Edward VI and Mary: A Mid-Tudor Crisis?* (1990) he wrote: 'The concept of a mid-sixteenth-century crisis in England is now considered to be difficult to maintain. This is certainly true if by "crisis" it is implied that the whole country, and all of the people, were experiencing a crisis continually between 1547 and 1558. Indeed, it is only really possible to say that the country as a whole and some sections of society underwent very short-lived crises at times between these dates ... at no time, even in 1549, was the country in danger of collapse, and for most people life went on as normal'.

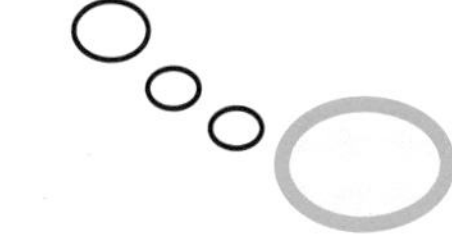

Nigel Heard

# 4 Does Kett's rebellion prove that 'rebellions of the belly' were really dangerous?

Tesco Morrisons Asda
Sainsbury's Waitrose

You may wonder what the names of modern supermarkets are doing in a book on Tudor England! The answer is that supermarkets are a reminder of one of the greatest differences between our lives and those of people in the sixteenth century. We can go to a local supermarket and choose our food from the shelves, including things from all over the world, either because they're out of season in the UK or because they're not produced here at all. In the 1500s, people depended on the food they managed to grow themselves or that they could buy from those who had grown it, in and around their locality. The staple diet of the lower classes was pottage, soup made in a pot over the fire. It was kept bubbling for days with peas and vegetables added as they could be scavenged and a chunk of bread as an accompaniment. The repetitive nature of this diet is captured in the rhyme:

> Pease pudding hot, pease pudding cold,
> pease pudding in the pot nine days old.

It may have been repetitive but at least people could survive on pease pudding. If the weather was unkind and harvests had failed, the little they had managed to grow or could afford to buy would have to be eked out further and further. If two or more harvests were poor, then there was a real danger of people starving to death. For much of this period there was little government support for the homeless or destitute. The monasteries which had provided some support for the poorest were dissolved in the 1530s and until the reign of Elizabeth those searching for employment and food were classed as vagrants who had to be moved on. Any who turned to stealing to feed themselves and their families risked being caught, tried and very probably hanged.

The situation in the 1540s was particularly bad because the cost of basic foods had risen so steeply that many people were unable to keep pace with prices. The root cause of this was the failure of agricultural production to keep pace with the steep rise in population. As demand increased so did the prices. In addition, people's opportunities to supplement the food they bought were under threat. The common land which had provided firewood, nuts, berries and rabbits was increasingly being enclosed by landlords eager to try new farming methods and so these extra sources of food were no longer available. Not surprisingly therefore, enclosures (and the gentry who put up these fences) were seen as the cause of the decline in living standards. In towns, the rising population and a periodic slump in industries such as the woollen trade meant there were not enough jobs to go round. Even for those in work, wages did not keep pace with the rising cost of food. The prospect of going hungry was very real and this caused great anger. In 1549 this anger boiled over into a major protest in East Anglia. It was led by a local landowner, Robert Kett, and like the Pilgrimage of Grace was remarkable for the quality of its leadership, its organisation and determination to persuade the government of the rightness of its cause.

## Enquiry Focus: Does Kett's rebellion prove that 'rebellions of the belly' were really dangerous?

In the early 1600s, the politician and historian, Francis Bacon, wrote in his book *The Essays or Counsels, Civil and Moral* that 'rebellions of the belly are the worst' and by 'worst' he meant the most dangerous to the government. Kett's rebellion gives us the chance to test the truth of Bacon's assertion by assessing just how threatening it was to the government, which was led at that stage of Edward VI's minority by the Protector, the Duke of Somerset.

To test Bacon's assertion use this graph to summarise your findings.

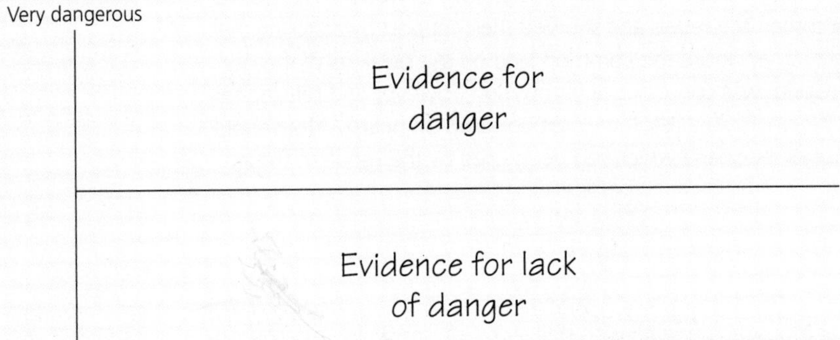
Very dangerous
Evidence for danger
Evidence for lack of danger
Not dangerous

1. As you read the account of Kett's rebellion on pages 74–81 jot down the evidence on a copy of this graph. This will give you an overall summary and you will be able to see clearly the pattern that's emerging.
2. Use the notes on the graph to complete a 'threat chart', like the example on page 12.
3. Make separate clear notes to justify your reasons for your grading of the six criteria.

However, before you begin, take time to think about the enquiry question and consider what the answer may be. We've already seen that the Pilgrimage of Grace and the Western Rising both frightened governments, but even with their very strong religious motivations and the support of some gentry they were defeated. Those who took part in what Bacon termed 'rebellions of the belly' were the common people and they were certainly feared by the ruling class as it was believed that hunger and desperation would drive the protestors to greater violence. These rebels would certainly be strongly motivated, but was it really just the commoners who took part in these rebellions and what would be the implications of that for success?

# Hunger, poverty and protest – the progress of Kett's rebellion

This very focused, well-organised and disciplined protest started in July 1549. This map shows how the unrest then spread rapidly, culminating in the establishment of Kett's camp at Norwich and its suppression by government forces at the end of August.

**1** There was widespread economic discontent during the early summer of 1549 with protests taking place in towns in Suffolk, Norfolk and Essex. Kett's rebellion started in the market town of Wymondham in Norfolk where the villagers were celebrating the annual festival at their abbey between 6 and 8 July. During the festivities a crowd decided to pull down enclosures which had recently been erected in the surrounding countryside. Robert Kett, a yeoman farmer who had himself enclosed land, agreed with the protestors that his enclosures should come down and accepted their choice of him to lead the protests.

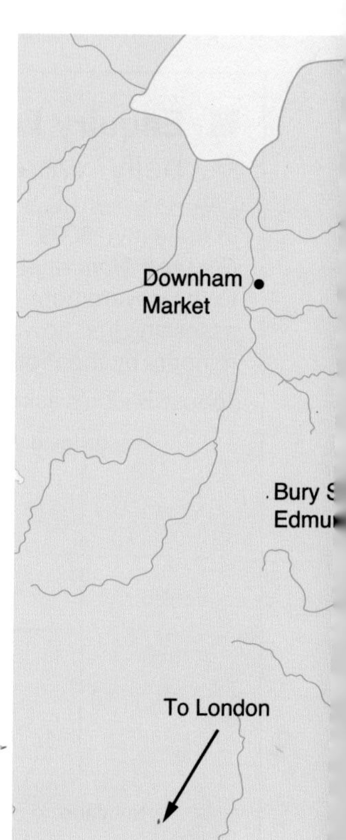
Downham Market
To London

**2** The rebels marched to Norwich which they reached on 10 July 1549. On the way they were joined by men from other villages and pulled down enclosures and attacked gentry property as they went. Norwich had a tradition of antagonism between social classes, largely due to extreme discrepancies of wealth. The poorer citizens therefore welcomed the rebels and showed their support by attacking the hedges which had recently enclosed the common land on the outskirts of the city. The mayor, Thomas Codd, was conscious of his position however and refused to allow the rebels into Norwich. As a result they set up camp on nearby Mousehold Heath, a wide expanse of moorland which had been used by the rebels in the 1381 Peasants' Revolt.

**3** Kett ran the camp at Mousehold Heath with staggering efficiency. He established a council with appropriate representation from both Norfolk and Suffolk which took responsibility for feeding and arming the increasing number of rebels, who reached a peak of around 16,000. Similar camps had by now been established at Downham Market and Hingham in Norfolk, Ipswich and Bury St Edmunds in Suffolk and further afield at Canterbury and Maidstone in Kent. The local ruling class was caught unawares; many gentry had obeyed a summons to Windsor by the Protector, the Duke of Somerset, to discuss these same economic issues. Fletcher and MacCulloch state that, 'Led by tradesmen and yeomen, the countrymen of Norfolk and Suffolk set up a quadrilateral of camps in July 1549, challenging the traditional rulers of these shires'.

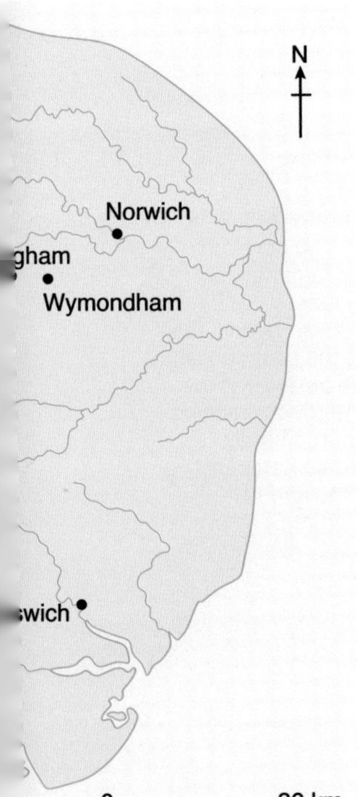
N
Norwich
gham
Wymondham
swich
0
30 km

**4** The presence of the rebel camp at Mousehold had divided the authorities in Norwich. In an attempt to prevent bloodshed they had initially agreed to provide the rebels with the provisions they requested. Kett meanwhile was busy drawing up a list of articles representing the rebels' grievances to present to Somerset. This calm was broken on 21 July however when a government herald appeared at the camp offering a pardon to all rebels if they dispersed. This and Kett's subsequent refusal to accept the pardon, on the grounds that he had committed no crime, encouraged the authorities to take a tougher stance. Provisions were withdrawn and the city's defences strengthened. The rebels attacked Norwich the following day, armed with pitchforks and spears and by evening the town was in their hands.

**5** Other camps in Suffolk were dealt with easily by the government because of the rebels' willingness to accept pardons in return for consideration of their grievances, but the protesters at Norwich were unwilling to disperse. The Marquis of Northampton was dispatched with a small force of 1500. Northampton easily re-captured Norwich but then dined and feasted with the deputy mayor of Norwich, allowing the rebels to capture and kill one of his mercenaries. After rapidly fortifying the city, Northampton repeated the offer of a pardon. Only twenty rebels accepted. Kett ordered a fresh attack and in the violent street fighting which followed 36 people were killed including Lord Sheffield, beaten to death by the rebels. Northampton retreated to London, leaving Norwich in rebel hands.

**6** Kett now held Norwich but his rebels were increasingly isolated as other camps disbanded. The government meanwhile assembled a much larger army of 12,000 men commanded by the Earl of Warwick. This entered Norwich on the 23 August. For the next three days the rebels staged daring attacks into the city, engaging the army in street fighting. They appeared to have gained the upper hand but on the 26 August Warwick's army was strengthened by the arrival of foreign mercenaries. When Warwick cut the supply lines between the city and the rebels' camp, Kett made the fatal decision to move his men from the higher Mousehold Heath to the valley of Dussindale where they were mown down by Warwick's cavalry. Three thousand rebels were killed. Kett was captured the following day and taken to London to stand trial for treason. In December he was returned to Norwich for execution and hanged from the walls of the castle.

1 What does this account of events suggest about the extent to which this rebellion threatened the government? Is 'rebellion' the best word to describe these events?

2 Check when the 1549 rising in the south-west took place. How might events in the south-west have affected government reactions to Kett's rebellion?

## Why did Kett's rebellion take place?

Begin by reading pages 76–81 quickly to gain an outline understanding, then read them more carefully, annotating your graph with evidence and summarising your conclusions in a 'threat chart' for Kett's rebellion. Remember to make more detailed notes to support the summary conclusions in your chart.

The economic and social hardships which you read about on pages 68–71 were felt across the country from the 1540s onwards, and you have seen their impact in the Western Rising in Chapter 3. They were particularly acute however in East Anglia. The diagram below summarises the causes of poverty and anger.

**rack-renting**
Increasing rents (to a level considered extortionate) paid by tenant farmers, often through threat of eviction

**Causes of poverty and anger**

**High rents**
The villagers were not only facing rising prices for food, many were also now paying increased rents. Fletcher and MacCulloch in *Tudor Rebellions* (1997) explain: '**Rack-renting** was felt to be a major and long standing grievance in Norfolk. ... Norfolk landlords had no difficulty in keeping pace with ... increased expenses ... and where landlords were harsh, their tenants undoubtedly suffered hardship'.

**Enclosures**
East Anglian landlords were keen to increase their profits by enclosing the common land in order to develop the more lucrative practice of sheep farming. The peasantry lost out in two ways. Firstly, there were fewer jobs as sheep could be looked after by fewer people than were required to till the land. Secondly, the common land could no longer be used by villagers to graze their own animals and to supplement their diets through trapping rabbits, picking berries and so on. It is hardly surprising that the third article issued by Kett's East Anglian rebels requested that, 'no lord of the manor shall enclose upon the common land'.

**Rising food prices**
All food prices were rising but the price of grain in particular was high. As Nicholas Fellows explains in *Disorder and Rebellion in Tudor England* (2001, p. 48): 'this had important consequences as bead was the staple diet of the masses, and the peasantry found themselves frequently in a state of poverty'. In such circumstances it was not surprising that, 'starvation in either the towns or countryside could soon turn into desperate violence and a challenge to either local or central government'.

**Inflation**
By the middle of the century inflation had doubled, largely as a result of the heavy taxation levied by Henry VIII to pay for wars and the Crown's policy of debasing the coinage in order to line its own coffers. Inflation meant the value of people's wages was less and that therefore they could afford less food.

The peasantry of East Anglia were in little doubt as to who was to blame for their poverty. Ruthless landlords were held responsible for the suffering of their tenants, whether by raising rents or by converting the common land (particularly in central and south-east Norfolk) to capitalise on the profits to be had from sheep farming. The poor were convinced that it was the greed of the gentry that had resulted in depopulated villages, unemployment and vagrancy, and hunger.

Relations between the landowning gentry class and their tenants were so strained in East Anglia that many historians have seen the ensuing Kett's rebellion as the product of a class war.

Although tensions in East Anglia between the classes had been simmering for some time, the trigger for the disturbances of summer 1549 appears to have been the policies of Protector Somerset towards enclosures which ironically gave the hard-pressed people hope. Andy Wood in *Riot, Rebellion and Popular Politics in Early Modern England* (2002), attributes the disturbances arising in East Anglia and elsewhere to:

> ... rumours that Protector Somerset's reformist government would establish a commission to remove recent enclosures. In June 1548, the anticipated government proclamation establishing an enclosures commission was issued. This both reiterated the widely held view of enclosure as a moral evil and assumed that the commons and the government had a mutual interest in its suppression.

A key feature of Kett's Articles was the belief that both rebels and the 'Good Duke', Somerset, were fighting the same war against a grasping gentry class.

### Edward Seymour, the Duke of Somerset, 1506–52

As the brother of Henry VIII's third queen, Jane Seymour, Edward Seymour rose rapidly to become a privy councillor and Earl of Hertford. He showed particular skills in conducting military campaigns against Scotland and France in the 1540s. On the death of Henry, Seymour was elected Protector by the Privy Council, became Duke of Somerset and was given the authority to run the country until his nephew, the new King Edward VI, was eighteen. Historians, and contemporaries, have described him as stubborn, obsessive, arrogant, rude, hesitant and greedy. His close relationship with the young King and his Protestant sympathies provided the basis of his power, but his inability to work well with fellow councillors and to act decisively against the commons in Kett's rebellion ensured his overthrow by the more astute Duke of Northumberland in 1549. He was executed in 1552.

# How threatening was Kett's rebellion?

## Robert Kett's leadership

Robert Kett has been credited with turning what was one of many local protests against social and economic grievances into a full-scale rebellion but, as John Walter argues in his article on Kett in the *Dictionary of National Biography* (2004), it is unlikely that he was the only leader: 'His signature always appeared first on the various commands and articles of the protesters, which makes it clear that Kett played a prominent role. But Kett was not, as he is sometimes portrayed, the only leader of the rebellion. The subsequent labelling of the events first as "Kett's camp" and later as "Kett's rising" probably exaggerates Kett's leadership and obscures that of others. In a letter written shortly before the final battle, the Duke of Somerset referred to "Ket and other Archtraitours".

It was the government's decision to focus on Kett and his brother in the trial after the defeat of the rebellion that both gave it Kett's name and ensured that successive governments gave him a hostile press, portraying him as an enemy of law and order. Kett underwent something of a transformation, however, in the nineteenth century when he was resurrected by Victorian historians as a folk hero, an early socialist and upholder of justice and equality. It seems most likely that Kett, like the leaders of the other camps, had some responsibilities within his local area and had become increasingly disillusioned with the activities of the local gentry who were expanding their own lands at the expense not only of the commons but of yeomen like himself. When the crowds from Wymondham began attacking his hedges therefore, he not only agreed with them that these enclosures should come down but was sufficiently convinced by the legitimacy of the villagers' grievances to agree to become their leader.

▽ **A summary of the main articles presented by Robert Kett to the government of Edward VI showing the rebels' greivances.**

- *3, 11, 17, 23 and 29 concern changes about the use of land including enclosures, loss of the common land and fishing rights and the landlords' exploitation of their position at the expense of the peasants.*
- *16, 27 and 28 express the rebels' frustration at the failure of the local nobility and gentry to run the county effectively on behalf of the central government.*
- *8, 15 and 20 refer to religious concerns but unlike the Western Rebellion welcome the recent Protestant reforms and request that the changes must ensure an improvement in the quality of spiritual life.*

Kett was encouraged by Somerset's apparent hostility to enclosures to believe that he had the opportunity to provide a sympathetic Protector with the means to initiate social and economic reforms. The Articles of 1549, drawn up by the council at Mousehold Heath, represented both a summary of wide ranging local grievances and a potential blueprint for a restructured local government at the expense of the gentry who Kett believed were inadequate as both Justices of the Peace and local government officials.

The articles highlighted in the scroll (left) make clear that the rebels saw a link between their poverty and the activities of the ruling classes. In the face of economic hardship many felt let down by those above them with responsibility for their welfare. The articles included an appeal to Somerset to 'give authority to such commissioners as your poor commons have chosen', so that they could put an end to local government which, 'hath been abused by your Justices of your peace, and other of your officers', and again return to the more halcyon days of Henry VIII's reign. Norwich, with its huge discrepancies between rich and poor with 6 per cent of the population owning 60 per cent of the land and goods, was particularly vulnerable to complaints against the ruling classes.

The articles also reflected the rebels' support for the religious changes introduced by Somerset and the young Edward VI. The rebels' camps were decidedly Protestant, using the new Prayer Book and listening to evangelical preachers. The rebels shared Somerset's desire for a highly educated clergy who could raise the standard of spiritual teaching and learning. There was no desire to stop the doctrinal changes or return to Catholicism which drove the Western Rising.

Once the rebellion was underway, Kett rapidly attracted support from a population who believed that the government shared their grievances and would bring about social reform. The march on Norwich attracted many along the way so that within a matter of days Kett's followers numbered about 16,000. People leapt at the opportunity to tear down the hated enclosures or vandalise the house of a local gentleman. Unsurprisingly the rebels had no support from nobles or wealthy gentry, but rather from small tenant farmers, lesser gentry, rural workers and unemployed craftsmen, many from the city of Norwich itself. In the week after 7 July, other rebel camps were set up throughout the Home Counties, the Thames Valley and East Anglia with what Fletcher describes as 'astonishing speed'. The outbreak of these different rebellions at the same time has led MacCulloch to argue that there must have been 'co-ordinated planning throughout the region'.

Like the other camps in East Anglia, the one at Mousehold was set up to make the point to the government that the ordinary people were capable of conducting business without the gentry. Rebels with previous experience of local government, such as bailiffs and constables, established a form of local government. Each of the **hundreds** that had men in the rebellion elected two governors to sit on the council. Under the authority of Kett and the council, written commissions bearing his name were sent out to purchase supplies of food and gunpowder. This council, meeting under an oak tree, dispensed justice and settled disputes. Kett's name again appears on one of the few surviving writs from this period.

**hundreds**
These were introduced by the Anglo-Saxons who divided large areas into smaller units based on one hundred homesteads for administrative, judicial and military purposes. Traditionally within each hundred there was a meeting place where men could discuss local issues and where judicial proceedings were carried out

Kett's aim was to negotiate with, not attack, the government because he believed he was helping Somerset by highlighting ineffective local government and also supporting Somerset's apparent intention to help the poor. This is why the rebels camped rather than marched on London, waiting until their continued presence pressurised the government into conceding to their demands. Given Somerset's approach this strategy seemed realistic. Kett also refused a pardon because he believed that would make him guilty of rebellion, a charge which he refuted. However his refusal pushed him into a political role that allowed the government to claim that he had; 'taken upon hym our royal power and dignitie and calleth himself M(aste)r and king of Norfolk and Suffolk', and so gave Somerset a way out of the predicament he found himself in.

Even so, the development of a government response took time. The camp at Mousehold became established because the local authorities were unable to deal decisively with it and Somerset's government seemed unaware of the seriousness of both the Western Rising and Kett's rebellion. Pre-occupation with invasion from France made it inevitable that the government resorted to offering pardons, a cheap strategy that did not tie-up forces that Somerset needed for his campaigns in Scotland. Throughout the summer of 1549 therefore there were negotiations between the rebels and representatives of Somerset based on the premise of a royal pardon. Even the dispatching of an army led by the Marquis of Northampton was to pressurise the rebels rather than engage them in armed combat. However, Northampton's failure signalled an end to negotiation and compromise.

By August 1549 both leaders had backed themselves into a corner. Kett continued to refuse a pardon although some of his followers would initially have accepted one. However, when the offer was repeated a second and final time, only 20 out of the 16,000 agreed. Somerset, meanwhile, had come under intense criticism from the Privy Council for showing leniency by negotiating with rebels – councillors such as Sir William Paget urging him to use the repressive measures employed by Henry VIII. Somerset's position was not strong enough for him to resist this pressure indefinitely or to antagonise the gentry by considering Kett's demands. Andy Wood summarises Somerset as a 'tragic figure, caught between the active politics of a rebellious commons, the guarded hostility of the gentry and nobility, and his own authoritarian reform agenda'. The dispatching of the royal army under Warwick shows the 'Good Duke's' eventual realisation that he could only stay in power by showing the rest of the Privy Council that he was capable of enforcing law and order.

△ The erection of the plaque on the walls of Norwich Castle to commemorate the 400th anniversary of Kett's rebellion emphasises the twentieth-century view of Kett as a leader of the common people in their struggle for social justice, who was ahead of his time.

## Concluding your enquiry

Kett's rebellion represented a considerable challenge to the workings of central government because its leadership, organisation and demands show considerable political sophistication. In this way it did not embody the characteristics of the typical food riot so feared by Francis Bacon. Nevertheless it was the harsh economic changes of the mid-sixteenth century and their threat to the living standards of the poor which provoked Robert Kett and the other leaders of the camps to demand better local government. They accused the gentry of not only failing to protect the poor in their area but, in many cases, of exacerbating hunger and poverty through enclosing land, driving up food prices and raising rates. In the camps across East Anglia they set up systems of self-government, which included the regulation of food supplies and aimed to show the government that there existed within the commons experiences and skills which could be better utilised and could act as a check on the perceived greed of local gentry.

Hunger and poverty undoubtedly provided the catalyst for the outbreak and spread of Kett's rebellion, given the social and economic circumstances prevalent in East Anglia. It was the third largest of all Tudor Rebellions and the presence of rebel camps across Norfolk, Suffolk and probably Essex effectively sealed off that area from the control of central government. The local nature of the grievances however and the lack of any intention to either march on London or attempt to overthrow the government makes it less threatening than some other rebellions. As part of your analysis you may therefore want to address the issue of 'threatening for whom'.

The response of the government does not show that it initially saw this 'rebellion of the belly' as very threatening. The government in 1549 was neither however united nor consistent in its reactions and made blunders, especially in its choice of Northampton which made the situation in Norwich worse. It also seriously underestimated the resolve and conviction of Robert Kett and the threat to the political status quo inherent in his articles.

'Rebellions of the belly' did not end in 1549. Food riots and protests against land use occurred sporadically throughout the century, such as the food riots throughout the last two decades of Elizabeth's reign in Ipswich, Gloucestershire, Hampshire, Somerset and Kent. They were usually dealt with by local gentry and nobility, as happened with all the camps in East Anglia except Mousehold.

In 1596 a planned uprising in Oxfordshire against enclosures failed when only four men turned up to seize the home of the local Lord Lieutenant. Despite these small numbers the government used considerable force to make its point and all four were executed. Unlike Kett's, these uprisings were undertaken by artisans and servants, did not win support from the middle classes of yeomen and gentlemen and had no leaders. Even so ministers still feared hunger and poverty, with William Cecil observing that 'there is nothing will sooner lead men into sedition than dearth of victual'. By the 1590s however, the strength of the Tudor monarchy and its close alliance with the gentry class meant that Elizabeth could work through central and local government to alleviate the problems of poverty and vagrancy through the introduction of Poor Laws.

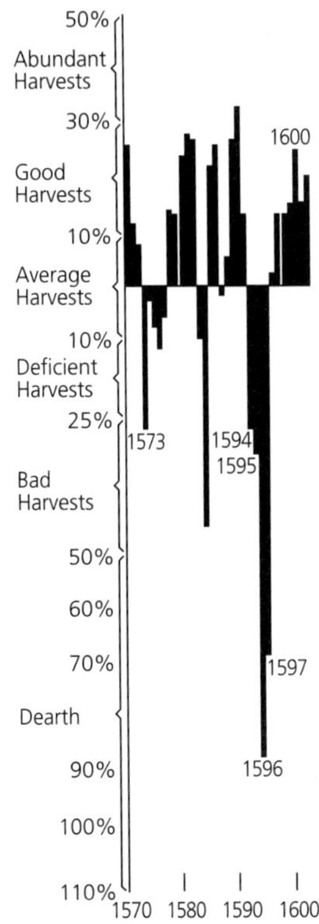
50%
Abundant Harvests
30%
Good Harvests
10%
Average Harvests
10%
Deficient Harvests
25%
Bad Harvests
50%
60%
70%
Dearth
90%
100%
110%
1600
1573
1594
1595
1597
1596
1570
1580
1590
1600

△ This graph shows how variable harvests were in the later sixteenth century. The sequence of poor harvests between 1594 and 1597 led to deaths from starvation and threats of disorder but no major protest risings. Perhaps Bacon and Cecil were wrong about the danger created by hunger?

## Concluding your enquiry

1. Complete your 'threat chart' (see page 12) to evaluate the threat from Kett's rebellion. Make sure you have detailed notes to justify your grading of the threat according to each of the six criteria.
2. Use your completed evidence graph to prepare arguments for and against the statement that Kett's rebellion supports Bacon's contention that 'rebellions of the belly are the worst'.
3. Place Kett's rebellion on your own version of the 'threat line' on page 13. Add brief annotations to give the major reasons for where you placed this rebellion.
4. You can now extend your research to consider whether social and economic grievances feature in any of the other rebellions described in this book. This will enable you to prepare a synopsis which evaluates their overall contribution to Tudor rebellions between 1485 and 1603.

# Context: Mary, Elizabeth and religious change

## Queen Mary Tudor (1553–58)

△ Born in 1516, Mary was the eldest child of Henry VIII by his first wife, Catherine of Aragon. Throughout her life Mary was deeply influenced by her mother's devotion to Catholicism. This portrait by Hans Eworth dates from 1554 when Mary had been queen for a year.

Mary's upbringing as heir to the throne came to an abrupt end in 1533 when Henry VIII divorced her mother, Catherine of Aragon, to marry Anne Boleyn. This had the effect of making Mary illegitimate, a fact which was reinforced by the later births of first Elizabeth and then Edward and confirmed by an Act of Parliament. For several years she was rarely invited to court and was sustained by her devotion to the Roman Catholic faith and links with her mother's relatives, particularly the Holy Roman Emperor, Charles V. She was horrified by the Break with Rome in 1534 and only took the Oath of Supremacy under threat of execution for treason. After 1540 relations with her father improved, Mary's claim to the throne was reinstated and she returned to court.

When Edward became king in 1547 Mary had to tread carefully. Edward's Protestant reformation meant that Mary became the potential figurehead for any rebellious Catholics, particularly as it was known she continued to celebrate Mass, despite royal orders to the contrary. Mary's religion was the reason why Edward, when his health deteriorated, agreed to exclude Mary from the throne, replacing her with the Protestant Lady Jane Grey. The story of how Mary fought for and won her throne is told in Chapter 5, but it was one of the tragedies of her reign that she believed her victory was an endorsement of her Catholic and Spanish adherences.

Mary had three priorities when she became queen in 1553. She was determined to restore Roman Catholicism and the Pope as Head of the Church, she intended to marry and have children to ensure the continuation of Catholicism and she wanted to strengthen ties with Spain, her mother's homeland. Six weeks after her coronation she announced her impending marriage to Philip II of Spain and within the year the English Church had been reconciled to the Roman Catholic faith and the authority of the Pope. The stage was set for the tragedies of her reign for which Mary is remembered: the burning of nearly 300 Protestant martyrs; the loss of Calais to Spain's enemy, France; and a profoundly unhappy marriage which failed to provide the heir who would have secured Mary's ambitions.

As preparation for Chapter 5 read pages 82–87 and then think about these questions:

- What do you expect to see as the main reasons for opposition to the two queens? In what ways might the queens themselves have been responsible for rebellions?
- Why were some nobles likely to rebel but not others?
- Were rebellions against Mary and Elizabeth more likely to threaten the Tudor's hold on the crown than the rebellions of 1536 and 1549?

## Queen Elizabeth Tudor (1558–1603)

Born in 1533, Elizabeth was the daughter of Henry VIII and Anne Boleyn. Like Mary, she had to endure the downfall of her mother and exclusion from her father's court. Her education, with its **humanist**/Protestant slant, made it unlikely Elizabeth would continue Mary's Catholicism.

Her father's treatment of his wives and her dangerous but exciting teenage flirtation with Thomas Seymour (subsequently executed for treason, see page 89) may have coloured her later views on marriage and relationships. Elizabeth's arrest and interrogation by Mary in 1554 on suspicion of involvement in Wyatt's rebellion put her life at risk and perhaps confirmed in her a lifelong need for caution and detachment.

On becoming queen in 1558 Elizabeth determined to establish a national Church that was uniquely English and would prove acceptable to the majority of her subjects by incorporating elements of the Protestantism of Edward VI's reign and the Roman Catholicism of Mary's reign. Her aim was to confirm the monarch as Supreme Head of the Church, rather than the Pope, and to combine Protestant doctrine with a traditional structure and Catholic ritual. The 1559 Acts of Supremacy and Uniformity established Elizabeth as Supreme Governor of the Church of England, a wording thought to be more acceptable to both Catholics and the more **radical Protestants**, and enforced a new Prayer Book based on the Protestant ones of Edward VI although with ambiguous wording around the communion service. Not all Catholics however were able to accept this compromise.

It was expected that Elizabeth would marry and produce an heir but she never did. Many reasons for this have been suggested: Elizabeth's childhood experiences; her relationship with Robert Dudley; her reluctance to share power; the lack of a suitable suitor; and the risks of embroilment within European politics. Without children of her own, Elizabeth's heir was her cousin, Mary Stuart, who was briefly Queen of France and, from 1561, Queen of Scotland. Mary was a Roman Catholic who believed that Elizabeth was illegitimate and that she, Mary, was the rightful queen of England. Mary's position as an alternative queen was to cause Elizabeth continuing anxiety.

**humanist**
An education with a humanist leaning stresses the importance of individual thought and evidence over established doctrines and faith. In the sixteenth century scholars would have been expected to acquire this learning through the analysis of Greek and Latin texts

Catholics maintained that the Pope was the Head of the Church while, for **radical Protestants**, only Christ could be 'head' of the Church.

▷ **The coronation portrait of Elizabeth I. From the start of her reign Elizabeth used biblical slogans to emphasise the advent of a new Protestant regime to contrast with the chaos of Catholic Mary's reign. She appears here as Deborah, the judge and restorer of the House of Israel, heralding in an age of light after a time of darkness.**

Insight

## Context: The importance of the ruling elite

By the reigns of Mary and Elizabeth the importance of the ruling elite in ensuring political stability in England was well established. The nobles and gentry had served the Tudors well in central and local government and in resisting rebellions. Nevertheless, some individuals had participated in recent rebellions: Lord Darcy, Robert Aske and Sir Humphrey Bigod in the Pilgrimage of Grace and Humphrey Arundell in the Western Rising. Their participation was dangerous because they brought status, authority and the ability to raise military forces to rebellions. More importantly, by siding with rebels they were not fulfilling their role as the ruling elite in putting down disturbances at local level before they got out of hand. Without a permanent army of their own, monarchs depended on nobles and gentry to provide the men to defeat rebels and the fact that they usually did so is a major reason why Tudor rebellions failed. The Dukes of Norfolk and Suffolk contained the rising against the Amicable Grant, the Earl of Shrewsbury stopped the Pilgrimage of Grace at Doncaster, the mayor of Exeter, John Blackaller, held that city against the Western Rising while Thomas Codd did the same in Norwich against Kett's rebels.

The rebellions between 1553 and 1568 and again in 1601 were all led by members of the elite who either feared a loss of political influence and status or had a specific grievance against the monarch's policies, usually related to religion. However, it took a lot for members of this class to rebel. They were transferring their allegiance from the monarch, their social superior, to rebels who were their social inferiors though perhaps it was easier to do this when the monarch was female. The elite also had the most to lose. Contrary to some preconceptions, they preferred peace to war and support for the monarch brought rewards of political office in the royal household, central government or local administration. Powerful and wealthy noble families such as the Howards in Norfolk, the Percy family in Northumberland and the Earls of Derby, Shrewsbury, Pembroke, Bedford, Westmorland and Cumberland were best able to protect their own interests through serving the monarch and avoiding conflict.

Members of the gentry were also crucial to the monarch in maintaining law and order and as a result saw their opportunities to better themselves expand. However, loyalty to the monarch was not just about self-interest and greed. Many of the ruling elite took great pride in holding the newly created offices of Lord Lieutenant and Justice of the Peace and took their duties and responsibilities very seriously. Alison Wall comments in *Power and Protest in England 1525–1640* (2000):

> Some men may have desired public authority selfishly for status, for advancing their own interests and harassing their rivals, as successive Lord Chancellors complained. However the private diaries and letters of JPs ... demonstrate astonishing devotion to duty by many gentry while they held local office.

Members of the ruling elite therefore seldom rebelled and only when the interests of a monarch no longer coincided with their own. This could arise when the monarch changed or when there was a more attractive alternative in the wings, but even then rebellion was the last resort of a desperate few. The case studies on pages 86–87 are included to deepen your understanding of the opportunities and dangers facing the ruling elite, of the crucial role they played in rebellions and of the vagaries of fortune as to who ended up on the winning side.

◁ Hardwick Hall in Derbyshire, built during Elizabeth's reign for Bess of Hardwick. Bess was the second richest woman in England (after the Queen herself). Power, influence and considerable wealth were the reward for loyalty to the Tudors.

| Position | Duties | Importance |
|---|---|---|
| Lord (and Deputy) Lieutenant | • Commanding local militia during emergencies.<br>• Assembling, inspecting and training local militia.<br>• Administrative and supervisory duties. | This post was created by the Tudors to formalise the role of leading nobles in the shires. Its holders were often also members of the Privy Council in London. These nobles tended to serve the Crown well, often out of a sense of responsibility and loyalty and also because they could see the financial benefits of office holding and patronage to supplement their incomes. |
| Justice of the Peace | • Enforcing government legislation.<br>• Providing the local militia.<br>• Investigating breaches of the law.<br>• Hearing cases in the Quarter Sessions and determining sentences.<br>• Administering the Poor Law, controlling sheriffs and licensing ale houses. | Their numbers and workload increased during the sixteenth century because legislation added to their duties and responsibilities. The gentry class valued this office for its prestige and social standing. The expectation of promotion ensured the loyalty and co-operation of much of the politically-active classes. The Tudors were aware of the need to cultivate this group and used all means available to do so. At times when they feared a clash of local sensitivities, as in the enforcement of religious laws, they used external commissioners instead. |

## Sir William Cecil and the advantages of political caution

William Cecil navigated his way through three changes of monarch, religious settlements and rebellions, emerging as Elizabeth's Principal Secretary in 1558. After a classical education at Cambridge and legal training at Gray's Inn, Cecil followed the careers of his grandfather and father (both excellent examples of men from the yeomen class who prospered through public service), becoming an MP in the 1540s at the end of Henry VIII's reign. His friendship with Roger Ascham and John Cheke, both religious reformists like Cecil, who were tutors to the new king Edward VI, probably helped him to secure a post in the household of Protector Somerset. Cecil's lifelong capacity for hard work and attention to detail ensured his promotion as Somerset's private secretary in 1548. When Somerset lost power in 1549, Cecil was imprisoned but in 1550 was appointed as Edward VI's Principal Secretary. He was also, by now, significantly helping the sixteen-year-old Princess Elizabeth run her estates.

Cecil served Edward VI and Northumberland well. Like most of the King's officers, on Edward's death Cecil signed the Device excluding Mary Tudor from the throne (see the Lady Jane Grey plot on pages 90–92), but received a pardon on her accession, although the price for this was conformity to Catholicism and the disapproval of his Protestant friends. In *The Cecils* (2012, p. 51) David Loades writes:

△ **William Cecil, Lord Burghley, Elizabeth's most loyal and capable adviser, probably painted in the 1560s. Cecil, like his father, benefited from loyal service to the Tudors, even when there were differences of religious opinion.**

> Cecil's religious conformity certainly saved him trouble with the authorities, but it may also have strained his conscience and additionally earned him reproach from some of his friends and relatives who had gone into exile ... clearly fearing that he had lost all sense of right and wrong. There are signs in his diary and other later documents that these reproaches troubled him deeply, but he was not made of the stuff of martyrs.

Although Mary did not appoint Cecil to any office, he remained a public figure and continued working with Elizabeth. As Mary's health worsened, Cecil became a regular visitor to **Hatfield House**.

The Spanish ambassador predicted, a month before Mary's death:

> I have been told for certain that Cecil, who was King Edward's secretary, will also be secretary to madame Elizabeth. He is said to be an able and virtuous man, but a heretic ...

Cecil survived the turbulence of the mid-Tudor period and took up the challenge of securing the fledgling government of Elizabeth I.

**Hatfield House** in Hertfordshire was Elizabeth I's childhood home, although after Mary became queen in 1553 she was kept there under house arrest. Famously, Elizabeth was sitting under an oak tree in the park of Hatfield when news was brought to her in 1558 that she was now queen.

## Thomas Howard, Fourth Duke of Norfolk and the perils of noble ambition

△ Thomas Howard, Duke of Norfolk. Howard's downfall, like others of his house, reflects the Howards' conviction that with a lineage stretching back to Norman times and as descendants of Edward I they outranked all others of noble birth.

While Cecil survived religious change other members of the elite did not. Some older noble families felt that their political influence declined during this period because of their opposition to Elizabeth's religious changes. The prospects of Thomas Howard, fourth Duke of Norfolk, living to a ripe old age were never good. His father, the Earl of Surrey, was executed for treason against Henry VIII in 1547. The eight-year-old Thomas was then brought up by his aunt and given a classical education with an emphasis on Greek. Thomas seems to have been an average scholar with no unswerving religious convictions but when his elderly grandfather, the third Duke, was released from imprisonment in the Tower of London at the start of Mary's reign, he ensured that fifteen-year-old Thomas was educated in the Catholic faith.

By the time Elizabeth became queen, Thomas had succeeded his grandfather as Duke and as the hereditary Grand Marshall of England. He was the foremost peer of the realm but the story of the following decade is a mixture of loyalty to the Queen, frustration at lack of personal recognition, glittering ambition and chronic indecision. Despite his role in securing peace with Scotland in 1560 and his elevation to the Privy Council, Norfolk let himself be persuaded that the best way to end the succession crisis caused by Elizabeth's refusal to marry was for him, as the leading English noble, to marry the heir to the throne, Mary, Queen of Scots. As Mary already had a son from a previous marriage, it was assumed that she would be bound to have another with Norfolk and so secure the succession on Elizabeth's death. Norfolk was also even persuaded that Elizabeth would come round to the idea of this marriage.

However, he was deceived by more skilful politicians and lacked the courage to act decisively. With Elizabeth opposed to the marriage, Norfolk became implicated in both the Northern Rebellion and Ridolfi Plot which aimed to replace Elizabeth with Mary, Queen of Scots with himself as Mary's husband. As Neville Williams wrote in his biography of Thomas Howard (1963):

> The proposal that he should marry the Queen of Scots was the turning point in his career, for lured by the chance of a crown he went to pieces ... for this he would dally with conspiracy and break his oath to his sovereign. He would refuse to heed warnings ... for nothing would distract him from the prize he had set his heart upon, and in the end he would be trapped into committing treason and compromising his religion.

That treason ended in Norfolk's execution in 1572.

# 5 Why did the elite conspiracies against Mary and Elizabeth fail?

The elite conspiracies have been regarded by some historians as particularly dangerous. Roger Turvey and Nigel Heard wrote in *Change and Protest 1536–88: Mid-Tudor Crises?* (2009) that:

> The dangers posed by elite rebellion were potentially more serious than those posed by popular uprisings ... Kett and the Western rebels never set out to destroy the government or change the monarchy ...

What similarities are there between the dynastic rebellions against Henry VII and the elite rebellions of 1553–1601?

The aims of the elite rebels brought a threat that was absent from the rebellions of the 1530s and 1540s which sought to reverse a religious or economic policy. In addition, those 'elites' who challenged the throne reduced the ability of the monarch, who relied on their military force, to suppress rebellions in their early stages. At a time when the crown had passed to a boy and then, in quick succession, to two females, and against a background of religious, social and economic change, the obvious question to be asked is why, if these elite rebellions seemed so dangerous, did they fail?

## Enquiry Focus: Why did the elite conspiracies against Mary and Elizabeth fail?

**1** Read the accounts of the four rebellions that follow:

- The Lady Jane Grey Plot of 1553
- Wyatt's rebellion of 1554
- The Northern Rebellion of 1569
- Essex's rebellion of 1601.

Summarise the reasons for the failure of each one on a mind map such as the one shown below.

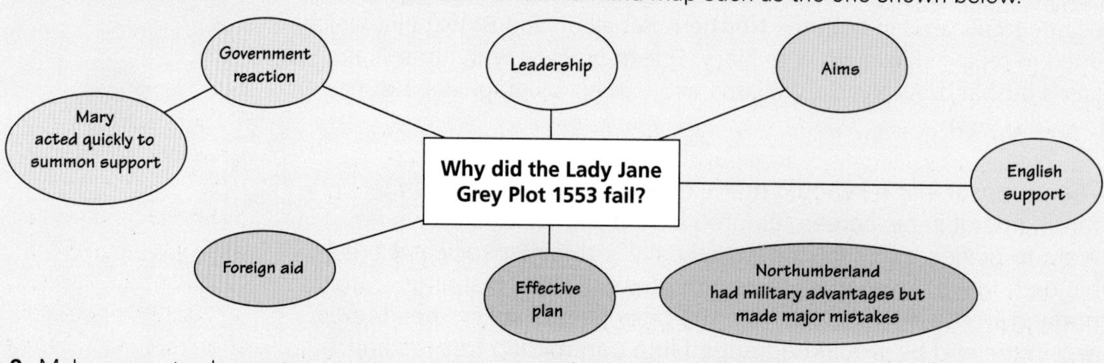
Why did the Lady Jane Grey Plot 1553 fail?
Government reaction
Mary acted quickly to summon support
Leadership
Aims
English support
Foreign aid
Effective plan
Northumberland had military advantages but made major mistakes

**2** Make separate clear notes to support your summaries on the mind map.

## The Lady Jane Grey Plot of 1553

Lady Jane Grey has been the focus of many novels and films eager to tell the tragic story of a young, innocent girl who was queen for just nine days, and whose short life ended on the scaffold, the victim of scheming politicians. Jane's political importance, as you can see in the family tree on page 5, lay in the fact that she was the great-granddaughter of Henry VII. Jane's claim to the throne made her a highly marriageable 'commodity'. As early as 1548, aged ten, Jane was sent to be brought up in the household of Katherine Parr and **Thomas Seymour**, the latter seeking to enhance his own status by arranging a marriage between Edward VI and Jane.

**Thomas Seymour** was the brother of the Lord Protector, the Duke of Somerset and uncle of King Edward VI. He married the widow of Henry VIII, Katherine Parr, but after her death in 1548 embarked on a dangerous plan to marry the 14-year-old Princess Elizabeth without the permission of the Privy Council. This was a treasonable offence for which he was executed in 1549.

△ **This anonymous picture of Lady Jane Grey (1537–54) was probably painted in the 1590s, towards the end of Elizabeth's reign.**

After Seymour's downfall Jane focused on her studies, acquiring a reputation as a scholar with considerable ability in Greek, Latin, French, Italian and Hebrew. Unusually, she had also been brought up in a Protestant reformist household. Her father, Henry Grey, Duke of Suffolk, corresponded with Swiss humanists and reformers and Jane had been encouraged further in this direction by Katherine Parr.

The plot to make Jane queen originated towards the end of Edward VI's reign and was designed to prevent Mary from succeeding her childless half-brother. Since Edward VI was only a minor he had relied on the ruling elite to govern on his behalf through a Council of Regency. This had been dominated initially by the Duke of Somerset and after his downfall in 1549 by the Duke of Northumberland, who as the Earl of Warwick had defeated Kett's rebellion. The turning point came at the beginning of 1553 when the health of Edward began to deteriorate with what was probably **TB**.

**TB**

TB or tuberculosis is a common and often lethal disease which is today more prevalent in developing countries. It usually attacks the lungs. TB is spread through the air and symptoms include chronic coughing and fever

Both the Succession Act of 1544 and Henry VIII's will stated that if Edward died without children then the crown was to pass to Mary. As a devout Catholic, it was expected that Mary would restore the Catholic religion if she became queen.

The Lady Jane Grey Plot, as you will see, is probably most like the dynastic rebellions of Henry VII's reign in that a leading noble (in this case the Duke of Northumberland) was trying to replace a Tudor with his own 'claimant' to the throne. However, what complicates this 'rebellion' is that the 'rebel' was already running the country and initially had the support of the Council and the government's armed forces while Mary, the Tudor monarch in-waiting, had to fight to win the crown by raising support from the countryside. It is therefore a unique Tudor rebellion.

My deuise for the succession. 217

1 For lakke of issu ~~masle~~ of my body ~~to the issu masle cumming of thissu femal, as i haue after declared~~. To the L Fraunceses heires masles, ~~For lakke of~~ if she haue any such issu befor my death to the L' Jane and her heires masles, To the L Katerins heires masles, To the L Maries heires masles, To the heires masles of the daughters wich she shal haue hereafter. Then to the L Margets heires masles. For lakke of such issu, To theires masles of the L Janes daughters To theires masles of the L Katerins daughters and so forth til yow come to the L Margets daughters heires masles.

2 If after my death theire masle be entred into 18 yere old, then he to haue the hole rule and gouernaunce therof.

3. But if he be under 18, then his mother to be gouuernres til he entre 18 yere old, But to doe nothing w'out thauise and agremēt of 6 parcel of a counsel to be pointed by my last will to the nombre of 20.

4 If the mother die befor theire entre into 18 the realme to ~~be~~ be gouuerned by the cousel Prouided that after ~~he~~ he be 14 yere al great matters of importaunce be ~~so~~ opened to him.

~~5. If i died w'out issu, and ther were none heire masle, then the L Fraunces to be gouuernres regent for lakke of her, the her eldest daughters and for lakke of them the L Margets to be~~

△ The 314 words written by Edward VI to alter the succession and make Lady Jane Grey queen. The first version was probably written by Edward in early 1553. The alterations made to the first clause in June when Edward's health was beginning to fail, leave the throne directly to Lady Jane rather than any male heirs born to the Grey family.

### John Dudley, Duke of Northumberland, 1502–53

Son of Henry VII's infamous minister of finances who was executed by Henry VIII, Dudley was brought up by Sir Edward Guildford whose daughter he married. He served the King successfully in wars in France and against the Scots and gained a reputation for military prowess. On Henry's death he became the Earl of Warwick and Lord Great Chamberlain. After defeating Kett's rebellion he moved against the Duke of Somerset, securing first his removal as Lord Protector and then his execution for treason. In January 1550 he became Lord President of the Council and the following year, Duke of Northumberland. He was a skilful politician but also ambitious and opportunistic.

## The escalation of the Lady Jane Grey Plot

Early in 1553 steps were taken to change Henry's succession arrangements by replacing the heir, Catholic Mary Tudor, with the future male descendants of Protestant Lady Jane Grey, the granddaughter of Henry VIII's sister. This diary of 1553 explains the sequence of events.

**January** Edward's health started to decline.

**March** Edward was well enough to carry out some duties.

**April** Plans were made to marry Lady Jane Grey to Northumberland's son, Guildford Dudley, one of three aristocratic weddings to take place in May, all of which boosted Northumberland's influence. Jane's sister married the son of the Earl of Pembroke and Northumberland's daughter married the heir of the Earl of Huntingdon.

Edward drafted notes to exclude Mary Tudor from the succession. He ignored the claims of both his half-sisters (Mary and Elizabeth), who had been declared illegitimate, in favour of any male heirs born to the Grey family, the daughter and granddaughters of Henry VIII's younger sister, Mary. The resulting 'Devise' to change the succession was signed by Edward and shown to Northumberland at the end of the month.

**7 May** Northumberland confided to the French ambassadors both his fears for Edward's health and his worries for the succession.

**25 May** Guildford and Jane were married, despite Jane's reluctance. There was a lavish ceremony and they were living together as man and wife by July. In a letter written later to Mary Tudor, Jane claimed to be ignorant of the plot to make her queen on Edward's death until 9 July when she was taken to meet the Privy Council who knelt before her.

**28 May** The Council received confirmation that France would not let the Holy Roman Emperor intervene on Mary's behalf if she were barred from the throne.

Edward's doctors informed Northumberland that Edward would not live beyond the summer. Over the next two weeks Edward altered the wording of the Devise to leave the throne directly to Lady Jane Grey, as she had as yet no male descendants.

**11 June** Edward met his councillors and expressed his concern that Mary would not only restore Catholicism but very possibly marry a foreigner.

**13 June** Edward's lawyers stated they were not prepared to change Henry VIII's Succession Act of 1544. The Lord Chief Justice argued that Mary had the legitimate claim and that Edward as a minor could not change the succession.

**15 June** Northumberland, with Edward, harangued the lawyers who were bullied into turning the Device into a legal document. However, although it was signed by the King, it was never endorsed by Parliament.

**21 June** All leading officials signed the will and swore in front of the King to uphold the Devise.

**6 July** Edward died before Parliament could change the Act of Succession which still named Mary as heir. He left the document, which named Lady Jane Grey as his heir, signed by the ruling elite but not yet law. The suddenness of Edward's death had not given Northumberland the time he needed to win over the people through a propaganda campaign. In particular, he lost the opportunity to capitalise on the fact that the Acts declaring Mary and Elizabeth to be illegitimate had never been repealed.

## Why did the plot fail?

Northumberland has been accused, for centuries, of having masterminded the Lady Jane Grey Plot to preserve his own position. Does this timeline suggest any alternative interpretations?

This plot was sanctioned by the strongest leadership in the land, the King and his regent, the Duke of Northumberland. That however neither made it legal nor popular. There was no guarantee that this plot to subvert the succession by excluding Mary Tudor, the daughter of Henry VIII, would happen peacefully, whatever Northumberland might have told himself and his fellow councillors.

When Edward died, Northumberland announced that Lady Jane Grey was now queen, as stipulated by the dying King and Council in the Device. Northumberland's position appeared very strong. According to David Loades in *Two Tudor Conspiracies* (1992):

> The Duke held the Tower, the treasury and arsenal of the kingdom; the Council was at his command; he had men, ships and artillery. There was little chance that one woman could prevail against such power, however legitimate her claim.

Given his power, Northumberland may have believed that Mary would go quietly. His subsequent actions certainly seem to indicate that he did not have a plan should Mary fight for her throne. He failed to prevent Mary leaving London which allowed her to reach her supporters in East Anglia, an area which had little love for Northumberland, the man who had forcefully suppressed Kett's rebellion there four years earlier. From her palace at Kenninghall in Norfolk, Mary sent letters to the council stating that she was now the legitimate queen.

Northumberland could now only 'win' by physically capturing Mary. The Council ordered sheriffs and justices to raise government forces. In reply Mary began mustering her troops. Even so, at this point the ambassadors to the Emperor believed that Mary would lose but then Northumberland made his second and even poorer, strategic error. Although he was by no means certain that he had the support of all the Council, he left London and led an army of 2000 troops into East Anglia. He had not mobilised all the troops he had at his disposal as he expected to gain more support on the way but this did not happen.

Meanwhile reports of vast numbers of people joining Mary, including nobles, gentry and some Protestants, began to increase the unease of the Council. Andy Wood attributes this support to continuing social antagonisms at local level rather than religious or political loyalty.

In Suffolk, where following Northumberland's coup some of the leaders of the 1549 rebellions had been executed, popular support for Mary's bid for the throne was strong ... In Great Yarmouth, the commons had their revenge upon the Protestant merchant elite of the town, and were enthusiastic in their support of Mary. Even overt Protestant opinion in East Anglia was consistently pro-Mary, so powerful was 'the memory of Northumberland's commanding role in the destruction of the Mousehold camp four years earlier.

In the face of this popular support the Council abandoned Northumberland. When the Earls of Pembroke and Arundel were asked to rally their own forces and march against Mary they drew back from such military involvement and instead persuaded the Council to switch its allegiance. The rebellion fizzled out quickly as Northumberland's own army began to desert. The Earl of Arundel set off for Cambridge to arrest Northumberland while the Duke of Suffolk had to tell his daughter, Lady Jane Grey, that she was no longer queen.

Londoners now celebrated the accession of the rightful monarch. Despite protesting that he was now the Queen's man, Northumberland was executed on 22 August, nineteen days after Mary entered London in triumph. David Loades summarises the failure of the plot in *John Dudley, Duke of Northumberland*:

From a historical distance it looks as though Mary had an easy victory, but contemporary outsiders were flabbergasted, and in fact it had been a close call. If the radical Protestants had not been alienated by his 'worldliness', if he had stayed in London after 13 July, or if he had had a couple of thousand reliable men, the outcome might have been different. It is misleading to speak simply of the legitimism of the English, or their religious conservatism, or even of Northumberland's unpopularity as being the main causes of Mary's success. The actual outcome was determined by human courage and human error. Northumberland's most serious error had been to rely on offices and money rather than men.

■ Now complete your mind map for the Lady Jane Grey Plot. The sketch on page 88 shows one way of building up the Jane Grey section of your mind map. You don't need to add lots of detail.

## Wyatt's rebellion of 1554

Less than a year after she entered London in triumph to claim the crown, Mary faced the possibility of losing that crown. In January 1554, 3000 men were marching from Kent to London, led by Sir Thomas Wyatt. They aimed to bring Mary's reign to an end and had already been joined by a force of Londoners sent to stop Wyatt who had swapped sides.

Wyatt's rebellion fits all the characteristics of an 'elite' rebellion in that it was planned by a group of courtiers. The men behind this plot and their aims are shown below.

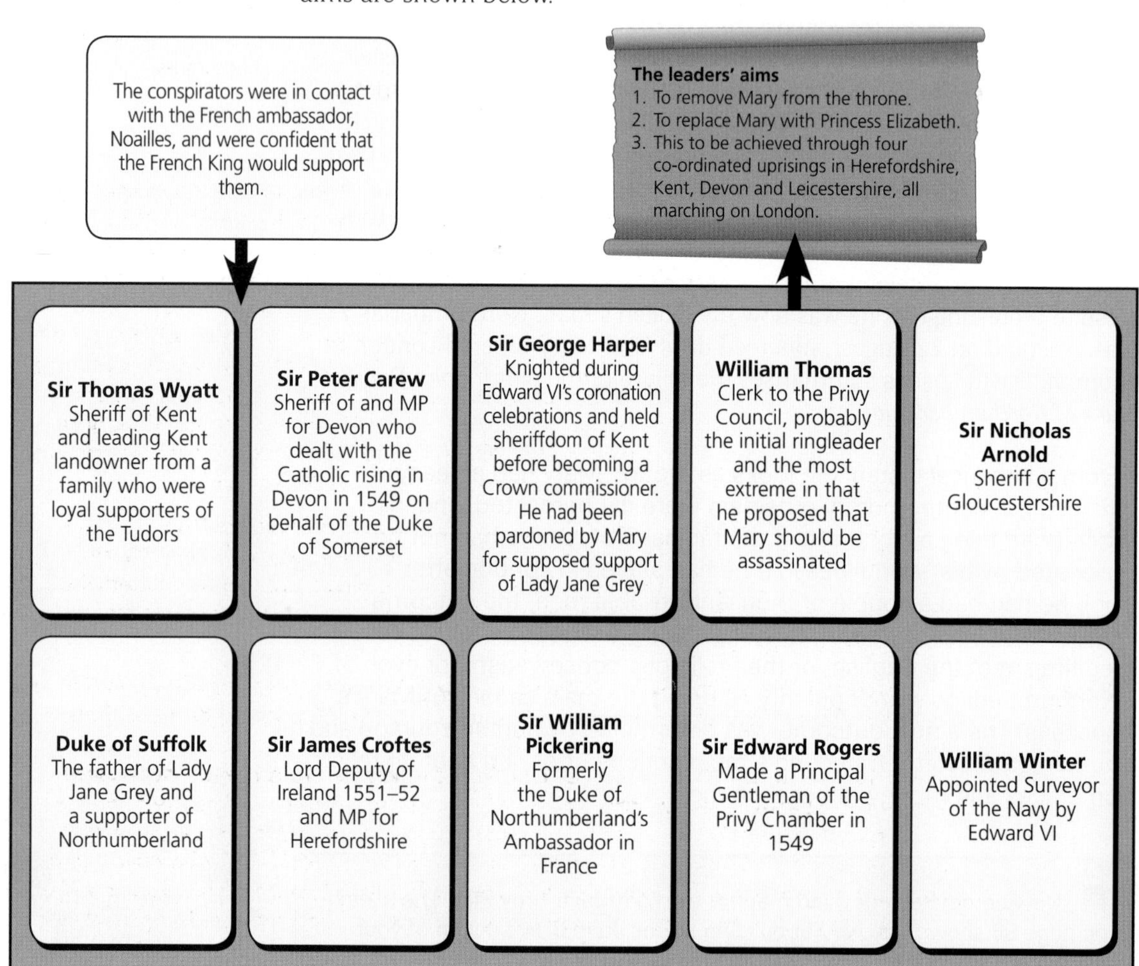

The conspirators were in contact with the French ambassador, Noailles, and were confident that the French King would support them.
The leaders' aims
1. To remove Mary from the throne.
2. To replace Mary with Princess Elizabeth.
3. This to be achieved through four co-ordinated uprisings in Herefordshire, Kent, Devon and Leicestershire, all marching on London.
Sir Thomas Wyatt
Sheriff of Kent and leading Kent landowner from a family who were loyal supporters of the Tudors
Sir Peter Carew
Sheriff of and MP for Devon who dealt with the Catholic rising in Devon in 1549 on behalf of the Duke of Somerset
Sir George Harper
Knighted during Edward VI's coronation celebrations and held sheriffdom of Kent before becoming a Crown commissioner. He had been pardoned by Mary for supposed support of Lady Jane Grey
William Thomas
Clerk to the Privy Council, probably the initial ringleader and the most extreme in that he proposed that Mary should be assassinated
Sir Nicholas Arnold
Sheriff of Gloucestershire
Duke of Suffolk
The father of Lady Jane Grey and a supporter of Northumberland
Sir James Croftes
Lord Deputy of Ireland 1551–52 and MP for Herefordshire
Sir William Pickering
Formerly the Duke of Northumberland's Ambassador in France
Sir Edward Rogers
Made a Principal Gentleman of the Privy Chamber in 1549
William Winter
Appointed Surveyor of the Navy by Edward VI


△ **'All men of substance and influence' – the elite plotters behind Wyatt's rebellion.**

The original plan was for four simultaneous, co-ordinated uprisings from the Midlands to the south-west. In the event only the rebellion led by Sir Thomas Wyatt in Kent took place. The trigger for rebellion lay in the growing hostility to Mary's proposed marriage to the Catholic King Philip II of Spain. The prospect of a Spanish King influencing or possibly directing policies was not welcome in England. Many of Mary's councillors wanted her to marry an Englishman and they proposed Edward Courtenay, the Earl of Devon who, although frequently described as both foolish and weak, was at least descended from Edward IV.

Mary was aware of the unrest her proposed marriage would cause so she agreed that the marriage treaty would limit Philip's powers as king. Only Englishmen were allowed to hold office and England's laws and customs were to be preserved. Philip would lose any rights to the English throne on Mary's death. Despite this, many in England believed that Philip would not sign this or, if he did, would break his word.

While Mary pressed ahead with arrangements for her Spanish marriage, often without the knowledge of her full council, the group of courtiers shown on the previous page met in November 1553. This group, though Protestant, were driven more by fear of possible loss of office and status to Spanish courtiers than by religious differences.

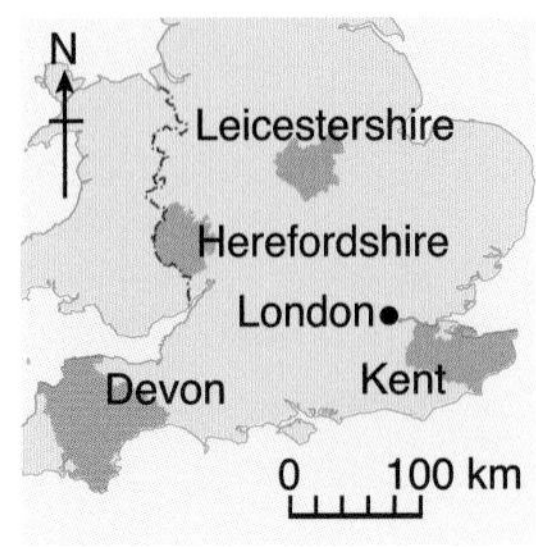
N
Leicestershire
Herefordshire
London
Devon
Kent
0
100 km

△ Attacks were planned from four counties.

## Why did the plan for a four-pronged attack fail in January 1554?

| | |
|---|---|
| **Leicestershire** | Mary was warned by the Imperial Ambassador that he had got wind of a plot centring on Courtenay and Elizabeth. When Courtenay was questioned by the Council in January 1554 he revealed the little he knew but this was enough to panic the rebel leaders. Summoned to Court, the Duke of Suffolk instead rode to rally support in his home county of Leicestershire. For this he was proclaimed a traitor and was accused of wanting to restore his imprisoned daughter, Lady Jane Grey, to the throne. The Earl of Huntingdon was sent from London to apprehend the Duke. The only men of substance to join Suffolk were his kinsmen and their retainers. He failed to capture his target of Coventry through a mixture of bad timing, over-estimation of the amount of support there and the propaganda of Huntingdon. The Leicestershire Rebellion was over within five days and its failure had an impact on the success of the wider rebellion. |
| **Herefordshire** | The intention had been for Croftes to call out his friends and neighbours in Herefordshire but he was in London when Courtenay confessed and stayed there to keep an eye on developments. As a result, this part of the rebellion never materialised. Croftes' communication with both Princess Elizabeth and Noailles convinced him an uprising could not now succeed. |
| **Devon** | Carew was more successful in winning support in Devon and alarming the Council in London. The people of Devon were genuinely concerned that Spaniards were about to land and ravish their wives and daughters. However, the attempts of Carew and his followers to capitalise on this panic backfired when the Devon gentry denounced these anti-Spanish rumours, and presumably those who were spreading them, as 'treasonable and malicious'. The revolt was ultimately thwarted by the diligence of another of the ruling elite, Sir Thomas Dennis, then Sheriff of Devon, who managed to stay one step ahead of the rebels, particularly by fortifying Exeter. Mary's dispatching of Sir John Leger to restore order finally ended the matter. The commons had shown no desire to stir, particularly against the man who had opposed the 1549 Western Rising. More significantly, the gentry, having thrown in their lot with the government in 1549, showed no enthusiasm for changing sides despite the majority being Protestant. The Queen, meanwhile, steadfastly refused offers of help from Philip II and the Holy Roman Emperor. She judged, probably correctly, that any intervention by the **Habsburgs** would increase **xenophobia** at home. |

**xenophobia**
Intense patriotism coupled with a hatred of foreigners

The **Habsburg** family dominated European politics for the first half of the sixteenth century. The grandson of Maximilian (see page 27), Charles V, became Holy Roman Emperor in 1519 having already inherited the Spanish crown from his mother, Joanna of Castile, in 1516. He ruled an Empire therefore which included most of central Europe, Spain and its territories in the Americas and Far East. Charles abdicated in 1556 leaving the Empire to his brother but it was his son, Philip, who became king of Spain and the husband of Mary Tudor.

## The escalation of Wyatt's rebellion, January–February 1554

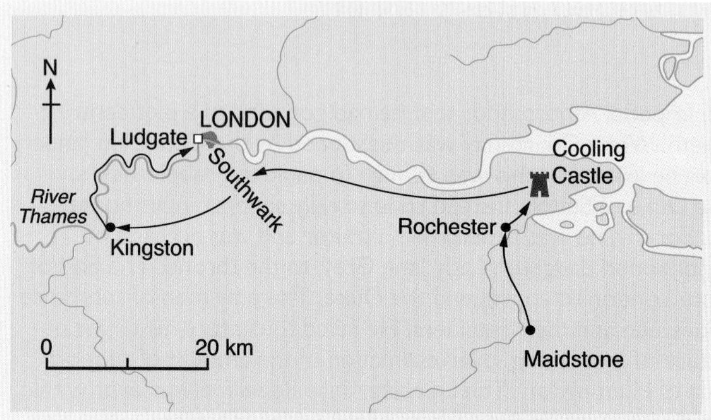
N
LONDON
Ludgate
Southwark
River Thames
Kingston
Cooling Castle
Rochester
Maidstone
0
20 km

△ **The route of Wyatt's rebellion from Maidstone.**

**25 January** Wyatt raised the standard at Maidstone, signalling the outbreak of rebellion.

**27 January** Mary named Wyatt and his followers as traitors and sent a force of 800 Londoners under the ageing Duke of Norfolk. At Rochester Bridge the core of Norfolk's army, the 'Whitecoats', deserted and joined Wyatt. He was also joined at Rochester by forces from other areas of the county who shared his anti-Spanish views. The rebel force now probably numbered over 3000.

**31 January** The Queen offered to review the rebels' grievances if they disbanded. As exemplified here, throughout the rebellion Mary repeatedly rose to the occasion, showing considerable political skill. When this offer was rejected by Wyatt she rallied the city with stirring speeches and, crucially, rejected the advice of her councillors to leave London. Wyatt was urged by his captains to march directly on London while the government was still unprepared but he allowed himself to be side-tracked first by Mary's offer of an investigative review and then by a diversion to Cooling Castle to collect Lord Cobham. In the meantime Mary ordered the strengthening of London's defences.

**3 February** Wyatt and his force of 3000 arrived at Southwark on the south bank of the Thames but had to cross the river to get to the centre of London. The bridge at Southwark was by now heavily defended against the rebels.

**6 February** Wyatt left Southwark and marched west to Kingston where he crossed the river virtually unopposed before marching on central London.

**7 February** The citizens of London were thrown into panic by the appearance of the rebels' army. However, Wyatt's guns got bogged down allowing time for the royal army under the Earl of Pembroke to take up its position. The royal forces under Pembroke outnumbered the rebels and were fresh and well armed. By contrast, Wyatt's followers were by now weary and demoralised and lacking in heavy artillery. Wyatt tried to storm the city gates at Ludgate but they held against him. As he retreated he was attacked by the royal army. Like the diversion to Cooling Castle, the failure to storm Ludgate was another turning point. The crowds who had been watching and waiting on events now joined in against Wyatt. Wyatt surrendered to avoid further bloodshed.

## Why did Wyatt's rebellion fail?

The plan of campaign had been based on the four-pronged attack from all sides of the capital. The weakness of the overall leadership was demonstrated by the fact that only Sir Thomas Wyatt was able to raise a force to march on London. Once Wyatt decided to go it alone, and particularly to take the rebellion outside Kent, his options were fewer. As David Loades suggests:

> ... to have succeeded in his real purpose without support from Leicester or Devon, Wyatt would have had to have done one of two things: either rely upon being able to raise a big enough revolt in South-East England to defeat any army that the government might be able to send against him, or use his local support in Kent for a rapid stroke.

Nevertheless, as Fletcher and MacCulloch have argued, Wyatt was well placed to lead a successful rebellion: 'The rising in the midlands was ineptly executed and that in the west was inadequately based. Only in Kent was the leadership sufficiently capable to make success possible'. Wyatt's family had served the Tudors faithfully and he was one of the largest landowners in Kent. He had experience in local government where he had acted as sheriff and been involved in drawing up military plans for the defence of the county in times of unrest. Wyatt therefore had the social standing and expertise to summon a militia rapidly. He also showed considerable ability in playing on people's anti-Spanish sentiment while avoiding too close an identification of the uprising with the Protestant religion. Wyatt's emotive proclamations appealed to national patriotism by stressing the danger to the country of Spanish control.

Wyatt was wise to focus on the threat from Spain and to emphasise that his aim was only to protect the Queen from unsuitable counsellors. When he did acknowledge to his captains that his real intention was the overthrow of the Queen, this caused unrest amongst even his most loyal followers. Similarly his refusal to turn the rebellion into a religious crusade showed strategic sense, as this enabled those Catholics opposed to the Spanish marriage to join him. Many landowners, including Catholics, feared that the restoration of the Papacy would mean having to return monastic lands that were now in private ownership. The leaders though were all Protestants and the religious policies of the Queen provided them with another justification for her overthrow, whatever they said in public. In the event neither anti-Spanish sentiment nor religious differences proved sufficient to attract support from beyond the leaders' immediate circle of influence.

Despite being forced to act more quickly than he intended, Wyatt raised a force of about 2500 in Kent. This support included a number of influential gentry but none of the nobility. The rebellion's lack of a noble 'big name' at its head reduced its popular appeal. The majority of Wyatt's rebels in Kent came from those three or four districts where the principal gentry lived. The commons here followed those of the ruling classes to whom they felt local loyalty and obedience, and in general agreed with their cause. Evidence is lacking for the commons being motivated by either the recent slump in the Kent cloth trade or religious grievances.

For all his local influence, however, Wyatt was not known outside of Kent. Leading national Protestants, in particular, did not join the rebellion. Nevertheless, the effectiveness of Wyatt's propaganda ensured that those gentry who should have raised forces to check Wyatt's progress through Kent refused to do so, allowing the rebels to reach London. David Loades sums up the somewhat limited nature of the rising:

> Although the men of Kent and their neighbours might be unwilling to fight against Wyatt, they were equally unwilling to fight for him. There were symptoms of disaffection everywhere, and yet the rebel leader could not raise sufficient force to press his advantage. It seems that most men were in standing water between loyalty to the Queen and dislike of her policies, so that their actions were effectively determined by the desire to keep their necks from the hangman, and their property from sequestration or plunder.

The success or failure of the rebellion also depended on whether the Queen would have sufficient support to defend London against Wyatt or whether its citizens would join the rebellion and open the city gates, especially as it became obvious to both sides that the much anticipated French support for the plotters was not going to materialise. The reaction of the government, particularly Mary's skilful handling of the situation, was therefore also key to the rebellion's failure. By diverting Wyatt with offers of discussions Mary gained the time she needed to build up London's defences and dispatch the royal army under Pembroke against the rebels. In many ways it was her finest hour.

The seriousness of Wyatt's rebellion can be shown best by Mary's actions following its defeat. She was still so unsure of her support that she did not order a whole scale execution of the rebels. Eventually, only 90 were executed including Wyatt and the Duke of Suffolk and the innocent Lady Jane Grey and her husband. Princess Elizabeth and Edward Courtenay were spared. Parliament went on to prevent the coronation of Philip of Spain and Mary also backed down from her intentions to disinherit the Protestant Princess Elizabeth and to insist on the return of the monastic lands to the Catholic Church.

Wyatt's was an elite rebellion led by members of the ruling class but it simply did not have enough members of this elite class, with their followers, to take a national fight beyond the borders of Kent. It is testament to the vigour of its leaders, and the lack of local opposition, that it got as far as it did and challenged London, but once the government was finally able to rally its forces the rebellion collapsed. Wyatt could only have won if the Queen had been unable or unwilling to muster a royal army to fight him and, although it was close, in the end she did.

■ Now complete your mind map for Wyatt's rebellion. Use the model on page 88 to help you.

# The Northern Rebellion of 1569

The trigger for the Northern Rebellion was the escape from her Scottish prison of Mary, Queen of Scots and her arrival in England in 1568. As a prisoner in England Mary became the focal point of plots against Elizabeth. Most were engineered either by nobles at court opposed to the anti-Spanish policies of William Cecil or by nobles in the north who feared the loss of their political status and wanted to restore the Catholic faith.

What made the Northern Rebellion seem dangerous was that it initially involved both nobles at court and nobles in the north. Together they hoped that the Duke of Norfolk, the leading English noble, would marry Mary, Queen of Scots. They believed this marriage would force Elizabeth to marry or to name Mary as her heir and would also lead to the downfall of Cecil. However, attempting to influence the succession was itself treasonous and the plan failed when Norfolk confessed and threw himself on the Queen's mercy.

The failure of the scheme to marry Mary to Norfolk ended the opposition of the court faction but left the Northern Earls, Westmoreland and Northumberland, hesitating about what to do. If Mary was not going to be named as Elizabeth's heir, then was the next step for her supporters to take the throne by force on her behalf?

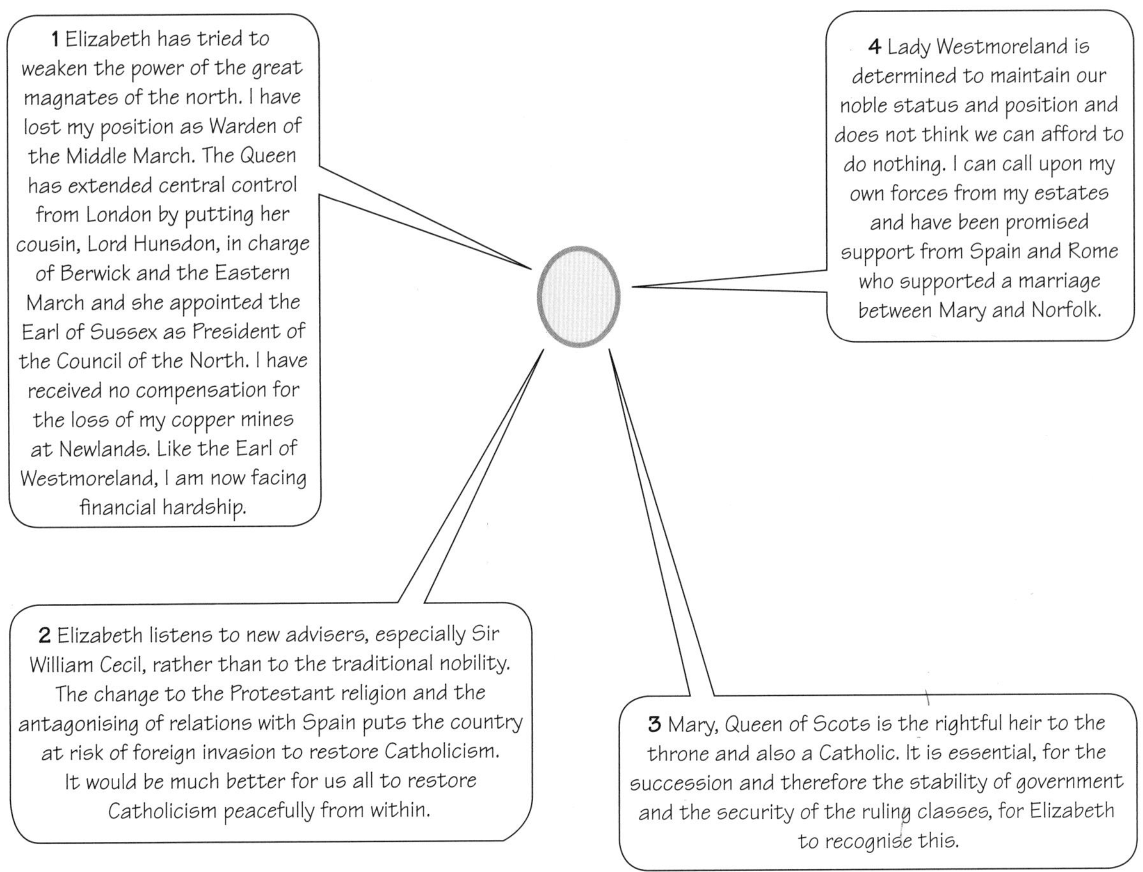
1 Elizabeth has tried to weaken the power of the great magnates of the north. I have lost my position as Warden of the Middle March. The Queen has extended central control from London by putting her cousin, Lord Hunsdon, in charge of Berwick and the Eastern March and she appointed the Earl of Sussex as President of the Council of the North. I have received no compensation for the loss of my copper mines at Newlands. Like the Earl of Westmoreland, I am now facing financial hardship.
4 Lady Westmoreland is determined to maintain our noble status and position and does not think we can afford to do nothing. I can call upon my own forces from my estates and have been promised support from Spain and Rome who supported a marriage between Mary and Norfolk.
2 Elizabeth listens to new advisers, especially Sir William Cecil, rather than to the traditional nobility. The change to the Protestant religion and the antagonising of relations with Spain puts the country at risk of foreign invasion to restore Catholicism. It would be much better for us all to restore Catholicism peacefully from within.
3 Mary, Queen of Scots is the rightful heir to the throne and also a Catholic. It is essential, for the succession and therefore the stability of government and the security of the ruling classes, for Elizabeth to recognise this.

△ The grievances of the Earl of Northumberland.

## Mary, Queen of Scots

Like Lady Jane Grey, Mary, Queen of Scots has become the subject of many historical novels and films focusing on the drama and tragedy of her life. Many historians however have been less impressed by her actions. In *England under the Tudors* (1991), G.R. Elton confirms:

> It remains impossible so to speak about Mary, Queen of Scots that all are satisfied; she had to the utmost the Stuart ability of attaching men's loyalties to herself despite the most outrageous and the most foolish of deeds. Of her famous beauty her surviving portraits provide little evidence. She was passionate, wilful, intelligent, given to violent moods of exultation and depression, and entirely without common sense.

△ Mary, Queen of Scots.

Much of Mary's life indeed reads like a historical soap opera. Married in her teens to the future King of France, Mary returned as a young widow to rule Scotland in 1561. Four years later she married Henry, Lord Darnley, a promiscuous drunkard who also had a claim to the English throne. Mary's close friend Rizzio was murdered in 1566 on Darnley's instructions, although Mary survived to give birth to the future James VI of Scotland. One year later Darnley died when his house was blown up, though he had first been strangled. Mary then married the chief suspect, the Earl of Bothwell. At this point the scandalised Scottish lords overthrew and imprisoned Mary. After enchanting her gaoler, Mary escaped, finally fleeing across the border and throwing herself on Elizabeth's mercy. Elizabeth imprisoned her and she remained behind bars for over twenty years until her execution for continual plotting against the Queen, including the Northern Rebellion. Like Lady Jane Grey, Mary represented a threat even when behind bars, her claim to the throne and religious beliefs always made her a figurehead for Catholic plots against Queen Elizabeth.

## The escalation of the Northern Rebellion

While the Earls dithered, Elizabeth grew uneasy. She ordered the Earl of Sussex, President of the Council of the North, to question the Earls and he assured Elizabeth of their loyalty. Elizabeth however was not convinced and in October 1569 she summoned the Earls to court. Backed into a corner, and persuaded by the more vocal and enthusiastic of their tenants, the Earls now ordered the ringing of bells to summon the men of their county estates to take arms against their Queen.

**9 November** The two Earls joined forces at Westmoreland's castle at Brancepeth to take arms against the Queen.

**13 November** Sussex sent out summons to raise a royal army of 1500 foot soldiers, forcing men to choose between their allegiance to their lord or their queen. Few dared join Sussex and the Queen.

**14 November** The Earls marched to Durham Cathedral, tore down Protestant images and celebrated Catholic Mass.

**15 November** The rebels marched south, gaining support from Westmoreland's tenants at Kirby Moorside and Richmondshire. However, appeals to Lancashire and Cheshire and the Catholic nobility were unsuccessful.

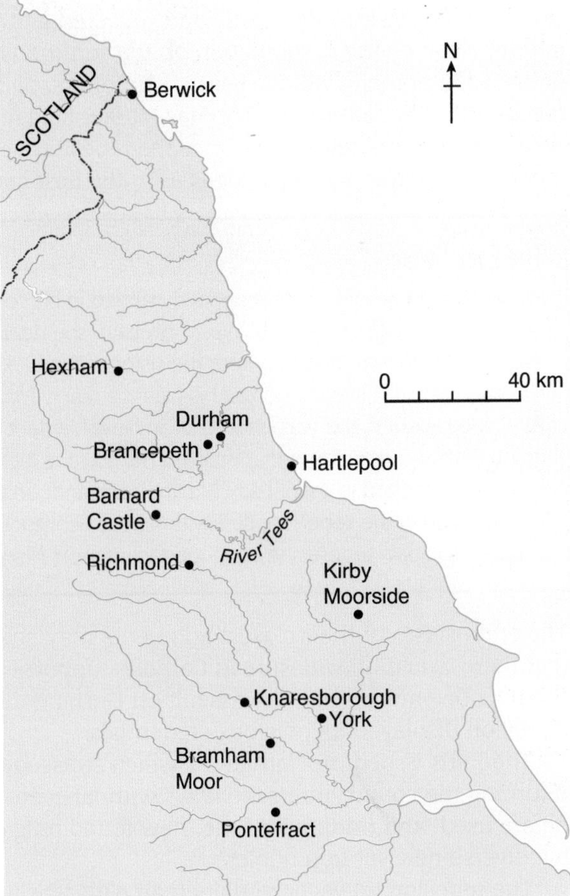
N
SCOTLAND
Berwick
Hexham
0
40 km
Durham
Brancepeth
Hartlepool
Barnard Castle
River Tees
Richmond
Kirby Moorside
Knaresborough
York
Bramham Moor
Pontefract

**22 November** The Earls reached Bramham Moor with 3800 foot soldiers and 1600 horsemen. The government however was preparing to move Mary from prison to prison and the Earls realised it was impossible to free her. Government officials such as Lord Scrope had also done exemplary work in containing the rebellion with the result that the rebels made no attempt to take the key towns of Pontefract, Berwick and York. Once rumours of a large royal army assembling at Warwick reached the rebels, the Earls decided to turn back.

**24 November** The rebels moved back north to Knaresborough.

**30 November** One rebel division attacked Barnard Castle, the other captured Hartlepool in the misguided anticipation of the landing of Spanish troops to support them.

**14 December** Barnard Castle surrendered to the Earls.

**16 December** The royal army of 10,000 reached the River Tees. The Earls did not attempt to face battle but fled to Hexham.

**19 December** A skirmish took place between the scouts of the two opposing forces. The Earls, desperate to escape, crossed the border into Scotland.

## Why did the Northern Rebellion fail?

On paper the leadership of the Northern Rebellion looked strong. The conspiracy involved the Duke of Norfolk, some of Elizabeth's courtiers and the Earls of Northumberland and Westmoreland. Noble birth-right in itself however was no guarantee of skilful and inspirational leadership. In the event none of these nobles impressed with either charismatic leadership qualities or outstanding skills in strategy and organisation. Norfolk's nerve collapsed when his ambition to marry Mary, Queen of Scots became known to Queen Elizabeth and he fled before throwing himself on her mercy. Northumberland and Westmoreland waivered and were only goaded into rebellion by the combination of: the summons from Elizabeth; the enthusiasm of their Catholic gentry supporters, particularly Richard Norton, the Sheriff of Yorkshire and Thomas Markenfield his son-in-law; and the determination of their wives. Once the rebellion began they continued indecisively with only vague ideas as to the best course of action.

### The Earls' wives

Although the Earl of Northumberland claimed in his confession to have been pushed into rebellion by Lady Westmoreland, she denied this to Cecil. Lady Westmoreland was Jane Howard, the sister of the Duke of Norfolk. As such, she was likely to have supported his plans to marry Mary, Queen of Scots. After the rebellion she was cleared of any involvement by the government and granted an annual income that enabled her to raise her daughters, although her husband remained in exile. Lady Northumberland, on the other hand, joined her husband in the rebellion, fled with him to Scotland and, after his capture, escaped to Spain where she continued to support Mary's cause.

The enthusiasm of their closest adherents may have convinced the Earls that there would be widespread Catholic support for their rebellion. From its beginning, with the assault on Durham Cathedral, the Northern Rebellion displayed its religious credentials.

The Earls issued proclamations which stressed their intention of returning the country to its old ways with 'ancyent customes and usages before used' and ridding it of the 'new found religion and heresie' enforced by 'diverse new set upp nobles'.

The rebellion however remained an elite rebellion, lacking the sort of popular spontaneous support seen in the Pilgrimage of Grace. The gentry who joined from the huge Neville and Percy estates provided the rebellion's strength, supplying horsemen and their tenants and servants, but they never amounted to more than 20 per cent of the total number of 5500 to 6000 rebels. The Nortons, Thomas Makenfield and the bishopric of Durham also contributed considerably to these armed forces. The bulk of the rebels however were recruited as the Earls proceeded south from Brancepeth, through Richmondshire and Yorkshire. This was partly achieved by belief in their cause, partly by the issuing of musters and sometimes by threats and the promise of daily wages. However, the Earls did not attract popular support from areas where they had no personal authority. The appeals made to the Catholic nobility completely failed. In particular, support from Lancashire and Cheshire was not forthcoming. The great majority of the ruling elite in the north remained loyal to the government.

The rebellion also lacked a realistic strategy. The original plan centred on freeing Mary, Queen of Scots from her prison at Tutbury. Success depended on moving south to free Mary or attacking London or both. Once the government however moved Mary to nearer Coventry, the Earls hesitated. Rumours of the advance of the Earl of Sussex with a large royal army may have convinced them of the weakness of their position and caused them to turn back at Bramham Moor.

The failure of the Northern Rebellion does not exempt the government from criticism. Christopher Haigh, in *Elizabeth I* (1988), argued that it was Elizabeth's misjudged summons of the Earls that precipitated rebellion when other tactics might have been wiser:

> Elizabeth had blundered: she forced the Earls to choose between flight and rebellion, when rebellion was still (just) a realistic option. They chose rebellion, because of the Catholic enthusiasm of their followers and the scorn of the Countess of Westmorland ... so the Earls rebelled, more in sorrow than in anger: men who had been planning a rebellion for weeks, even months, were forced into an unplanned rising.

The Queen had no problem in raising funds and issuing musters for a huge army to march north but her commander in the north, the Earl of Sussex, saw things differently, as Fletcher and MacCulloch relate:

> A desperate lack of armour and horsemen still detained him in York. The southern army was slow in coming north and with 10,000 men was unnecessarily large and expensive anyway as Sussex and Hunsdon continually pointed out to Cecil. In vain they pressed the government for 500 horse and 300 shot that they might pursue the rebels, but the Lord Admiral, writing from Lincolnshire, could only offer 100 horsemen.

The upshot of this was that the Northern Rebellion continued for longer than might otherwise have been the case.

Sussex was fortunate. He was served by capable men such as Lord Scrope who kept key towns for the government. In the event there was no battle, although that did not prevent the government from exacting savage reprisals. Elizabeth was determined to use the defeat of the Northern Rebellion to bring the north into line. She ordered the execution of 700 rebels, although because of the bad weather and her officials' reluctance, the number killed was probably nearer 450. The Earl of Northumberland was handed over by the Scots and beheaded, although the Earl of Westmoreland escaped abroad. The power of these great northern magnates was destroyed and the north remained quiet for the remainder of Elizabeth's reign.

■ Now complete your mind map for the Northern Rebellion. Use the model on page 88 to help you.

△ Essex was charming and brilliant but also greedy and ambitious. By the late 1580s when he was aged twenty he had become the favourite of the 55-year-old Queen.

## Essex's rebellion of 1601

This final Tudor rebellion never came close to success. It also, unlike the other elite conspiracies, did not aim to overthrow the monarch. Paul Hammer in *Elizabeth's Wars* (2003) claims:

> Although Essex himself oscillated between anger and despair at his fate (i.e. house arrest in 1600), a group of die-hard supporters plotted to see him restored to power and sweep his rivals away, while some hostile government officials sought to frame treason charges against Essex to destroy him completely.

The closing years of Elizabeth's reign, like the mid-Tudor period, were characterised by faction as a weak monarch was unable to control the ambitions of powerful groups of nobles and courtiers who saw an opportunity for self-promotion. Faction was a major factor in Elizabethan politics in the 1590s and Essex's rebellion needs to be analysed within this context.

Elizabeth was now approaching 70. Many of the councillors who had served her so loyally throughout the reign had died. Political power was passing to a new generation although Elizabeth still refused to name her successor. Throughout the 1590s the Queen had been spending much time with her new favourite courtier, the Earl of Essex, the stepson of Robert Dudley, Earl of Leicester (perhaps the one man Elizabeth may have wanted to marry).

Essex's pathway to rebellion was as follows:

**Robert Cecil** became Elizabeth's leading minister after the death of his father, William, Lord Burghley, in 1598. His great organisational skills brought him high office but he clashed repeatedly with the more flamboyant Essex. Their rivalry split the court.

| | |
|---|---|
| **1593–96** | Essex repeatedly advocated an aggressive foreign policy against Spain which would provide him with opportunities for military glory. This approach brought him into conflict with the faction led by **Robert Cecil** who increasingly favoured negotiating a peace with Spain. |
| **1598** | During a particularly heated debate in the Privy Council on who should be sent to Ireland as the new Lord Deputy, the Queen humiliated Essex by slapping his face. |

**1599** Essex was sent to Ireland as the new Lord Deputy. This was against his wishes as he believed his enemies would strengthen their position in his absence. His campaign against the Earl of Tyrone was a disaster. He dispensed honours to his friends and failed to engage the rebels in battle, negotiating a truce instead. In a last desperate attempt to regain his standing with the Queen, Essex deserted his command and disobeying a direct order from Elizabeth, fled to London and burst unannounced into her bedchamber to plead his case. Instead he was banished from court by a furious Elizabeth and put under house arrest.

**1600** Essex was now disgraced and deprived of all his government offices. The precariousness of his financial situation was further revealed by the Queen's withdrawing his **patent** for sweet wine which plunged him deeper into bankruptcy.

**1601** Feeling he had nothing left to lose, Essex determined to seize power by capturing Whitehall Palace and the Tower of London, aiming to seize control of Elizabeth, remove the Cecils from office and then win the favour of James VI of Scotland who was next in line to the throne. Essex had, however, overestimated the amount of popular support he was likely to attract and, although many of the elite ruling class shared Essex's dislike of the Cecils, they were not prepared to join a military revolt and risk losing their power and money.

**patent**
Granted by the sovereign, this gave the holder exclusive rights and prevented others from the selling or importing of sweet wines

The planned coup turned out to be more of a demonstration as Essex and about 300 supporters marched into the city of London. Ironically this rebellion enjoyed the greatest number of participating nobles but most were young and poor like Essex. His plans had also become known to the government so the Sheriff of London had fortified the city with barricades and Essex was declared a traitor. The revolt was over in twelve hours. Essex's small band was soon surrounded and he had to fight his way back to his own house. Once there however the government ordered the use of artillery from the Tower and Essex surrendered with the promise of a fair trial.

## Why did Essex's rebellion fail?

Essex was not a powerful feudal magnate like Northumberland or Westmoreland but a courtier whose position rested on the support of the Queen. He did not have tenants or men at arms that he could summon to fight his cause. Essex had no clear plan. His motives and aims changed frequently between 1599 and 1601 but were always personal. He was consistent only in wanting to keep himself in power and to ensure financial rewards for himself and his followers. As his plans were thwarted he became increasingly desperate and detached from reality with little support outside his immediate friends and followers. Although, like others before him, Essex claimed to be acting to save the Queen from evil counsellors, few Londoners were motivated to join him. Essex's impulsive

Now complete your mind map for Essex's rebellion. Use the model on page 88 to help you.

and egocentric behaviour was unlikely to convince many that he had the strategic leadership qualities necessary to spearhead a successful rebellion against the monarchy. Although strategically this was another rebellion that struck at the heart of London, it was a farcical attempt. Even so, the response of Elizabeth's government was severe. Essex was executed for treason. Despite the age of the government and the confusion over Elizabeth's successor, most of the ruling elite still had more to lose than gain from rebellion. This class were now far more likely to raise their grievances through Parliament than to turn to force.

## Concluding your enquiry

You now have a complete set of mind maps summarising the reasons for the failures of the four rebellions.

1 Use the maps and your notes to complete a threat chart (see page 12) for each rebellion. This will consolidate your understanding of each rebellion.

2 Your mind maps should help you to identify the factors which were most important in determining the failure of these rebellions. Now use a factors chart like the one below.

   **a)** Draw your own version of the factors chart with the most important factors closest to the question in the middle. Use distance from the question as an indicator of the significance of each factor in the failure of these rebellions. For example, if a factor was highly significant in the failure of all four, then place it right at the centre of the diagram.

   **b)** Now add lines linking any factors that were closely linked in explaining the failure of the rebellions. Add notes to explain these links.

3 Your chart and notes should enable you to plan an answer to the enquiry question:

'Why did the elite rebellions against Mary and Elizabeth fail?'

4 Place each rebellion onto the relevant threat line in the activity on page 13 and make notes to justify these placements.

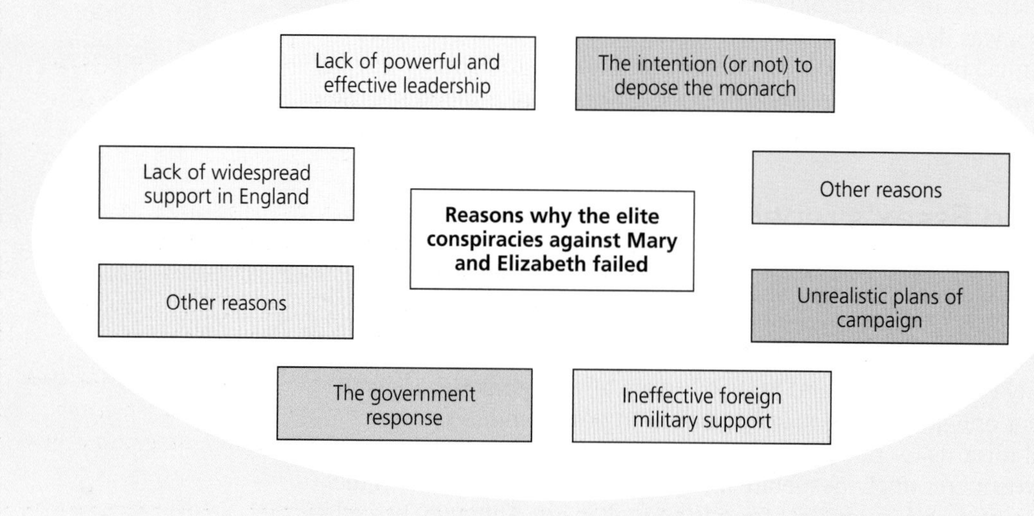
Lack of powerful and effective leadership
The intention (or not) to depose the monarch
Lack of widespread support in England
Other reasons
Reasons why the elite conspiracies against Mary and Elizabeth failed
Other reasons
Unrealistic plans of campaign
The government response
Ineffective foreign military support

# 6 Why did Irish rebellions never threaten English control of Ireland?

The Tudors' control of Ireland had some similarities with their governing of remoter parts of England such as Cornwall and the north where they failed to hide their basic contempt for subjects living beyond the south-east. The Irish, in particular, were seen as, in the words of Polydore Vergil, 'savage, rude and uncouth', or 'wild men of the woods'. Even so, the Tudors had to find ways of working with the leading noble families to maintain control of Ireland. None of these ways was completely successful because of Irish hostility to being ruled from London and the many internal rivalries amongst leading Irish families. Tudor strategies towards Ireland were usually triggered by a rebellion and often precipitated another one. After 1534, Tudor control was seen as threatening not only the Irish language and customs but also Ireland's adherence to the Catholic faith and led to the rebellions shown below.

### Summary of Irish rebellions

**Henry VII** Individual Irish lords did become involved in dynastic rebellions against Henry VII. In 1486 the Earl of Kildare, head of the Geraldine family, provided a force for Lambert Simnel's invasion of England. Nine years later Perkin Warbeck gained the support of another Anglo-Norman noble, the Earl of Desmond, but this time Kildare and the key town of Waterford remained loyal to the King. However, neither of these events challenged English control of Ireland.

**Henry VIII** In 1534 Thomas Cromwell detained the Ninth Earl of Kildare in England and removed him as Lord Deputy of Ireland. This sparked a revolt in Ireland led by his son 'Silken Thomas'. Thomas also justified his rebellion by claiming to be leading a Catholic crusade against a heretic king.

**Elizabeth I** James Fitzmaurice Fitzgerald led two rebellions in 1569 and 1579 against the harsh policy of Plantation, introduced in the reigns of Edward and Mary, which forcibly dispossessed native Irish and replaced them with English settlers. In 1579 Fitzgerald was aided by soldiers financed by the Pope who was attempting to enforce the Papal Bull of Excommunication against Elizabeth.

In 1594 the Earl of Tyrone, Hugh O'Neill, reluctantly became the leader of what became a nine-year rebellion against the Queen, where his leadership united the Irish in a common cause to expel English settlers and administrators and win independence.

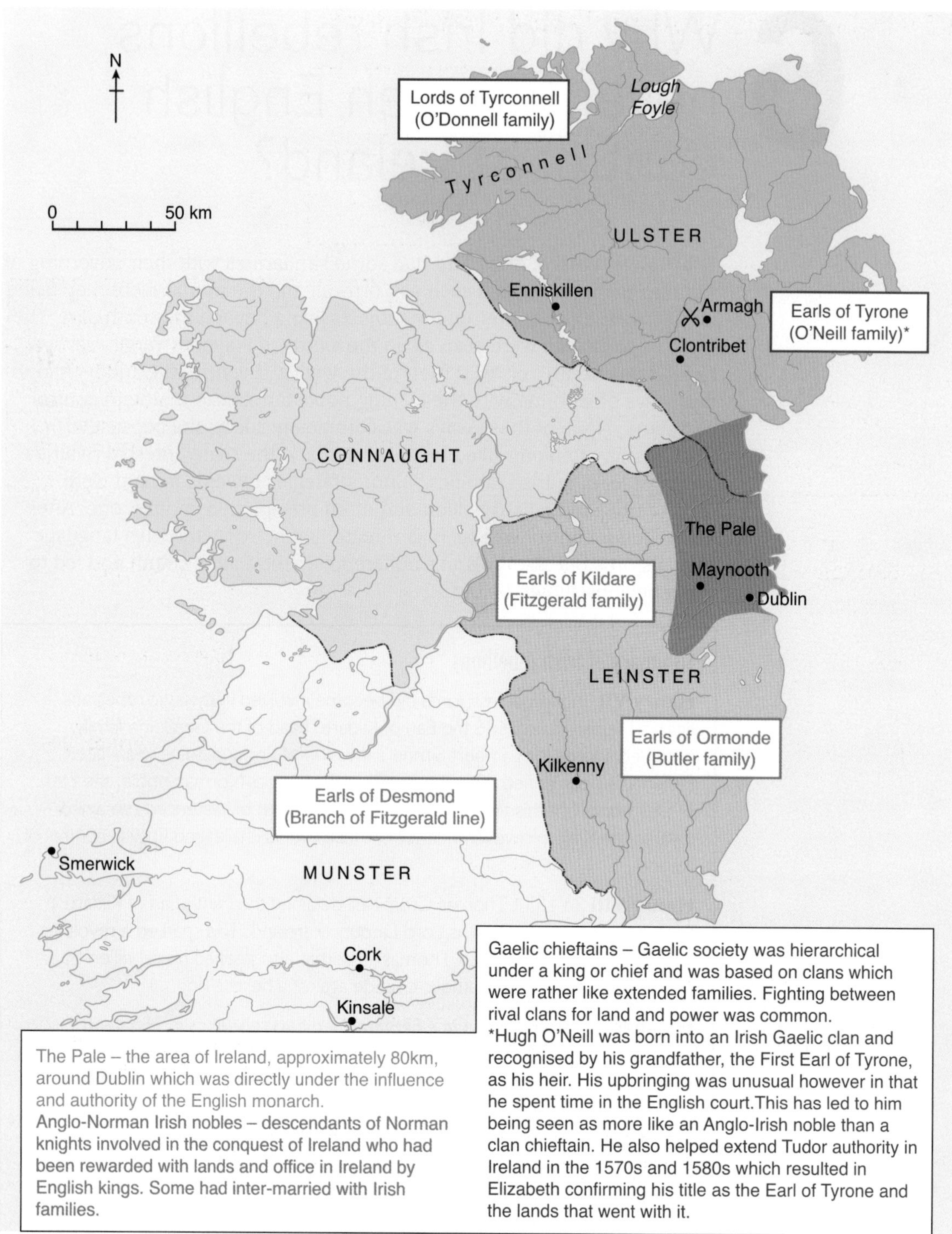
N
0
50 km
Lords of Tyrconnell
(O'Donnell family)
Lough
Foyle
Tyrconnell
ULSTER
Enniskillen
Armagh
Clontribet
Earls of Tyrone
(O'Neill family)*
CONNAUGHT
The Pale
Maynooth
Dublin
Earls of Kildare
(Fitzgerald family)
LEINSTER
Earls of Ormonde
(Butler family)
Kilkenny
Earls of Desmond
(Branch of Fitzgerald line)
Smerwick
MUNSTER
Cork
Kinsale
Gaelic chieftains – Gaelic society was hierarchical under a king or chief and was based on clans which were rather like extended families. Fighting between rival clans for land and power was common.
*Hugh O'Neill was born into an Irish Gaelic clan and recognised by his grandfather, the First Earl of Tyrone, as his heir. His upbringing was unusual however in that he spent time in the English court.This has led to him being seen as more like an Anglo-Irish noble than a clan chieftain. He also helped extend Tudor authority in Ireland in the 1570s and 1580s which resulted in Elizabeth confirming his title as the Earl of Tyrone and the lands that went with it.
The Pale – the area of Ireland, approximately 80km, around Dublin which was directly under the influence and authority of the English monarch.
Anglo-Norman Irish nobles – descendants of Norman knights involved in the conquest of Ireland who had been rewarded with lands and office in Ireland by English kings. Some had inter-married with Irish families.

△ The Irish Provinces and their leading families in 1500. The north and west were Gaelic, sharing a common legal system and social and cultural institutions. Politics was highly localised around Gaelic chieftains. Dublin and the south followed English laws and customs while the Pale was garrisoned by English soldiers. Even here there was evidence of Gaelic practices and speech. English landowners tended to live in fortified houses.

# How Ireland was governed under the Tudors

**Lord Deputy**
The monarch's representative who had royal powers over the government of Ireland and a responsibility to defend the Pale from attack. For most of the early sixteenth century the position was held by the earls of Kildare.

**The Irish Council**
Advised the Lord Deputy and had administrative and judicial functions. It was made up of six key offices all appointed by the monarch: Lord Chancellor, Vice Treasurer, Chief Justice of the Court of King's Bench, Chief Justice of the Court of Common Pleas, Chief Baron of the Exchequer, and Master of the Rolls.

**The Irish Parliament**
Comprised of three separate houses: peers and bishops; gentry and merchants and the lower clergy. Its role was to assess the payment of taxes, pass new laws and resolve disputes. After Poyning's Law, introduced by Henry VII in 1494 to increase English control over Ireland's administration and institutions, the Irish Parliament met less frequently and tended to 'rubberstamp' legislation from England.

## Enquiry Focus: Why did Irish rebellions never threaten English control of Ireland?

**1** To gain an overview of the reasons for the failure of the Irish rebellions from 1534 onwards use a chart like the one below to summarise your conclusions.

**a)** Draw your own copy of the chart, perhaps on A3 paper.

**b)** As you read pages 109–114 note on your chart how each factor contributed to the failures and any links you can see between factors.

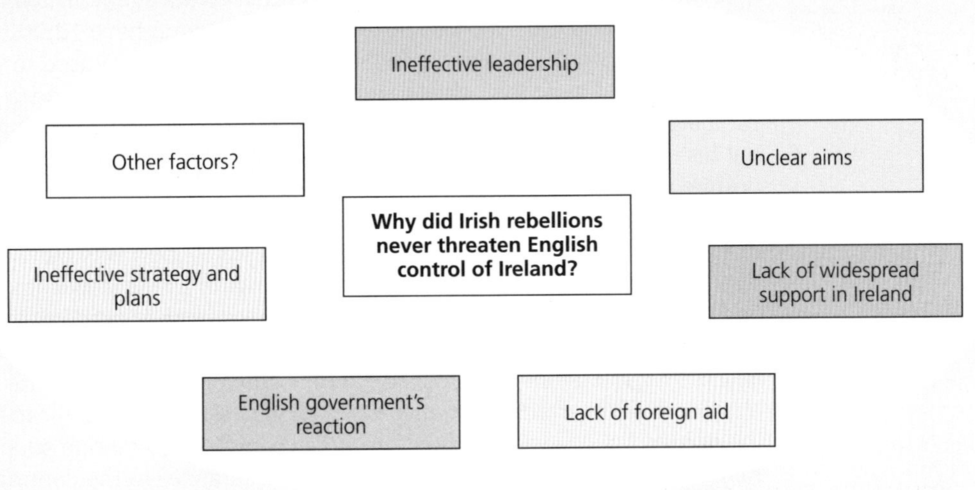
Ineffective leadership
Other factors?
Unclear aims
Why did Irish rebellions never threaten English control of Ireland?
Ineffective strategy and plans
Lack of widespread support in Ireland
English government's reaction
Lack of foreign aid

**2** To support this chart make detailed notes identifying the impact of each factor on the rebellions.

## The rebellion of 1534

In the early 1530s relations with Ireland grew more complex. The rejection of Papal authority to gain an annulment of Henry's marriage to Catherine of Aragon brought the issue of religion into the relationship between the two countries. In September 1533, the King summoned the then Lord Deputy, the elderly Earl of Kildare, to London to assess his ability to enforce the Break with Rome in Ireland. On hearing that his father had been lodged in the Tower of London, Kildare's son Thomas raised 1000 men in Munster and invaded the Pale in June 1534.

Thomas Fitzgerald (who became the tenth Earl of Kildare on the death of his father in London in the summer of 1534) was nicknamed Silken Thomas because his horsemen had silk fringes on their helmets. Colm Lennon in *Sixteenth Century Ireland* (2005) has evaluated his leadership skills more positively than the image conveyed by his nickname:

> Silken Thomas was not the immature and headstrong fop of legend: the 'silken' epithet was a piece of bardic whimsy; his twenty-one years made him older in 1534 than **Charles V** was when assuming the ruling of an empire and he already had martial experience.

**Charles V** was head of the royal houses of Habsburg (see page 95), Burgundy and Spain. He was elected Holy Roman Emperor in 1519 and was a determined opponent of the Protestant reformation. As the nephew of Catherine of Aragon, Charles was hostile to Henry VIII's Break with Rome.

Before the outbreak of the rebellion in June, Thomas had been given pledges of support from the allies of the Kildares, including the Earl of Desmond, and he showed considerable skills of leadership in deploying his forces. His original motives were political, aimed at the disruption of the government of the country to pressurise the King into restoring his father to power, but once Thomas became earl himself, he also saw the advantage of claiming to lead a crusade on behalf of the Pope and Catholic Church against a heretical king. The impact of religion was potentially most helpful in attracting foreign support. Charles V's agent visited Ireland in June 1534 and Earl Thomas believed he would soon have 12,000 Spanish troops at his disposal. As his support at home increased through alliances with Gaelic Irish chiefs and the Church, he at first led a successful campaign, gaining control over the bulk of the area ruled by the English, but his lengthy siege of Dublin and its castle gave Henry time to respond despite all his other pressures.

By late summer Henry had denounced Kildare as a traitor and dispatched a force under Sir William Skeffington. Dublin was quickly restored to the authority of Sir William Skeffington as the new Lord Deputy and then Kildare made a tactical error by retreating to Maynooth, losing the opportunity to capitalise on weaknesses in the English army such as illness over the winter months. When the campaign resumed in the spring, Maynooth fell to the English after just a six-day siege. Kildare escaped but the garrison of 40 was executed. Without the promised foreign support, Kildare surrendered in August and, despite assurances to the contrary, he and his five uncles were beheaded the following February. Henry VIII was determined to destroy the House of Kildare for good.

After the defeat of Kildare, Cromwell pressed ahead with his administrative reforms for Ireland. He intended that Ireland be ruled directly from London, with a local administration presided over by an

Englishman, a permanent English garrison and a bureaucracy comprising some English officials. The major Acts of the Break with Rome were passed through the Irish parliament, thus putting the Church of Ireland under the control of the English king and Archbishop of Canterbury. During the lengthy Lord Deputyship of Anthony St Leger, 1540–47, the Irish monasteries were dissolved, enriching not only the crown but the English in Ireland who received titles and lands. In 1541 Henry also changed Ireland's constitution. The Act of Kingly Title named him as King of Ireland and made all the Irish his subjects, under the jurisdiction of the crown.

## The rebellions of 1569 and 1579

The Duke of Somerset took the first significant steps towards colonisation by introducing English settlers into the counties of Leix and Offaly. Mary continued this policy and created two new shires through a policy known as **Plantation** which played its part in stirring rebellions against Elizabeth.

In 1569, James Fitzmaurice Fitzgerald sparked a revolt with an attack on lands earmarked by the Lord Deputy, Sir Henry Sidney, for English settlers. Fitzmaurice (cousin of the Earl of Desmond) had the personality and status to rally all nobles and gentry who feared loss of their lands and status. A renowned swordsman, his charisma and military prowess won him support from the Fitzgerald family and their affiliated feudal lords. Like Silken Thomas, he broadened his appeal and aims by embracing the rhetoric of a Catholic campaign against a heretic monarch, thus winning support from the Gaelic chiefs of the south-west. Fitzmaurice then embarked on a fruitful campaign to capture key towns in Munster. By July 1569 the rebels numbered 4500 and were laying siege to Kilkenny.

The government's response came in October when Sidney left Dublin with an army of 600 men but it was the governor of Munster, Humphrey Gilbert, who quelled the revolt savagely and efficiently by capturing 23 castles and slaughtering all their occupants. In *Tudor Ireland* (1985) Steven Ellis draws comparisons between this and the Northern Rebellion which took place in England the same year: 'very probably however, the revolts of 1569–70 were an Irish manifestation of the court intrigues which culminated in the northern rising of 1569–70. Two northern rebels later joined Fitzmaurice'. Any analysis of the government's response needs to be aware of the impact of two rebellions in the same year, both in areas distant from London.

Fitzmaurice remained at large, the focal point for all malcontents for the next six years until he fled to France. Once abroad he visited both the Spanish and Papal courts to gain foreign support and the Pope gave him 1000 Italian swordsmen, under the leadership of the English adventurer, Thomas Stukely. Although this force was side-tracked to fight in Morocco where Stukely was killed, Fitzmaurice and a smaller force landed at Smerwick in July 1579 and proclaimed they were fighting a holy war sanctioned by the Pope. This 1579 rebellion coincided with the arrival of the Jesuits, Robert Parsons and Edmund Campion in England on a mission to strengthen the Catholic community's allegiance to the Pope. The two events, and involvement of the Pope in both, would have increased the government's concern. This time the rebels were joined by the Earl of Desmond who had refused to surrender all his authority to the crown after his brothers had murdered the English constable of

**Plantations** were established throughout Ireland by the Tudors from Henry VIII onwards. Lands, usually in Ulster and Munster, were confiscated from the Gaelic Irish and granted by the crown to settlers from England who therefore colonised them. These settlers eventually formed a new, and Protestant, ruling class in Ireland.

Dungarvan and provost-marshal of Munster. The rebellion spread through Munster, Leinster, Ulster and Connaught, although Fitzmaurice himself was killed in a skirmish in August. In 1580 Elizabeth sent Lord Arthur Grey with an army of 6500 men to quash the rebellion. Grey's brutal tactics included the massacre of the garrison at Smerwick – composed mainly of reinforcements sent from Spain – despite them having surrendered. There were also widespread executions, the harvest was burned and cattle slaughtered. Grey was finally recalled by Elizabeth, once it became clear that his actions had alienated even the traditional supporters of the government in the Pale. However, by forcefully depopulating much of the two provinces, Grey had paved the way, at considerable cost to the Irish, for the successful colonisation of Desmond's lands in Munster and Connaught.

## Tyrone's rebellion 1594–1603

Tyrone's rebellion in Ulster from 1594 to 1603 is also known in Ireland as the Nine Years' War.

The policies followed by the Tudors in Ulster were not dissimilar from the rest of Ireland and had enjoyed limited success but the province remained intensely Gaelic and hostile. Elizabeth's government expected Hugh O'Neill, Earl of Tyrone, to help drive through their policies of reform in Ulster, partly because of his skills in negotiation and partly because he was an Anglicised Irishman, a regular visitor to the English court as the second Earl of Tyrone, and a Gaelic chieftain, O'Neill of Tyrone. Instead he was gradually drawn into leading a rebellion against the English.

Little is known about Tyrone's personal religious convictions. Although he was born and died a Catholic, he did not object to attending Protestant churches while in London. Therefore, while religious differences between Protestantism and Catholicism may have added to the growing animosity between Tyrone and the government, the principal cause of his rebellion was, according to Colm Lennon:

> The operations of the English settlers in the province did not auger well for his continued ascendancy, let alone a presidential function … Tyrone wanted for himself an exclusive commission to govern Ulster, but when this was withheld he determined to join the rebellion.

Thus Tyrone increasingly believed that the security of his position was best secured by rebelling against the authority of the English government in Ulster rather than by allying with it.

Tyrone never completely gave up efforts at diplomacy in order to secure a peaceful settlement which would establish him as ruler of Ulster, but as the war progressed he increasingly acquired almost cult status as the leader who would deliver Ireland from English occupation. He also, more significantly, provided military expertise and support. Tyrone had built up an army of 2500 cavalry and infantry combined, comprised of native mercenary soldiers trained by veteran English and Spanish instructors. This force included some survivors from the Spanish Armada, shipwrecked on Ireland's coast. The army was equipped with up-to-date weapons including pikes and muskets and supported by a supply network which provided the growth and transport of food and the importing of munitions. Tyrone also had the advantage of 'playing at home' and was able to use the landscape of Ulster to plan a campaign of surprise attacks and ambushes when the 'war' broke out in June 1594.

## Timeline of events of Tyrone's rebellion (the 'Nine Years' War')

**1594** Hugh Maguire, another Gaelic Lord in Ulster, besieged his castle of Enniskillen and after nine days won it back from the occupying English force, although the castle was retaken by the English six months later.

**1595** Tyrone seized the English fort on the Blackwater, captured Enniskillen Castle and defeated the English at Clontribet.

**1597** Following a pardon from Elizabeth, Tyrone defeated the English garrison at the Battle of the Yellow Ford, using the natural features of the terrain to his advantage.

**1599** The Earl of Essex was sent to Ireland with a huge army of 17,000 men but failed to confront Tyrone and disobeyed orders by returning to London to seek an audience with the Queen.

**1600** Essex was replaced by Lord Mountjoy who was given far greater military support.

**1601** Spanish forces landed at Kinsale to join O'Neill. Mountjoy prepared a three-pronged attack from Armagh, Lough Foyle and Tyrconnel. In December Tyrone's forces failed to defeat Mountjoy in a surprise attack on the English camp.

**1602** The English reduced Tyrone's power base through the building of new fortresses and control of food supplies which resulted in famine conditions in the winter.

**1603** Tyrone's negotiated surrender came six days after Elizabeth's death.

The response of the government to Tyrone's rebellion was inconsistent and often influenced by both finance and relations with other hostile European powers, particularly Spain, with whom England had been at war since 1588. William McCaffery in *Elizabeth I* is one of many historians critical of Elizabeth's Irish policy:

> To these problems of geographic distance, money, greater urgency of other problems and a lack of long-term goals Elizabeth contributed nothing. So far as possible she avoided them; invariably resorting to the cheapest remedy which would buy a short-term solution … she was incapable of balancing short-term costs against long term advantage.

The initial English response was characterised by a poor chain of command, delays in troops arriving from England and other problems common when maintaining an army in what was essentially a foreign field, such as illness, lack of supplies and negative effects upon the local inhabitants.

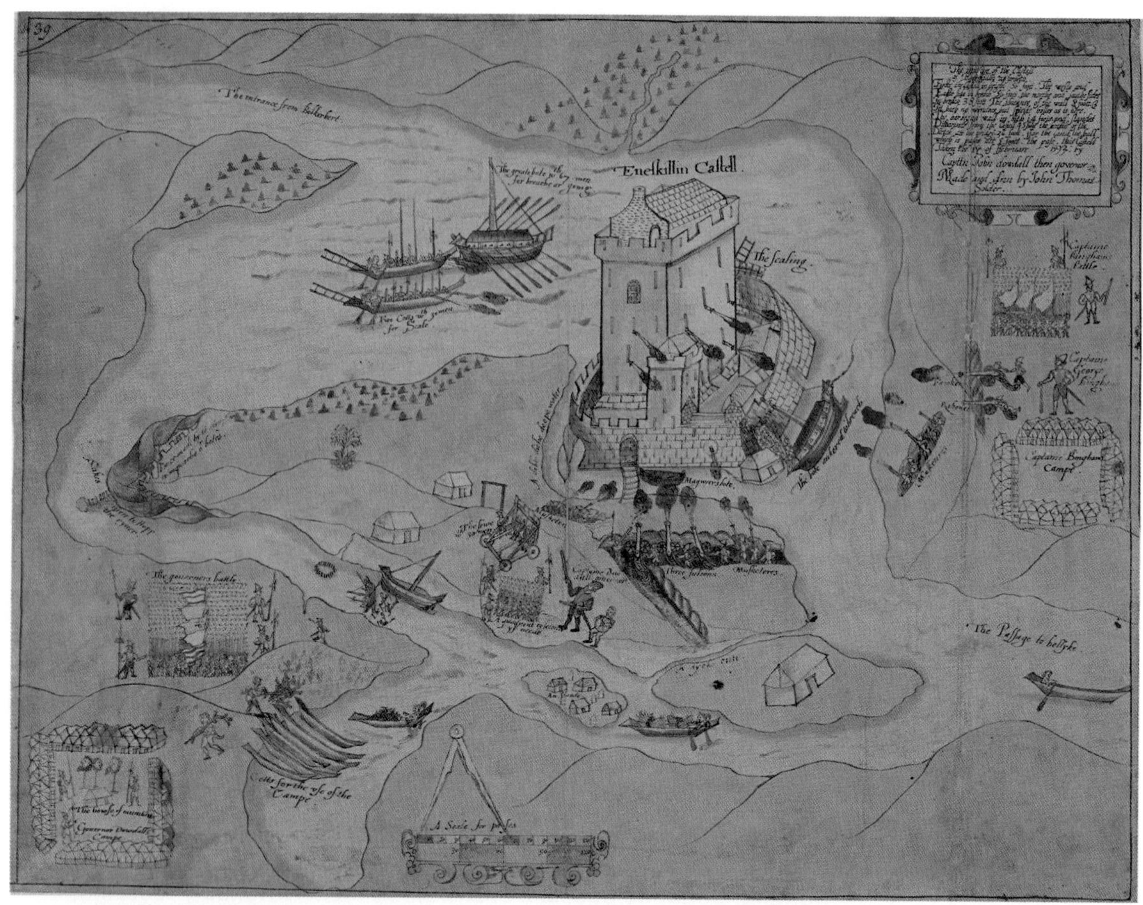
Eneſkillin Caſtell

△ Enniskillen Castle was the stronghold of the Maguires but strategically vital to the English for keeping Ulster under control. Control of the castle passed backwards and forwards between Maguire and government forces until its final capture by the English in 1607. This picture, painted in oils by John Thomas in 1594, shows the massive government siege of 1594 at the beginning of Tyrone's rebellion.

Outwardly, Tyrone's aims were similar to many rebel leaders in England who professed allegiance to the crown while defending by force their freedom of conscience, retention of traditional authority, both political and religious, and the curtailing of unpopular policies which extended royal control. At first Tyrone focused on Ulster and confined his military campaigns to that province. However, after his success at Yellow Ford, Tyrone was seen as an inspiration by all Irish who were hostile to government policies and fighting broke out in plantation settlements throughout the provinces colonised by the English. With the failure of Essex's campaign, Tyrone seems to have accepted his role as a national leader and led his forces to central and southern Ireland in 1599.

The debacle of Essex's campaign was however a turning point for both sides. Tyrone now made the restoration of the Catholic religion, as well as political and economic independence, his rallying cry against the English. In this he was successful in attracting foreign support from Philip II who saw the opportunity of opening up another front from which to attack England. In 1601 a Spanish contingent of 3400 landed at Kinsale. Elizabeth had at last been convinced of the necessity to send the experienced military commander, Mountjoy.

When Tyrone surrendered in 1603 he was granted a royal pardon and restored to those powers which he had held before the rebellion. However, the defeat of this rebellion came at a price, as Steven Ellis shows:

> Undoubtedly, the planning, preparation and execution of Mountjoy's campaign was an extraordinary feat of government. Yet it placed an enormous strain on the English economy and the crown's limited financial resources – the cost of victory was unexpectedly high. Large parts of Ireland had been devastated, crops burned, cattle slaughtered, or buildings razed. Ulster was almost a wilderness, Munster west of Cork almost uninhabited, trade disrupted, the coinage debased, towns ruined or declining, and the population decimated by famine.

## Concluding your enquiry

Although Henry VIII and Elizabeth defeated rebellions in Ireland, neither was successful in establishing the government control achieved throughout England and Wales. As a result they bequeathed to succeeding centuries a country still dominated by Catholicism and powerful nobles, but now suffering from social and economic distress and smarting from the injustice of foreign occupation.

Use your completed factors chart to plan an essay with the title: Why did Irish rebellions never threaten English control of Ireland?

You should also be able to assess whether these rebellions failed for the same reasons as those in England by a further analysis of the 'threat criteria'. There is also scope for independent study comparing rebellions in England and Ireland and the ways in which they were dealt with.

# 7 Review: Why were some rebellions perceived to be especially dangerous to the monarch?

The main focus of this book has been to evaluate the threat from each rebellion and by now you will have completed the activity below (introduced on pages 12–13) to compare the threats posed by the rebellions. You may have decided that Lambert Simnel's was the most dangerous because it was an invasion led by relatives of a ruling dynasty supported by foreign troops who succeeded in forcing Henry VII to fight for his crown. Alternatively, you may have decided that Kett's rebellion was more dangerous because he set up an alternative system of local government in East Anglia at a time when central government was riven by faction. Or perhaps you chose the Pilgrimage of Grace because much of the north was up in arms, forcing Henry VIII to play for time while he summoned his own forces in response.

As preparation for the main activity in this chapter, make sure you have completed this summary activity, placing each rebellion according to the extent of its threat.

**Rebellions that aimed to depose the monarch**

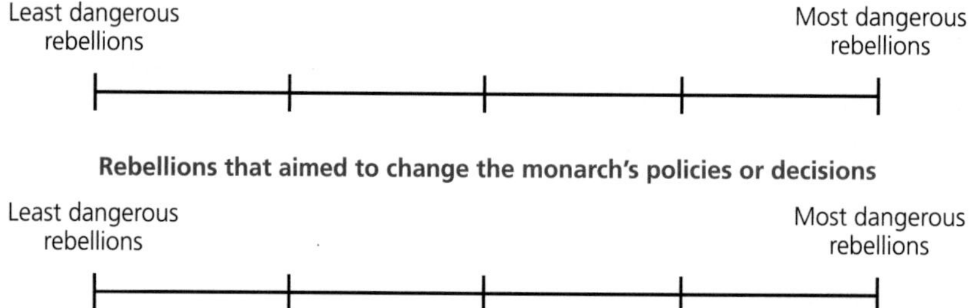
Least dangerous rebellions
Most dangerous rebellions
Rebellions that aimed to change the monarch's policies or decisions
Least dangerous rebellions
Most dangerous rebellions

## Focus route: Why were some rebellions perceived to be especially dangerous to the monarch?

We introduced this question and activity on pages 62–67 when you had studied about half of the rebellions. The aim then was to help you start thinking about this question, a vital question for creating a good synoptic overview of the topic of Tudor rebellions. Now that you have studied the rest of the rebellions it's time to finalise your answer, using the knowledge you have built up. On pages 117–121 you will find some examples of how each of the factors on the cards opposite may have helped some rebellions feel so threatening. You should be able to analyse these in more depth and pick out further examples of rebellions when, for example, English support or foreign aid was perceived as especially dangerous. Of course the perception of the monarch was not necessarily accurate.

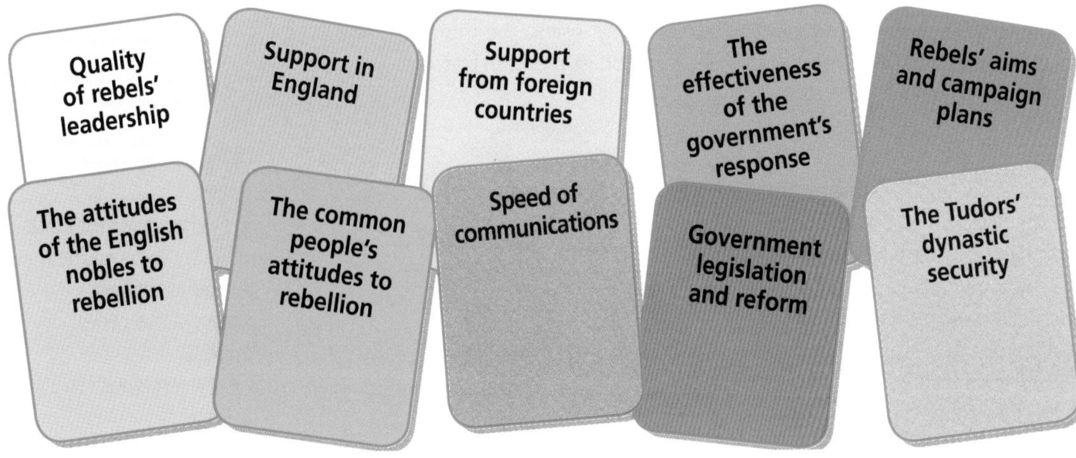
Quality of rebels' leadership
Support in England
Support from foreign countries
The effectiveness of the government's response
Rebels' aims and campaign plans
The attitudes of the English nobles to rebellion
The common people's attitudes to rebellion
Speed of communications
Government legislation and reform
The Tudors' dynastic security

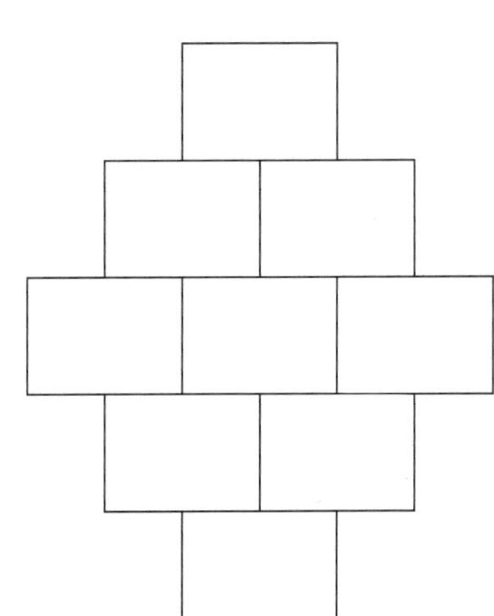

1. Make brief notes explaining how each factor created a sense of danger. Make sure you include examples from the rebellions you have studied, including those earlier in the period.
2. Create your own set of factor cards. Lay them out in a circle on a sheet of A3, then draw lines between any that you think are linked and write brief notes on the lines to explain the links.
3. Organise the cards into a pattern in which the factors that were most important in creating a sense of threat are at the top and those least important at the bottom.
4. Use this pattern and the links to answer the question 'Why were some Tudor rebellions perceived to be especially dangerous to the monarch?'

Synoptic Chapter

## How each factor created a sense of danger

### The Tudors' dynastic security

Henry VII was particularly anxious, seeing dangers around every corner, because he knew his own claim to the throne could be seen as weak. Both he and Henry VIII continued to be aware that there were surviving members of the House of York with theoretical claims to the crown. This insecurity increased when religion came to play in the fortunes of the monarchy. Mary's restoration of Roman Catholicism and Elizabeth's establishment of the English Church meant both women had additional dangers to fear from the rebels fighting to overthrow the monarch's choice of national religion.

1 Which rebellions took place at times of greatest dynastic insecurity?
2 Do the events of 1536 and 1549 suggest that the Tudor dynasty was insecure in the minds of the commons?

## The quality of rebels' leadership

The Tudors faced rebel leaders whom they perceived as dangerous but for different reasons. Some leaders appeared threatening because they were noblemen with the potential to raise and lead an army against the monarch. The presence of the Earl of Lincoln, for example, with Yorkist blood in his veins and some military training, added to the threat posed by Simnel's rebellion. In Elizabeth's reign, the Earls of Northumberland and Westmoreland possessed huge power and influence in the north with armed followers on horseback who were ready to fight if led effectively. Henry VIII faced a different kind of threat from the leadership of Robert Aske who, during the Pilgrimage of Grace, was able to unite disparate groups across the north, to articulate their diverse grievances and capture and govern York. Aske, however, refused to take up arms against the King. Robert Kett posed similar dangers in 1549 as he rallied support across East Anglia, captured Norwich and set up an alternative government but again did not attempt to march on London or challenge the monarch's right to wear the crown.

△ **Perkin Warbeck was one of the pretenders who threatened Henry VII. Did leadership by pretenders undermine the threat they posed?**

1 What different kinds of leadership qualities can be identified amongst the rebel leaders?
2 Which kinds of leadership may have appeared most threatening to monarchs?
3 Why is it difficult to be certain how much impact leadership had on the course of many rebellions?
4 How important a role did leadership really play in creating a sense of threat?

## Support from foreign countries

The dangers posed by experienced foreign mercenaries landing in England to support rebellions against the monarch are not difficult for us to imagine. Henry VII was particularly aware of these from his own experience in 1485. In 1487 when Lambert Simnel landed in the north-west he was supported by 2000 German mercenaries led by Colonel Schwartz and provided by Margaret of Burgundy and 6000 Irish soldiers sent by the Earl of Kildare. The threat from Perkin Warbeck appeared all the greater because of the possibility of his winning foreign military aid. However, it was possibly the rebellions in Ireland that the Tudors would have perceived as particularly dangerous in their potential to harness support from Catholic Europe. In 1534 Thomas Fitzgerald, tenth Earl of Kildare, believed that Charles V would send 12,000 Spanish troops to support his rebellion against Henry VIII. Elizabeth was faced by Papal backing of a small force of mercenaries that landed in support of James Fitzmaurice Fitzgerald in 1579 and, most dangerous of all, a Spanish contingent of 3400 sent in 1601 by Philip II to fight with the Earl of Tyrone against English rule in Ireland.

1 Which rebellions appeared most dangerous because of foreign military support?
2 Why did some rebellions but not others receive foreign aid?
3 Was the perception of the danger from foreign military support greater than the reality?

## Support in England

Pure numbers can be misleading. The largest rebellion by far was the Pilgrimage of Grace with 40,000 rebels, followed by the 1497 Cornish Rebellion with 20,000 and Kett's rebellion with 16,000. All the other rebellions numbered fewer than 10,000 each at a time when the population was around three million. This does not seem to suggest that support in England was either particularly great or threatening. As always in history though, empathy and context are key. In the prologue to *The Pilgrimage of Grace*, Geoffrey Moorhouse paints a picture of how the danger might have been perceived by Henry VIII in October 1536:

> Royal scouts have been sizing up the rebel army for days and the prospect is intimidating. Something like 30,000 men have been advancing in extended order across Yorkshire towards Doncaster, where scarcely more than a token force is said to be deployed in time to obstruct their further progress south. Even when all the troops that Henry VIII has at his disposal are mustered together, they will be outnumbered by more than two to one – and they are not together: we hear that they are scattered across the Midlands almost haphazardly, the biggest and the nearest contingent consisting of no more than 6000 men. Unless something is done quickly, the rebels will have a walkover, picking off Henry's ill-equipped, unpaid and increasingly demoralised army in one isolated battalion after another. Then the way will be open to London.

We of course have the luxury of hindsight, of knowing how much English support actually materialised and the nature of that support. Tudor monarchs, however, just had to wait anxiously for the next report to arrive. How would Henry VII have perceived the news that Lambert Simnel had invaded and was marching from the coast to link up with unknown numbers of sympathisers in northern England? How would Elizabeth, lacking an heir and with a newly established Anglican religion, have perceived the dangers from a rebellion in the Catholic north where support for the succession of Mary, Queen of Scots could well be high?

1 What kind of English support was most threatening?
2 Why was it difficult for monarchs to be sure of the extent of support for rebels – and for themselves?
3 Which was more dangerous – 60,000 men in arms across the north of England or 3000 attacking the centre of London?
4 What kind of rebellions mustered the most support – and were these the rebellions that most threatened the monarch's hold on the crown?

## The attitudes of the English nobles to rebellion

Monarchs knew their nobles personally and were well aware of the dangers they posed in terms of their military power and territorial influence. Therefore the involvement of nobles in rebellions might well be perceived as a particular sign of danger. Henry VII owed his victory at Bosworth to Sir William Stanley's support and showed his fears when Stanley plotted against him by launching an extensive and cruelly executed investigation and show trial. A nobleman could also weaken the ability of the monarch to put down a potential rebellion in his region, simply by not supporting the crown. In 1536 Lord Darcy failed to hold Pontefract Castle against the 'pilgrims' and then, having decided to join them, was instrumental in organising the region around the castle to ensure it could withstand any forces sent by the King. Henry's panic in 1536 was no doubt intensified by the fact that he had ignored the defences of castles such as Pontefract and had done little to secure a good relationship with Darcy.

1 Did any rebellions receive particularly strong support from nobles?
2 Why was noble support for rebellion so dangerous?

## The effectiveness of the government's response

The monarch's perception of the danger he or she was in was compounded by their awareness of the speed with which they could respond to the threat. This response would be coloured by the efficiency of their communications and their ability to raise a royal army of necessary size. Thus in 1497 Henry VII knew that he was exposed by the arrival of the Cornish rebels on Blackheath because he had just sent Daubeney's army north to Scotland. In 1536 Henry VIII was caught out by the spread and size of the Pilgrimage of Grace and was forced to play for time by promising pardons and redress of grievances which he had no intention of keeping. Similarly the Duke of Somerset was slow to respond to both the Western Rising and then Kett's rebellion because he was preoccupied with economic issues and war against Scotland. When he did finally perceive the danger of his position his panic was clear in his choice of harsh military measures and employment of foreign mercenaries.

1 Why do we need to understand what other events were happening at the same time in order to assess the effectiveness of a government's response to a rebellion?

2 Did any rebellions become a greater threat because the government was slow to respond?

3 How is this factor linked to the role of the nobility in assessing the danger from rebellions?

## Rebels' aims and campaign plans

There is little doubt that monarchs would have perceived those rebellions that sought their overthrow as the most dangerous. Thomas Wyatt, however much he kept it hidden from his followers, planned to replace Mary with Elizabeth and to seize the government in London in order to achieve this. In 1569 the Northern Earls aimed to free Mary, Queen of Scots from imprisonment in England to ensure her place on the English throne and end the Tudor dynasty. However, we cannot assume that monarchs saw those rebellions in which leaders professed their loyalty, claiming to be only protesting about policies or ministers, as far less dangerous. Henry VII may have believed that the Cornish rebels' aim was to overthrow him rather than complain about taxes. Henry VIII saw the pilgrims as threatening his royal policies and ministers and endangering both his authority and ability to govern the country, especially in the north.

1 Were protests for removal of policies or ministers really dangerous to the monarch?

2 Which rebellions had a clear enough plan to pose a genuine threat?

3 To what extent were the beliefs of those involved a major factor in bringing about or sustaining the rebellions? It might be helpful to determine whether such beliefs were religious, political or moral (maintaining the natural order).

## The common people's attitudes to rebellion

The common people were most likely to protest against heavy taxation and in times of economic hardship, hunger and depression. Both Kett's rebellion and the Pilgrimage of Grace took place against a background of hunger and economic depression. All authorities were alert to the potential for such unrest. Henry VIII was so aware of the dangers that could arise from heavy taxation that he backed down when faced with the rising against the Amicable Grant and cancelled it. Commoners tended to react angrily to changes by, for example, pulling down fences or attacking local officials, but were unlikely to want to travel from their home or to challenge the monarchy directly, as opposed to those who protested at a policy. Deference was deeply ingrained but this did not stop monarchs from fearing the dangers posed by a 'hungry mob'.

1 Why were the ruling class afraid of the possibility of rebellion by the commons?

2 Was it the aims of commons' protest or simply sheer numbers that made them appear threatening?

## Speed and accuracy of communications

**Communication in August 2011**

4 August Mark Duggan was shot and killed by police attempting to arrest him
6 August Peaceful march to Tottenham police station, was joined by 120 people and rioting broke out
7 August The spread of news and rumours sparked riots in London
8 August Looting, arson and violence took place in areas across England including London, Birmingham, Bristol, Gloucester, Gillingham and Nottingham.


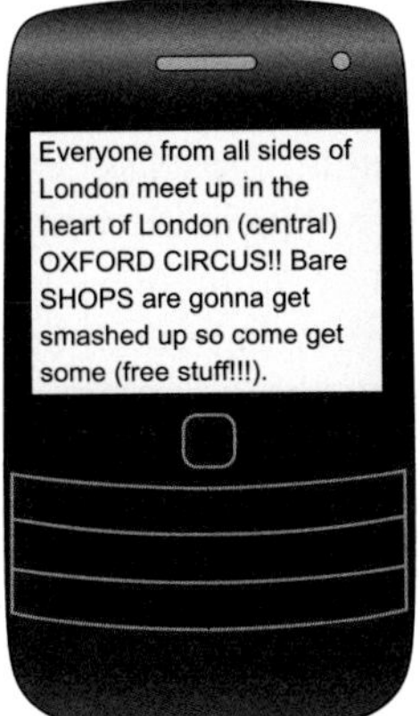

Everyone from all sides of London meet up in the heart of London (central) OXFORD CIRCUS!! Bare SHOPS are gonna get smashed up so come get some (free stuff!!!).


**Communication in August 1536**

| | |
|---|---|
| 1 October | *Inflammatory sermon was preached at Louth, Beacons were lit along the Humber. Leaflets were nailed to church doors warning of more attacks on churches and increased taxation. Ringleaders rode throughout the area to encourage rebellion. Church bells were rung to summon people to muster and swear allegiance to the rebels. Visible force of over 200 men was now able to attract more recruits.* |
| 12 October | *Whole of Wensleydale now in revolt.* |

The slow speed of communications in the sixteenth century, exemplified by the comparison above, increased monarchs' sense of danger as they waited for information about what was happening or how many were involved. This extract, from David Loades' *Two Tudor Conspiracies*, gives us an indication of what this must have felt like for Mary Tudor during one of the uprisings before Wyatt's rebellion:

> The news that reached London was not altogether reliable, for although it was known that Carew was the centre of a conspiracy in the south west, it was not known who adhered to him or what progress had been made. The only official communication which had been received was the Justice's letter of the 10th, which does not seem to have been very explicit, and which aroused suspicions that the whole county was disaffected. About the 20th it was rumoured in the capital that '… Sir Peter Carew … with dyverse others wer uppe in Devonshire resisting of the king of Spaynes coming, and that they had taken the city of Exeter and castell ther into their custodye' … while there is nothing particularly surprising in rumours being spread, it is surprising that the Council should have been so short of reliable intelligence that it believed them.

1 Why was news likely to be vague or inaccurate?

2 Why was the slow speed and uncertainty of information so likely to increase the sense of danger from rebellions?

## Government legislation and reform

As the sixteenth century developed, with the Tudors more firmly established on the throne, government authority was extended and centralised using a range of institutions, officials and laws. (These are detailed in full on pages 129–134.) It has been argued therefore that the Tudor state actually grew stronger as a result of rebellions, this in turn reducing the likelihood of future ones. The threat to political stability engendered by rebellions gave monarchs a justification for ridding themselves of awkward opponents, exacting savage reprisals and enacting harsher treason laws. At the same time rebellions showed the gentry class that they were better off supporting the monarch and may even have given some monarchs pause for thought. Not all the reactions to rebellion were aggressive. Monarchs and governments did listen to the people's grievances and as the century wore on, they increasingly saw the advantages in alleviating the causes of these through social and economic reforms.

# Concluding your enquiry

On several occasions rebellion seemed about to bring the government to its knees. In 1487 an army aiming to depose the monarch invaded with foreign support and marched south to meet Henry VII in battle. In 1536 the north of England seemed beyond the control of Henry VIII and his ministers in London. Thirteen years later widespread protests occurred across southern England in response to economic hardship, fuelled by the religious policies of a minority government led by an increasingly embattled regent. In 1554 Wyatt's rebellion succeeded in penetrating the centre of London, forcing Mary Tudor to appeal directly to Londoners to remind them where their loyalty lay.

These were very different rebellions. There was no one factor which made one more serious than the others. The causes and aims varied as did the quality of leadership, the extent of their support and the government response.

## Analysing themes

There is more than one way to construct a synoptic essay. The title of this chapter requires you to evaluate the relevant criteria and give a wide range of examples to produce a substantiated hypothesis. For other essay titles you may be required to focus in depth on a given theme, for example, 'How far do you agree that rebellions with foreign support posed the most dangerous threat to Tudor governments?', before contrasting and comparing it with other criteria to evaluate its relative significance. It is the selection of evidence that is of paramount importance. Once you have finished your notes on 'Why were some Tudor rebellions perceived as especially dangerous to the monarch?' you could extend your synoptic analysis further by completing a chart like the one below for all the rebellions. By colour coding each of the criteria in line with your supporting evaluation you will be better prepared to plan the second type of synoptic answer. One has been completed for you as an example but you do not have to agree with these judgements. You may also feel encouraged to refine further your synoptic overviews by evaluating:

- the aspects of rebellions that were the most and least threatening
- the combination of factors that appeared most threatening to monarchs
- whether aspects increased/decreased over time
- any discrepancies from the norm.

| Rebellions | Lovell and Staffords | Lambert Simnel | Yorkshire Rebellion | Warbeck's rebellion |
|---|---|---|---|---|
| The quality of rebels' leadership | | | | |
| Support in England | | | | |
| Support from foreign countries | | | | |
| The government's response | | | | |
| Rebels' aims and campaign plans | | | | |
| The attitudes of the English nobles | | | | |
| The common people's attitudes | | | | |
| Speed and accuracy of communications | | n/a | | |
| The Tudors' dynastic security | | | | |
| Government legislation and reform | | n/a | | |

## Comparing the danger from different types of rebellion

In Chapter 1 (page 11) we talked about the categories to which historians have assigned the rebellions. These were based on the rebellions' **causes**, for example religious, social/economic, desire to change the dynasty and so on. However, your work on the rebellions will have alerted you to the fact that although a rebellion may predominantly belong in one category, it may nevertheless contain elements of another.

To complete your synoptic analysis of the threat posed by Tudor rebellions you should reach a judgement as to the dangers posed by each category of rebellion in order to show whether, for example, social and economic rebellions were the most threatening. A chart analysing all the categories, like the one started below, should help you towards your verdict.

| Category | Which rebellions? | The nature of the threat and the degree of threat? |
|---|---|---|
| Social and economic | 1489 Yorkshire – taxes<br><br>1497 Cornish – taxes<br><br>1525 Amicable Grant – taxes<br><br>1549 Kett's rebellion – enclosures, inflation, unemployment<br><br>Also a secondary factor in:<br><br>1536 Pilgrimage of Grace – high prices, enclosure, high rents, Subsidy Tax, debasement<br><br>1549 Western Rising – high rents, debasement, inflation | None of these rebellions aimed to overthrow the monarch but instead sought a change of policy. 1489 and 1525 were easily suppressed but the other two were not. This is largely explained by the quality and determination of the leadership, despite the fact that both lacked strong noble presence. Both Flamanck (1497) and Kett were prepared to fight and die for what they believed in, and had the presence to convince many of their followers to do the same. Ultimately their grievances failed to maintain huge support outside their own area, although they did in some cases (for example, the 1525 rebellion) lead to a change of policy by the government. However, in the short term they were defeated partly because their aims did not envisage the overthrow of the monarch who thus had time to build up an armed response. |

The Tudor dynasty, itself the result of a successful rebellion, managed to survive intact on the English throne despite these rebellions. Although, as shown by your threat evaluations, some rebellions were strong in some areas, all had flaws and weaknesses. The strengths and weaknesses differed from rebellion to rebellion, some had good leaders but little tactical or military strength; others had a clear strategic plan but lacked sufficient popular and foreign support to implement it. Some faced an informed and prepared monarch while others did not but failed to exploit their opportunity, and so on. All the rebellions, however, had to deal with aspects of English society and government which made successful rebellion difficult and it was their inability to overcome these, as you will see in the next chapter, which ultimately spelled their downfall.

Synoptic Chapter

# 8 Review: Why did the rebellions fail?

The Tudor dynasty had to justify its existence and proved tenacious in fighting to keep what it had seized by force. Political propaganda is not commonly associated with the sixteenth century but the Tudors used all means at their disposal to glorify and publicise the majesty of their position and its semi-divine nature. Suppressing rebellions also allowed the Tudors to justify their more despotic actions; enemies and opponents could be executed and more importantly made an example of, whether or not they had actually taken arms against the monarch. In this way both Henry VII and Henry VIII disposed of surviving members of the House of York. Revenge exacted against a whole region, as seen after both the Pilgrimage of Grace and Northern Rebellion, created opportunities to bring in new men and improved institutions of direct government control. Rebellions themselves, therefore, played a crucial part in ensuring the Tudor dynasty remained on the throne. Rebellions also enabled the Tudors to centralise their powers still further, as in the extension of the Treason Laws, in order to prevent similar opposition arising in the future. Each time a rebellion failed it became that much harder for the one following to succeed.

## **Enquiry Focus:** Why did the rebellions fail?

This chapter returns to the second synoptic question you began thinking about on pages 62–67. Now it is time to create firmer conclusions, using the additional knowledge you have built up in Chapters 4–6.

However, there is one difference between this enquiry and those in earlier chapters. Previous chapters each provided a framework activity, which enabled you to keep track of your overall answer to the enquiry question while also compiling detailed notes. Without such a framework activity it is all too easy to become overwhelmed by detail and lose sight of your core answer. So, now you are near the end of this study of Tudor rebellions it is time to hand the initiative in creating a framework activity over to you.

1. What kind of activity will you use to keep that overall answer in view throughout the chapter? It will help to think about the nature of the question and look back to earlier chapters to see how framework activities are matched to questions.
2. Make a list of the factors you think played a part in explaining the failure of the rebellions.
3. Create an initial hypothesis in answer to the question, explaining which of the factors you listed were most significant in explaining the failure of rebellions.

## Introducing failure

The threat criteria which you have used through Chapters 1–6 have enabled you to analyse each rebellion's particular strengths and weaknesses. You will know by now therefore that the rebellions did not all pose an equal threat; an assessment which you could confirm by completing a chart like this one started below:

| Threat criteria | Strength | Weakness |
|---|---|---|
| Leadership | Lincoln. Aske. Kett. | Northumberland. Westmoreland. |
| | | |

The Tudor rebellions do not constitute a homogenous whole. We are not comparing like with like. The circumstances of each one in terms of its aims, leadership and support were very different. The rapidly changing political, religious and social/economic scene that was sixteenth-century England meant each rebellion took place within a different context. You have seen this already, for example, in studying the response of each government. External to the rebellions however were a set of factors, common to all of them, which they were unable to overcome and which form not only the basis of this last chapter but the last piece of the jigsaw explaining why Tudor rebellions failed.

Chief amongst the factors which all the rebellions had in common was the ability of the Tudors to deal with them. In reality, after Henry VII's success at Bosworth Field in 1485, no rebellion came close to destabilising the Tudor regime. The aims of the rebels were limited. Most sought to redress grievances, hardly any outwardly declared an intention to overthrow the monarch. The leaders often did not see themselves as rebels and showed little awareness of the political realities which surrounded any granting of their demands, or indeed what would happen afterwards. All the leaders made errors. If any of the rebellions had received significant military support from foreign powers, which would then have drawn support from discontented English, then the picture would have been very different. However, the rulers of Spain, France and the Empire were rarely moved to do more than make overtures to rebels in order to embarrass the ruler of England. As it was the Tudors were able to:

- benefit from generic weaknesses
- extend and centralise their authority.

> Compile a list showing where each of the rebel leaders made an error which cost them victory.

## Generic weaknesses of rebellions

### Communications and the impact of localism

The comparative difficulty of communications played a part in the failure of the rebellions in a variety of ways.

- Rebels found it difficult to communicate their aims and strategies to others beyond their locality. For example, in the Northern Rebellion the Earls were unable to convince the Catholic nobility of Lancashire and Cheshire to join them.

- The time it took to build major support reduced the prospect of taking the government by surprise.
- Rebels did not know in advance who else might rally to them and this affected how they planned to achieve their aim.
- The accuracy of reports was difficult to double check. For example, the diversion of the Northern Earls to Hartlepool to meet promised Spanish aid in 1569 was based on a letter which the Earl of Northumberland later claimed had been a ruse to encourage the Earls to rebel in the first place.

The impact of communications is closely linked to the problems caused for rebels by people's strong sense of locality. The reasons why people joined a rebellion and then stayed with it to its often bloody conclusion or turned back and went home are mostly unknown to us because sources providing insights into individuals' choices are extremely rare. What does seem clear is that local grievances often provided both the trigger and the core support for religious and economic rebellions, but could also limit that rebellion's appeal further afield and so stacked the odds heavily against success. Rebels, especially the commons, may have been happy to join a local protest but were more reluctant to leave their homes, families, crops and animals to travel beyond their locality. As Andy Wood has argued in *Riot, Rebellion and Popular Politics in Early Modern England* (2002):

> Early modern labouring people constituted their political identities within strong senses of locality. As inhabitants of a particular place, early modern plebeians frequently laid claim to legally meaningful local customs ..., often the subject of fierce conflict in early modern England.

Localism also affected many gentry who took part in rebellions because they too were likely to be responding to economic or religious changes in their locality. Thomas Flamank (1497), Robert Aske (Pilgrimage of Grace), Humphrey Arundel (1549) and Sir Thomas Wyatt gave rebellions strategic organisation, but were unable to extend their support outside the affected region partly because they were not well-known beyond their localities. In addition, grievances in one area were not always felt as acutely elsewhere. The attack on the monasteries was resented far more in the north than in the south, the loss of chantries was felt most keenly in the south-west, while enclosures were not a major factor in rebellions in the north but the political status of the old feudal families was.

> In what ways did the local nature of rebellions work against their success? Is localism linked to any other factors which help to explain their failure?

## The attitudes of the nobles

While the gentry were the workhorses of Tudor government, the nobility too played their part. Many became Lord Lieutenants responsible for implementing militia reforms in their county. More importantly, very few joined or led rebellions but instead commanded the crown's armies to suppress rebellion. Most of the nobility were with Henry VII in 1487 during Simnel's Rising and other examples of nobles leading royal forces against rebels include Lord Russell (Prayer Book Rebellion, 1549), Earl of Warwick (Kett's rebellion, 1549), Earl of Pembroke (Wyatt's rebellion, 1555) and the Earl of Sussex (Northern Rebellion, 1569). The importance of the royal army in defeating rebellions cannot be over-estimated. Although it took time for orders to go out and for the nobles to equip and muster their retainers, once a royal army had gathered under its commander there was only going to be one winner. As Geoff Woodward states in *Rebellion and Disorder under the Tudors* (2010): 'lack of funding for rebels resulted in inadequate cavalry, weapons, ammunition and supplies, whereas government troops could bide their time until they were ready to attack'.

The few nobles who led rebellions, such as Lord Audley (1497), Lord Darcy (Pilgrimage of Grace) and the Earls of Northumberland and Westmoreland (Northern Rebellion), did so at least partly because their influence was under threat from the centralising policies of the Tudors. However, although their power over their estates enabled them to summon armed support, the often highly personal and localised nature of their individual grievances against the crown made it unlikely that others of their class would join them. Nobles had the most to lose from taking arms against their monarch and, in reality, it was often the actions of nobles in support of the crown that ensured a rebellion did not get further than the local area.

1 How far was the nobles' overthrow of the Duke of Somerset in 1549 and the Duke of Northumberland in 1553 caused by rebellions? What conclusions can you draw from this?

2 How important was noble support for the monarchy in explaining the failure of rebellions?

## The commons' reluctance to rebel

These were turbulent times when few were immune from the impacts of population growth, inflation, changes in land ownership, the centralising policies of the Tudors and, above all, the enforcement of the Protestant reformation. There was much grumbling and complaining yet none of the rebellions attracted huge, popular, national support. One major reason was that the notions of deference and obedience were deeply engrained. Everyone was expected to keep their place and respect their social superiors. State and Church worked together to ensure that the implications of challenging authority were well understood. Draconian sanctions for rebellion must have warned off many potential rebels while the rewards of local and national offices kept the loyalty of others. Although the authorities always feared popular discontent and took savage measures to suppress it, it is perhaps the lack of rebellion in a period of such great change that may be more surprising. Another key component of the answer is that, as in all periods of history, many people of all classes simply wanted to live peaceful lives and do the best for themselves and their families.

1 Given the commons' preference for a quiet life, why did rebel leaders believe they could persuade them to fight? Explain how and why some leaders were more successful in achieving this.

2 Was the commons' reluctance to rebel more important in the failure of some rebellions than others?

## The absence of effective foreign support

Well-trained foreign forces were a major reason why Simnel's rebellion appeared threatening, yet other rebellions received no foreign help, even though Thomas Wyatt and later the Northern Earls expected it. In truth, European rulers only helped English rebels when it was in their own interests to do so. In 1487, for example, the French hoped that Henry VII would help them against Brittany and so did not give aid to Simnel. However, Margaret of Burgundy did provide Simnel with mercenary forces because of her personal crusade against Henry VII (she was the sister of the Yorkist kings).

There were several reasons for this lack of foreign support for English rebellions. The more established the Tudor dynasty became, the harder it was to dislodge. In addition, the Tudors forged good relations with foreign powers as part of their statecraft. Thus Henry VII established a strong link with the Spanish monarchy through the marriage of his son to Catherine of Aragon.

More importantly the focus of European politics changed. In the late fifteenth century north-western Europe was dominated by the three-sided struggle involving France, Burgundy and England. However, this focus faded by the early 1500s as the major political rivalry moved to southern Europe as Europe was embroiled in the conflict between the Holy Roman Emperor Charles V and the kings of France. This meant that England was now geographically less central and, in terms of armed power, relatively weak.

Foreign interest in English affairs was therefore more limited than in the late 1400s. In 1536 Robert Aske's pilgrims appealed to Charles V for money, guns and 2000 cavalry, hoping that as a staunch Catholic Charles would send aid. However, Charles faced a range of other, more important issues. He and Francis I of France were fighting over the strategically vital area of Italy, particularly over Milan. Charles also faced threats in the south as Muslim Ottoman Turks and Barbary corsairs challenged his territories in Spain and Italy and threatened trade in the Mediterranean. As Holy Roman Emperor, he also had to defend Christendom against Muslim forces. Finally, he was hoping to secure a marriage alliance between his family, the Habsburgs, and Henry VIII's daughter, Mary. Therefore the pilgrims received no aid from Charles.

This focus on mainland Europe and a determination not to drive England into the arms of enemies continued to reduce the likelihood of foreign intervention in English affairs in the second half of the sixteenth century. During the planning of Wyatt's rebellion (provoked by the Spanish marriage of Mary Tudor), the French ambassador, Noailles, was in touch with the conspirators but the French King, Henri II, when he had the opportunity, showed a reluctance to risk men or money in support of rebels whose country liked him little better than the Spanish. Therefore Henri did not invade England in support of Wyatt, preferring to distract England by strengthening his traditional alliance with Scotland.

The pattern of relationships changed again in Elizabeth's reign. Tensions over trade, religion and maritime expansion meant that Spain replaced France as England's major enemy. English and Spanish forces clashed in the Netherlands, the New World and the English Channel and Philip II's ambassadors were involved in plotting treason with the Northern Earls in 1569. However, self-interest overcame even Philip's championing of the Catholic faith. Overthrowing Elizabeth and replacing her with Mary, Queen of Scots was not in Philip's interest because of Mary's strong links with France. When he did launch the Spanish Armada, a Catholic crusade against England in 1588, growing loyalty in England to the Church of England and an increasing sense of nationalism combined to minimise the likelihood of many English Catholics supporting the Armada. Those Catholics who did 'invade' England from the seminaries in the Netherlands did so as individual priests with orders not to get involved in politics and not to incite rebellion.

The one exception to the lack of foreign intervention in the sixteenth century is of course Ireland, although intervention did not lead to success. Diarmaid MacCulloch summarises in *Reformation* (2004):

> Plantation provoked major warfare in Ireland in the 1570s and 1590s; the Gaelic aristocracy now allied with agents of the Counter-Reformation and with England's Catholic enemies in mainland Europe, principally Spain, which made repeated if unsuccessful attempts to aid Irish Catholics with military forces ... (forced to) choose between allegiance to Elizabeth or allegiance to the Pope ... increasing numbers chose the Pope.

How crucial was the lack of effective foreign support in explaining the failure of Tudor rebellions?

# Extending and centralising Tudor government

## The development of royal security and propaganda

Chief amongst the weapons employed by the Tudors was the awe and majesty of monarchy itself. The Tudors stressed that their powers were given by God and that rebellion therefore was a sin, a message reinforced by churches on a weekly basis across the land. The Tudors also used the 'media' of the sixteenth century to project an image of both the monarchy's power and its care for its subjects. This made it doubly difficult for the people to resort to rebellion and explains why many rebels proclaimed their loyalty to the monarch while protesting against policies or ministers.

- Henry VII asserted that he was descended from King Arthur, created the symbol of the Tudor Rose and spent lavishly on the royal court, greatly impressing foreign dignitaries.
- Henry VIII threw lavish tournaments where he excelled at jousting, ensured the image of majesty reached the biggest number of people through his portrait on coins, built magnificent royal palaces such as Greenwich, Richmond and Hampton Court, and employed Holbein as his resident artist (see page 67).
- Edward and Mary continued the use of paintings and images on coins to counteract the weaknesses of their age and sex respectively, although Edward was luckier in that he still had Holbein as his artist.
- Elizabeth used carefully constructed portraits and miniatures to convey images and messages, took advantage of all opportunities for celebrations (including her accession day and its subsequent commemoration), pageants and processions and went on progresses so she could be seen by her subjects (although they were mainly in the south).

Which groups in society were most likely to be influenced by the various forms of propaganda? Why would they be less likely to rebel?

Tudor rose – the emblem of the Tudor family, it shows Elizabeth's regal status and her right to the throne.

Fleur-de-lis – the royal emblem of France, it symbolises Elizabeth's claim to the throne of France which she did not renounce, despite the loss of Calais.

Pelican pendant – legend has it that the mother pelican pecks at her own breast and feeds her young on her own blood so that they might live. Elizabeth, as the mother pelican, will sacrifice her life for her people and for her Church.

△ Like her father, Elizabeth I used portraits to convey the power and aspirations of the Tudor monarchy. The Pelican portrait was probably painted by Nicholas Hilliard around 1575 when Elizabeth was in her forties, one of many portraits and miniatures he painted. All showed the wealth and magnificence of the Queen through elaborate clothes and jewels and the richness of the colours. The message in the different emblems would be clearly understood by the people.

■ How do you think Elizabeth wanted her subjects to see her

## Changes in local government

Most major disturbances took place in the furthest regions of the kingdom, in the north, the south-west, East Anglia and Ireland. These areas were traditionally hostile to central government. Some had cultures and languages of their own and, after 1534, were the centres of support for the Catholic faith. Nevertheless, the Tudors oversaw from London a system of local government set up to contain riots and disturbances and which was, in the main, successful in preventing the development of rebellions into something more widespread and threatening. The major work of government, in terms of enforcing law and order, was therefore carried out at local level where each shire had its own officials and local courts and the key figures were the local gentry who were bound to the Tudors through rewards of lands, positions and patronage.

The most important local official was the Justice of the Peace. You have seen on page 85 how their duties expanded during the sixteenth century and how the post carried status which made it much sought after by the expanding and rising gentry class. The importance of JPs was reflected in the rise in the number of Justices per shire from an average of ten per county in 1500 to over 50 by 1600. All local officials were charged with carrying out the wishes of the monarch and central government, whether expressed in royal proclamations, council circulars or parliamentary statute. The majority of these edicts aimed at ensuring peace and stability. Local officials' administrative roles therefore included both law enforcement and informing central government on potential or actual threats.

A continuing problem for the monarchy was the lack of a permanent standing army which could make the crown vulnerable and explains why, when faced with rebellion, it so often played for time in order to summon its forces. Historically the nobles had provided the crown with its army, but the Tudors strengthened their own position by tightening up the system of training and recruiting soldiers at a local level. Under the Militia Act of 1572, Lord Lieutenants were responsible for ensuring that all men between the ages of 16 and 60 were to receive ten days training a year in the use of firearms, with equipment provided by the county. Nicholas Fellowes concludes in *Rebellion and Disorder under the Tudors*:

> Lord Lieutenants and their deputies worked closely with the JPs and gentry and were a pivotal link in the chain of command between the crown and county administration responsible for ensuring the country remained stable and peaceful. The absence of any major rebellion after 1570 in Elizabethan England does not prove that they were an effective deterrent against popular disorder, but a permanent crown appointee in each county enabled the government to be better informed of local issues and undoubtedly better placed to resolve issues before they became too serious.

■ Using this information, and that on page 85, explain how significant the changes in local government were in preventing and defeating rebellions.

## Changes in central government and Parliament

Vital as local government was in the maintenance of law and order, it was central government and, in particular, the monarchs who had to respond to challenges. Rebellions failed partly because of the machinery of state available to the monarchy. Monarchs proved adept (if occasionally slow) at implementing strategies and changes which made maximum use of their resources.

Royal success depended on the ability to enforce the law throughout the realm, particularly in those areas remote from London. The strengthening of central institutions in the distant/border regions, such as the Council in the North, Council in the Marches and Wales, and the government of Ireland, was crucial to the centralisation of Tudor authority and thus the security of the dynasty. Tudor monarchs also continued the work of restoring the great law courts of the land started by the Yorkists, which helped to reinforce the impression of a country where law breakers would be brought to justice and punishments meted out.

After the 1530s Parliament grew under the Tudors to become a major tool in reducing the threat from rebellions and promoting stability. This was done through legislation aimed at reducing the power of opponents, increasing penalties for disobedience or removing some of the causes of unrest, as this chart shows.

| Aim | Acts | Main details |
|---|---|---|
| Reducing the powers of the nobles | Acts of Attainder | 138 were passed during Henry VII's reign, enabling the crown to seize lands of disloyal nobles. |
| | Acts v Retainers 1485 and 1504 | Although Henry saw these private armies of gentry following their noble lord as a threat to his authority, his aim was to limit them through licensing, not to abolish them. Further acts restricted the wearing of nobles' badges or uniforms (livery). The crown still needed these retainers to control unrest at local level. |
| | Star Chamber Act 1497 | Henry created a tribunal where his councillors and judges could enforce the law against those who considered themselves above it, the so-called 'over mighty subjects'. |
| Protecting the life of the monarch | Break with Rome 1532–34 | Henry VIII and Thomas Cromwell used oaths as a test of loyalty to the Tudors. The Act of Succession included the oath recognising the children of Henry and Anne Boleyn which was enforced on all office holders. |
| | 1583 Bond of Association | This was established by Elizabeth's councillors during a plot against her by Mary, Queen of Scots to ensure that, in the event of Elizabeth's assassination, none of those associated with the crime could benefit from it. |
| Ensuring the support of the gentry | Acts for Dissolution of the Monasteries 1536 and 1540 | By ensuring that the gentry, many of whom were MPs, benefited from the sale of monastic lands, Cromwell was linking their fortunes to those of the crown, and thus gaining their support both in Parliament and in keeping the peace in their own districts since many MPs were also JPs. |

| Aim | Acts | Main details |
|---|---|---|
| Extending the definition of 'traitor' | 1534 Treason Act | Following the Break with Rome this act introduced the death penalty for all those who wanted the King dead, whether through actual plotting or simply words or writing.<br><br>After 1534 all Tudors feared the voicing of popular dissent and ensured that meetings and materials which advocated criticism of the monarch or policies were treasonable. |
| | 1571 and 1581 Acts | The former made it high treason to deny Elizabeth her title as queen. The 1581 Act redefined treason to include anyone who drew the allegiance of English subjects away from their queen or Church. |
| Reducing unrest over economic grievances: enclosures | Enclosure Acts of 1489, 1533, 1549–50, 1555, 1563 and 1597 | All the Tudors were aware of the unpopularity of enclosures and passed acts to prevent the conversion of arable land to pasture, the engrossment of farms and the destruction of common rights. There were also five commissions of enquiry to check illegal enclosures. |
| Reducing unrest over economic grievances: food supplies | Acts to limit export of grain and encourage imports were passed in 1534, 1555, 1559, 1563, 1571 and 1593 | Much of this government legislation empowered JPs and town councils to tackle the problems of poor food supplies and starvation locally. |
| | Acts to prevent the hoarding of grain were passed in 1527, 1544, 1545, 1550, 1556 and 1562 | The Privy Council also issued Books of Orders giving detailed advice on how to deal with food shortages. |
| Reducing unrest over economic grievances: unemployment | 1563 Act of Artificers made seven-year apprentices compulsory in all crafts | Trying to create employment and tie men to their trade showed the Elizabethan government's pre-occupation with the notion that unemployment meant vagrancy, which in turn meant social unrest. |
| Reducing unrest over economic grievances: beggars and vagrants (the 'itinerant poor') | Acts of 1572, 1576 and 1598 set up the administration of poor relief based on the parish, where the impotent poor were given housing and the able-bodied poor provided with work, financed by the poor rate | Many town authorities were ahead of the government and levied their own poor rate.<br><br>Thomas Cromwell had distinguished between the 'impotent' poor and the 'idle' poor and the need to treat them differently, but it was not until the reign of Elizabeth that the government really accepted responsibility for the poor and laid down the principles for poor relief that were to last 400 years. |

Much of the strengthening of central government was the work of Thomas Cromwell, chief minister of Henry VIII from 1532 to 1540. Cromwell made fundamental changes to the way the country was run which strengthened the position of the monarchy and made opposition more difficult.

In what ways did central government reduce the likelihood of rebellions taking place or succeeding?

**How Thomas Cromwell strengthened Tudor government in the 1530s**

He used visitations and commissions to investigate local events. Those in the 1530s examined the state of the monasteries while Edward ordered reports on enclosures and Elizabeth required details as to likely opposition to the Church of England. In all cases the reports which were sent by crown officials to the Privy Council kept the monarch informed of local feelings and helped maintain stability in the country.

He worked ceaselessly, writing countless letters by hand, personally investigating many cases of treason and making himself responsible for all matters of internal security (a role continued by Sir Francis Walsingham under Elizabeth). Both ministers oversaw a network of informers. Royal correspondence was also used to generate obedience and terror. Cromwell constantly reminded JPs of their duties, as did William Cecil in Elizabeth's reign.

He utilised the printing press to publish pamphlets in what has been described as a 'full-scale propaganda campaign'. The pamphlets of the 1530s were written in easily understandable language and included warnings against rebellion. The majority of people were illiterate but pamphlets were read out in churches and marketplaces. The emphasis on the respect for authority was stressed in works such as Thomas Cranmer's 'Homily on Obedience' which continued to be heard throughout the second half of the century.

He used Injunctions, issued on his own authority, to enforce the major religious changes of the 1530s by issuing directives to clergy which included, for example, instructions on the content of sermons. Cromwell also introduced a nationwide scheme for licensing preachers and ordered bishops to take action against any clergy who were not supporting the government's line. In subsequent reigns the role of the Church in supporting the crown and maintaining stability was continued, for example, by the work of Matthew Parker as Archbishop of Canterbury in the 1570s.

## Concluding your enquiry

By reviewing your notes on the rebellions and your answers to the questions in this chapter, you should now be able to create a detailed and well-supported explanation of why the rebellions against the Tudors did not succeed.

As further guidance, think about the following:

- Are there any other factors, beyond those discussed in this chapter, which help to explain the failure of the rebellions?
- What connections can you see between factors?
- Which factor or factors seem to have been the most significant in explaining the failure of rebellions?
- How certain can we be about the answer and how should answers be worded to reflect this degree of uncertainty?

**What connections can you see between factors?**

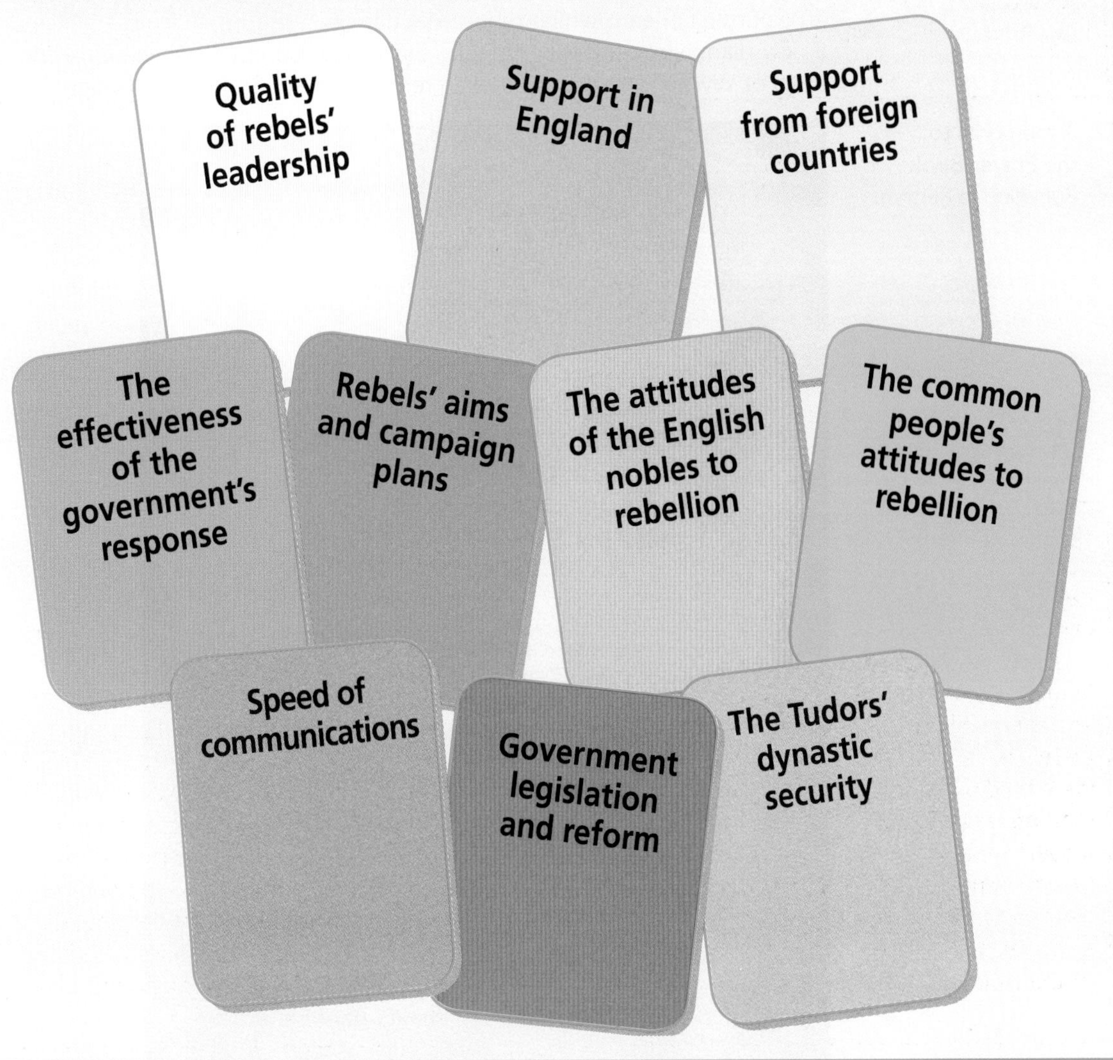
Quality of rebels' leadership
Support in England
Support from foreign countries
The effectiveness of the government's response
Rebels' aims and campaign plans
The attitudes of the English nobles to rebellion
The common people's attitudes to rebellion
Speed of communications
Government legislation and reform
The Tudors' dynastic security

# Conclusion: How should we remember Tudor rebellions?

In June 2007 the Bishop of Truro publically condemned the Church of England for the role it had played in suppressing the Cornish Prayer Book Rebellion 450 years earlier and apologised for the deaths of so many Cornish people. The Prayer Book Rebellion was also commemorated in the memorials pictured here. The one below was erected at Penryn in 1999 to commemorate those killed. This is far from being the only modern commemoration of individual rebellions against the Tudors. We have already seen some of them (on pages 33, 57 and 80) and another, to Kett's rebels, can be found on the road leading from Norwich to Hethersett. There, an oak tree beneath which rebels met has been preserved from 1549 and a new plaque was unveiled in 2006 by Norfolk County Council, while the town of Wymondham continues to remember Robert Kett on its sign.

Prayer Book
Rebellion
HEMM A GOVHA AN KOLL A
GOLLJI GLASNEDH HA'N
MERNANS A VILYOW A
WLASKARORYON GERNEWEK YN UNN
DHEFENDYA A GA FYDH, YETH
HA DEVOSOW KELTEK
THIS COMMEMORATES
THE LOSS OF GLASNEY COLLEGE
AND THE DEATH OF
THOUSANDS OF CORNISH PATRIOTS
IN DEFENCE OF THEIR FAITH, LANGUAGE
AND CELTIC CUSTOMS.
1549 - 1999
KERNOW ARTA

▷ A memorial to the Prayer Book Rebellion in Penryn.

On Whit Monday 1549
SAMPFORD COURTENAY
people killed a local farmer
WILLIAM HELLYONS
and then joined the Cornish in
the Prayer Book Rebellion which
ended in defeat by the King's army
outside this village

△ A memorial plaque in Sampford Courtenay.

In such places the impact of a Tudor rebellion has reverberated down the centuries, colouring an area's collective history and by adding to its identity it has proved worthy of a permanent memorial. But are the Tudor rebellions worth remembering more widely than in an individual locality?

One way of answering this is to ask: 'Did they achieve anything?' In assessing their success it is important to go back to the aims of each rebellion and to remind ourselves of what exactly each set out to achieve. From this perspective it becomes clear that the greatest degree of success was enjoyed by rebellions that included protests against taxation imposed by the crown. After the 1489 rebellion against the collection of the new Subsidy Tax in Yorkshire, Henry VII made no attempt to collect the tax and did not impose any fines on the rebels. The 1497 Cornish Rebellion, provoked by a new war tax levied to provide defence for the north of England from Perkin Warbeck and the King of Scotland, caused Henry VII to relieve the Cornish of having to pay the tax. Although the county was heavily fined, the King did not attempt to introduce new taxes there again. The most successful of all the rebellions was the 1525 protest in Suffolk and Essex against the Amicable Grant. The widespread unrest across all social classes forced Henry VIII to cancel the tax, blaming it on his minister, Thomas Wolsey. As a result no one paid any tax, no benevolences were requested by the royal treasury and the partially collected Subsidy Tax was re-assessed at lower levels. The rebels were pardoned.

Other rebellions were successful in moderating royal policy, although this only became obvious in the years after their defeat. After the alarm created by the Pilgrimage of Grace, Henry VIII's religious decrees became noticeably more conservative, though the rebellion was not the only reason for this. The 1539 Act of Six Articles confirmed the traditional Catholic sacraments of **transubstantiation**, private Masses and the hearing of confession by priests, while banning the Protestant practice of allowing priests to marry. The agrarian complaints voiced in the pilgrims' articles led to a royal commission which regulated unlawful enclosures and excessive entry fines. Thomas Cromwell's unpopular Statute of Uses which was virtually a tax on aristocratic landed inheritance was repealed in 1540, the same year Henry sanctioned his minister's execution for treason. Similarly in the wake of Kett's rebellion the government of Edward VI introduced legislation repealing the Subsidy and Vagrancy Acts. A new Enclosure Act was passed to protect villagers from any future enclosing of woods and common lands. Further acts sought to reduce economic hardship by fixing grain prices, prohibiting exports and maintaining arable land in its present state.

**transubstantiation**
The belief held by Roman Catholics that during the sacrament of Holy Communion the bread and wine become the body and blood of Jesus Christ when they are blessed

The longer term achievements of the Tudor rebellions, in terms of both their legacy and place in the context of rebellions, are harder to trace, not least because they were so varied in nature. They show little which foreshadows **the Levellers**' desire for equality in the seventeenth century or later demands by the Chartists and Suffragettes for the expansion of the franchise. At heart however, like these other rebellions and the ones described at the beginning of this book, the Tudor rebellions were triggered by a sense of injustice, for example, that heavy taxes had been imposed, religious doctrines and ritual overturned, local politics and traditions ignored or social classes divided by economic differences. The biggest legacy was not in terms of shaping the rebellions which followed but in the growing English way of addressing such grievances, through Parliament and discussion, which was to influence the direction of English politics from the sixteenth century onwards, the ignoring of which by Charles I caused not just rebellion but civil war between 1642 and 1652.

**the Levellers**
A political movement during the English Civil War who wanted to extend the vote and make sovereigns more accountable to their subjects. They also believed in religious tolerance and equality before the law

However, another reason for remembering these rebellions is not because of their long- or short-term successes, but because of the bravery and actions of the many thousands of individual people who took part in them. These rebellions may be varied in their causes and outcomes, methods and extent of support, but they brought together many principled people who were prepared to stand up for their local traditions and customs and to challenge unfairness and injustice. They were often unwilling rebels, slow to take violent action but determined to make their voices heard. In this, the men and women who took part in many of the rebellions of the 1500s did have a great deal in common with the protesters of later centuries and of today.

## Activity: Summing up the rebellions

**1** What is your overall impression of the Tudor rebellions? Can you suggest a phrase or a set of six words that sums up how Tudor rebellions should be remembered and commemorated?

**2** Which of these views would you feel most comfortable in defending?

- All the rebellions were doomed to fail because the Tudor state was so strong.
- The leaders of the rebellions were misguided and often seeking personal advantage. (In considering this, think about whether the leaders can be seen as inspirational, with courage and conviction.)
- Tudor England was a country of unruly and warlike people, spoiling for a fight.
- Tudor monarchs showed themselves to be cruel and despotic in their responses to rebellions. (In considering this, think about whether the monarchs should actually be admired for their tenacity in staying on the throne.)

# Index